UCD WOMEN'S CENTER

D0763835

THE
WOMAN-CENTERED
ECONOMY

IDEALS,
REALITY,
AND THE SPACE IN BETWEEN

EDITED BY
LORAINE EDWALDS AND MIDGE STOCKER

 Third Side Press
CHICAGO

Copyright © 1995 by Third Side Press, Inc. All rights reserved.
This book may not be reproduced in part or in whole by any means, except in
the case of reviews, without permission of Third Side Press. Copyright to
individual articles held by their authors unless otherwise indicated.

Cover art copyright © 1995 by Ursula Roma
Cover design by Ursula Roma, Little Bear Graphics

Text design and production by Midge Stocker

Printed on recycled, acid-free paper in the United States of America.

Permissions acknowledgments are printed on page 333. Page 333 is hereby
incorporated as part of the copyright page.

ISBN: 1-879427-06-0   paper $15.95
ISBN: 1-879427-16-8   cloth $29.95

Library of Congress Cataloging-in-Publication Data
The woman-centered economy : ideals, reality, and the space in between
 / edited by Loraine Edwalds and Midge Stocker.
     p. cm.
   Includes bibliographical references (p.   ) and index.
   ISBN 1-879427-16-8 (cloth : acid-free paper) — ISBN
1-879427-06-0 (pbk. : acid-free paper)
   1. Women— United States—Economic conditions. 2. Women in
business—United States. 3. Women-owned businesses—United States.
4. Lesbian feminisim—United States. 5. Sex discrimination against
women—United States.   I. Edwalds, Loraine. II. Stocker, Midge,
1960-   .
HQ1421.W652 1994
305.42—dc20   94-23364
                                    CIP

Third Side Press, 2250 W. Farragut, Chicago, IL 60625-1802

First edition, March 1995
10 9 8 7 6 5 4 3 2 1

UCD WOMEN'S CENTER

THE WOMAN-CENTERED ECONOMY

IDEALS, REALITY, AND THE SPACE IN BETWEEN

"The woman's movement rests not alone on her larger personality, with its tingling sense of revolt against injustice, but on the wide, deep sympathy of women for one another. It is a concerted movement, based on the recognition of a common evil and seeking a common good. . . . In the economic world, excessive masculinity, in its fierce competition and primitive individualism; and excessive femininity, in its inordinate consumption and hindering conservatism; have reached a stage where they work more evil than good."

—*Charlotte Perkins Gilman,* Women & Economics, *1898*

CONTENTS

Lesbian Riches, *Karen Williams* 179
Feminist Bookstores, *Theresa Corrigan* 181
A Tale of Two Feminist Businesses, *Alice Lowenstein* 189
Feminists and Health Care, *Karin Kearns* 199
Good Business Vibrations, *Joani Blank* 205
Nan's Rent-A-Bob, *Loraine Edwalds* 209
Creating and Sharing Woman-Centered Space, *Eleanor Morton* 211
Consumer Ethics in the Woman-Centered Economy, *Margaret VanArsdale* 215
Playing to the Highest Common Denominator, *Toni Armstrong Jr.* 219

PART 3 REAPING OUR HARVEST 231

I'll Show You Mine If You'll Show Me Yours, *Toni Armstrong Jr.* 233
Lilies of the Field, *Sonia Johnson* 243
Third World Diva Girls, *bell hooks* 265
You CAN Kill the Spirit, *Laura Burrows* 281
Lesbian Economy, *Janet Miller* 287
The Philosophy Behind Stonehaven, *Genevieve Vaughan* 293
Aunt Lute Books, *Jamie Lee Evans* 299
An Alternative to the Economics of Threat, *Mary Kay Blakely* 305

RELATED READING 317

CONTRIBUTORS 319

INDEX 325

PREFACE

MIDGE STOCKER

I am in the somewhat peculiar position of being both publisher and coeditor of this book. It is usually only in small-press publishing that this phenomenon occurs because in larger publishing corporations, there are many layers of management and workers. In small-press publishing, and therefore in most feminist publishing, there are very few, if any, layers.

As publisher at Third Side Press, I have to consider how the book fits in with the rest of the books the press is publishing and how I go about marketing it so that the people who will find it fascinating will be able to find it at all. I also have to make sure that the production details all work—that the book works out to be the right number of pages (a multiple of sixteen), that I've set the type properly and there aren't too many mistakes, that the computer keeps running while I'm putting the books together, and of course that there's money to pay for the printing. Then I have to keep track of how the printing schedule is going and be ready to unload the books, one box at a time—rain, snow, or shine—from a tractor-trailer truck that pulls up in the alley behind a rented garage where I store them. I have to prepare mailing labels of the people (including the book's many contributors) to whom I will send review copies of the book—copies that I unpack, personally, from the cases, repack, label, and ship. I have to keep track of how the sales of the book are going—and hope that they're going well so that there will be money to publish subsequent books. I spend one day a week doing nothing but accounting and financial work. And I do all of those things, and more, because I am committed to the work of Third Side Press, the work that I have chosen, the work of making women's voices public, of making change in the world by helping women consider and sometimes change the framework of their lives.

But I have to be practical, which means "I have to figure out how to make the press make enough money to keep itself going." And toward that end I've decided to try keeping a relatively balanced list, publishing about half fiction and half nonfiction. There is a strong market for quality lesbian fiction, but it's hard to make sure that good new books by first-time authors—like *On Lill Street* by Lynn Kanter and *The Sensual Thread* by Beatrice Stone—get found. The market for feminist health books is a little easier to find, I think, as long as the issues are clear: *Cancer as a Women's Issue* and *Alternatives for Women with Endometriosis* will stand as important books in their areas and be readily marketable for a long time to come. Selecting which books to publish is a very hard part of my job. I want to make as many risky choices as I can and still keep the press going, because it's those risky choices that raise issues that will make people think and argue and struggle to define themselves. And that sounds great philosophically, but in truth I have to make some safer choices, some more surely popular choices, for the press to make enough money to keep bringing out those otherwise unheard voices.

And then there's being editor. What does that mean exactly? When I'm working on a novel or a book of nonfiction written entirely by one other person, it means lots of careful reading, thoughtful commenting, and sometimes negotiation. When I'm working as editor or coeditor of an anthology, it means all of those things multiplied by twelve or twenty or so.

Why am I telling you all of this? Because it is these threads, all of these little details that are kept track of by women, all of these important tasks that are the stuff that keeps the wheels of business oiled—and they're oiled by women, whether the companies in question are owned by women or not. Look around at any bank. Who do you see working? It's women, many of them minority women. And who do you suppose is making most of the decisions? I'll answer that question with another question. How many women loan officers do you suppose there are in the United States with authority to approve loans of more than $10,000? Not many!

This book is largely by and about women who have authority. Authority that they have taken. No one gave them their businesses. No one handed them the kind of ethical theory they abide by and said, "Do it this way." Most of the women in

this book are "Americans," i.e. women living in the United
States, and many of them come from middle-class backgrounds.
So this is not a book about turning capitalism on its ear,
though many of the women writing here might like to do just
that. This book represents women who have thought for
themselves and who are in the process of building themselves
new ways of being and of conceptualizing how they make their
way in the world.

We solicited articles through calls for manuscripts in feminist
newspapers and magazines, such as *off our backs* and *Feminist
Bookstore News*. We handed out flyers at the National
Women's Music Festival and at the Michigan Womyn's Music
Festival. We talked it up at chorus rehearsals and writing
workshops. We searched for articles through our own reading,
and we are deeply grateful to the authors and publishers who
have allowed us to reprint previously published work. But that
does not mean we attracted or discovered pieces from every
part of the community. We hope that the articles included here
provoke you to think of the many other aspects of the
woman-centered economy that are not discussed here, because
in this as in so many areas of women's lives silence speaks
volumes.

ACKNOWLEDGMENTS

We have been working on collecting materials for this book for three years now, and we have many people to thank. We hope that anyone we forget to name here will forgive us and accept our thanks personally.

First rather than last, we thank our partners, Luanne Adamus and Jane Murtaugh, who indulged our absence on many occasions as we were working together to bring this book into being, who discussed and debated with us various points of contention that sprang up along the way, and who provide us with a particular kind of loving touchstone.

Beyond our partners, the community of women who have encouraged us has been a wide one, spreading from our home community among the Artemis Singers of Chicago through women in the National Women's Music Festival organization and the Feminist Bookstore Network, across the U.S. and Canada, to individual women in various parts of the woman-centered economy who have offered us suggestions, advice, materials, writing, criticism, and laughter.

For suggestions about women and topics and perspectives we should approach, we thank Mary Byrne of the National Women's Music Festival, Carol Seajay of *Feminist Bookstore News*, Nett Hart of Word Weavers, Janet Miller, and all of the authors whose work is in this book. Many of you have no idea what else is in the book other than your own writing. You have been very patient with the long time span between when we approached you about contributing to this book and the time the book was published. We hope *The Woman-Centered Economy* exceeds your expectations and that you are proud to have your work included.

For their help on this book and with many other Third Side Press tasks, we thank the Alice Lowenstein, Ann Morris, Deb Lewis, Eileen Lynx, Kim Ainis, Michaeline Chvatal, Mary

Hauck, Mary Wallace, Vada Vernee Woods; intern Eleanor
Morton who kept the project moving through the summer of
1993; and indexer Joyce Goldenstern.

For goading and prodding (sorry, make that encouraging and
gently insisting) us to remember that the work we are doing is
really important and that we really can get it done, we thank
Meta Hellman.

For listening to us as we struggled through the process of
sorting ideas and trying to finish this book, we thank all of our
friends and many of our acquaintances.

Finally, for having the love and patience and courage to see it
through, we thank each other.

INTRODUCTION

LORAINE EDWALDS

If you're like most women, you probably don't think of the
economy as being particularly woman-centered. The economy is
about getting and spending money, about trudging to a job,
about being out of work, about paying bills. For most of us,
the economy has nothing to do with loving women, with being
politically committed to women, with chosing to spend our
time and energy with women.

Or so it seems.

Money has always been an aspect of the women's movement,
which I am defining here as the organizations and individuals
that are working to further the rights and freedoms of women,
improve the lot of women, and create culture that comes from
a woman's perspective for the enrichment of other women's
lives. Because improving women's lot in life often means
improving their economic status, and because women's paths of
improving economic status have often been blocked by men,
the women's movement is often seen by the mainstream as
seeking mainstream recognition and dollars for feminists.
Certainly some feminists have achieved mainstream success,
without becoming any less feminist, and they are to be
applauded. Ultimately, what the women's movement is striving
to create is fair treatment in the mainstream, and community
for women alongside the mainstream. *Community* can get to be
a pretty big word, encompassing music festivals, choruses, bars,
sports teams, bookstores, potlucks. The women's movement
empowers, enriches, enlivens, entertains, educates.

Feminists have long recognized that our power as women is
determined in some part by our economic power. In this book,
we explore how our identities as women within the economy
and as women within the women's community relate to each
other. Various authors explore our ideals, our history, our
present reality, and our future.

WHAT IS THE WOMAN-CENTERED ECONOMY?

It's easy to look at the economy of the middle class of the middle United States and think that everything about the economy revolves around women. Images of women are used to sell cars, soap, magazines, perfume. Women are constantly encouraged to buy clothes, food, makeup. Women actually are a very important part of the mainstream economy: women are constantly bringing profits to men.

The *woman-centered economy* is what was born out of the realization that much of what women do is bring profits to men. Women have dreamed, and have worked, to make their labor and money bring profits to women instead of men. This book explores how and why this has happened over the past 25 years.

We discuss the woman-centered economy as

- ▲ the financial aspect of the women's community
- ▲ a segment of the world economy
- ▲ businesses run by women who have primarily women as customers
- ▲ how feminists and lesbians spend their money

It became clear early in the process of working on this book that focusing on money was not going to cover the topic accurately. The woman-centered economy is rooted in an emotional investment in women that cannot readily be paid for with cash. (Not that anyone has tried.) Possibly because women have less money, or because of the ways we have been socialized, we recognize that costs are not only money but also time and energy. So the woman-centered economy is also made up of

- ▲ women creating and being a part of organizations that give definition to our community and our culture
- ▲ women changing the way things are done in the mainstream to benefit other women

The woman-centered economy covers a wide territory. It is not a clearly defined market segment, ready for targeted mass mailings; nor is it a single way of thinking about money. It does not include all women-run businesses, or even all lesbian-run businesses. Most women-run businesses do not view themselves as part of the women's community. But those that do, and the women who support them, are part of the woman-centered economy, whether they are included in this book or not. Our hope is that naming the financial aspect of the feminist community "the woman-centered economy" will help us acknowledge money as a part of our power and our continued growth, as individuals and as a community.

EXPLORING DIFFERENT VIEWPOINTS

This book reflects the thinking of many women about the money we have and what we do with it. We raise awareness about how money influences the politics of our community and vice versa. We reinforce the idea that we can and do make a difference, economically as well as socially and personally, in the world around us.

Seeing beyond the band of economic reality that is ourselves and our personal friends to the rest of the women's community is more difficult than you might think. Much of our community has been built with a commitment to equality and access that would alarm the mainstream. This has, however, given many of us a false sense of sameness.

I, for example, am a white, 37-year-old, upper-middle-class lesbian with a middle-management job in a medical association. I've been out as a lesbian for 16 years. I have a college education and am saving money to go to graduate school in business. I co-own a small house in Chicago with a woman who earns more money than I do. I don't think I live lavishly; but I know only a few lesbians who have more access to money than I do. And during the time I've been working on this book I was laid off and remained unemployed for four months. These aspects of my own life influence how I view the economy as a whole, including the woman-centered economy.

Because so many women lack money, it is easy to get the impression that we all lack money. The perception of poverty has affected our expectations for ourselves and our organizations. Possibly it has intimidated wealthy women, encouraging us to be closeted about money, pretending to be a little more strapped than we really are. Many women in our community are seriously underemployed, and attempts by feminist organizations to make events or goods more affordable often don't reach these women. On the other hand, being at a large event where hundreds or thousands of women have paid $10, $20, $100, $1000 to be there can give the impression that we are a community rolling in spare cash. Clearly one of the challenges to the woman-centered economy is making room for both of these realities and all the space in between.

CELEBRATING WHAT WE HAVE DONE

Many of us are introduced to the politics of the women's movement in a moment of outrage: We must not allow men to continue to take advantage of us! But outrage is not an emotion you can sustain for long before you get exhausted. So eventually the outrage fades, and economic oppression becomes as much a part of womanhood as breasts and periods. For many feminists, the fact of less money has become, like breasts and periods, not just a curse but also a blessing. Our difference from men has allowed us to think more creatively about how we can affect change. It has made us think of ourselves as a group, rather than as individuals; it has helped us to understand how other groups are oppressed.

Many feminists have defined their priorities in ways that do not emphasize money. For some, this is necessity; for others, it is a choice we are glad we can make. Having the freedom to think differently about money leads us to new ways of looking at power, at leadership, at organizational structure. This book explores and celebrates the alternatives to the mainstream that feminists have created and continue to create.

We have created real places that are not utopias but that are safe, loving spaces for women nonetheless. We have kept alive institutions that support women. But we have also had to close noble businesses and organizations for lack of money. This book describes both successful and failed businesses, and shows how the politics that the mainstream ridicules both keep us together and tear us apart.

The feminist movement may have been declared dead by the mainstream many years ago. But the women's community is still alive. And the woman-centered economy keeps breathing it new life.

PART 1

GETTING TO THE ROOTS:
ACCESS AND SURVIVAL

At the heart of the woman-centered economy are the issues of access, fairness, and autonomy. As feminists, we have tried to create a world that provides what each of us individually defines as accessible, fair, and responsive to our own and other women's needs. Much of the struggle with developing a woman-centered economy has come from the differences uncovered when what is accessible to one woman seems unfair to another; or when what provides autonomy for one woman denies access to another.

Part 1 of *The Woman-Centered Economy* explores the access women have to the things that money buys, the attitudes women have toward and get from the mainstream economy, and the history of some women's ideas about how to change the economy.

HOW OTHERS SEE US

Let's look at some stereotypes of women in the economy.

▲ The woman executive carries a briefcase, works long hours, wears expensive suits, earns what men do, acts like a man too. She's the one who runs into the "glass ceiling"—she wants and deserves the highest jobs in the economy, but can't get them because the men in charge won't promote her.

▲ The working mother drives around in her mini-van, taking her children to day care, going to work, buying gifts on her lunch hour, exhausted. She's not looking for a promotion now because frankly she's got too many responsibilities as it is.

▲ The wealthy suburban housewife is decorating her lovely home, shopping, volunteering with the church and the PTA. Her life is set up as an ideal, although she is completely dependent on a man for her survival. She is seen as a consumer, not a producer.

▲ The blue-collar woman works long hours, spends what money she earns as she gets it, is bossed around by her husband, her boss, her children. She is lucky to have a job at all, what with the economy the way it is.

▲ The poor woman lives on AFDC and food stamps, buys lotto tickets and junk food, lets drug-addicted men share in whatever meager food and shelter she is able to get. Her life and health are bleak.

These mainstream stereotypes share more than just cartoonish simplicity. They deny the existence of lesbians and the reality of non-executive single straight women. They reinforce ruttedness for women of all economic classes. They reinforce the existing class structure. These are the definitions of women that the women's movement has been working to get rid of. Now, here are the stereotypes of lesbians in the economy:

▲

OK, so there aren't really any stereotypes of lesbians in the economy. Within our own community, the following stereotypes exist:

▲ Big tough tradeswomen who live in plain apartments and drive trucks

▲ Professional women who earn money in the mainstream and spend it on therapy, crystals, and Olivia vacations

▲ Independent contractors who are earning a living somehow but still have time to volunteer and run women's organizations

▲ Closeted, spinster schoolteachers who are totally absorbed in their dedication to special-needs children

▲ Celebrities who earn their money performing and spend it on advanced outfits

These stereotypes also reflect a very limited view of the lesbian and feminist worlds. Fortunately, women in our stereotypes have a lot more independence. But there's little recognition of many women's realities: for example, women who are supported by someone else, women who manage offices, women who take care of children. In this section, we turn away from both sets of stereotypes. We explore how women have broken off from the mainstream and why they continue to do so, how our community has strived to avoid the racism and classism of the mainstream, and the special difficulties that we have placed on ourselves in working toward this paradigm shift.

ACCESS

In "Surveying Ourselves," Janet Miller shares her survey of lesbian separatists, in which she asked not just how much money women make, but what they have access to: food, shelter, transportation, health care. In this way, she shifts the focus of economic reality away from raw dollar numbers of salary and net worth towards an open-minded recognition of different living standards.

Of course, most feminists and feminist organizations have struggled with money itself. Although money is not the huge central issue that men would have you believe it is, money is still very important. In many ways, our experience with money parallels our fight for equality, with women striving to treat all others as equals but at the same time acknowleging the differences that race, class, and economic status make.

Minnie Bruce Pratt, in "Money and the Shape of Things," shows how difficult it is for women who have made a commitment to the community to break free of the mainstream. She addresses privilege from both sides of the coin: what we as women are living without, and what privileges make it possible for some women to live more woman-centered lives.

One of the problems that has vexed the woman-centered economy for many years is racism, which has resulted in inadequate representation of women of color. Gloria Joseph interviewed many Black women about the women's movement to write "White Promotion, Black Survival" for the anthology *Common Differences* in 1981. In updating the article for this

book, she interviewed many of the same women, plus some
new ones. Although her discussion of economic issues is
tangential, her article analyzes why Black women's needs are
not met by the women's movement, an analysis vital to change.

HOW THE MAINSTREAM WORKS IS NOT GENERALLY IN OUR FAVOR

One of the unfortunate aspects of working in the mainstream is
that most men are not going to give up money any more readily
than they are going to give up power. This means that the
economics of feminism is as much of a struggle as the politics
of feminism.

Several articles in this section discuss the many different ways
that the mainstream economy holds us particularly as women
and to a lesser extent as feminists and lesbians down. Although
freedom to chose one's sex partners has always been an
important part of feminism, sexual orientation remains a
divisive issue in the woman-centered economy. In the
mainstream, straight women are smack dab in the middle of
the economy and lesbians are outside. But in the
woman-centered economy, lesbians are in the middle and
straight women are on the edge. This can be seen as an
unfortunate weakness in our community; after all, our need to
create businesses and culture of our own is largely due to our
experiences as women, not specifically as lesbians. In reality,
straight women may make up more of our economy than many
of us think, because they are not visible as straight women.
This would be a good thing, as recent surveys show lesbians to
be only a small portion of the population (1.4% !), so to survive
economically we need straight and bisexual women to be
included.

In this way, the natural segmentation and competition of the
mainstream have worked against us, discouraging coalition
building with women-run businesses that are not a part of the
feminist community. Being on the margin, it has often been
difficult just to find one another and work together.

BRAVE CHANGES: SOME IDEAS AND HOW THEY'VE WORKED

Some of the women who started woman-centered businesses and organizations in the 1970s, as Carol Seajay and Phyllis Chesler note in their pieces in this section, hoped to move feminists away from the mainstream, to protect ourselves from the patriarchy. That these ventures were largely not successful is due in part to women lacking the base materials to create an economy completely separate from men. A printing press run by women to publish writing by women must be purchased from men, and the paper and ink that run through the press must be purchased from men. Woman-centered banks lacked of course for sufficient deposits but also for sizable growing businesses to loan money to. Even women willing to farm their own land must buy tractors and seed from men. So the basic level of access women hoped for did not become a reality.

Nett Hart's "Taking a Slide" explores one of the ways that feminists have attempted to increase access to women's events and services: the sliding scale. The theory that some women have more money, and therefore can and should pay more, so that women with less money can pay what they can afford, has a lot of egalitarian appeal. But breaking a pattern of paying the price marked that carries us through the rest of our lives has proved more difficult to change than many thought.

Many other women have set up charitable, political and arts groups for women with the hopes of raising money from other women, and many have succeeded. Others have not. In "Feminist Fundraising Phobia," Karen Rudolph discusses some of the attitudes within the women's community that make fundraising, even for causes that many feminists support, difficult.

Another factor in the demise of some enterprises, mentioned somewhat wistfully throughout the book, is that our vision sometimes exceeds our physical and economic abilities. But even the women who lost money in these ventures would probably say that having the vision to create these alternatives is as important as making money at them.

SURVEYING OURSELVES

JANET MILLER

The survey whose questions follow this article was designed as an economic survey of the lesbian separatist community.* The survey grew from my conversations with three lesbian friends. Over a four-month time span, each of them (who are of varying income levels) stated that she was sure that *her* income level was "about what most dykes make." One thinks that is around $12,000 per year, another $29,000 per year, and the third believes most U.S. lesbians make about $50,000 per year.

It was clear that not all of them could be correct in their perceptions. That made sense given the sensitivity of the subject. Most people, dykes included, are not open about their economic situations. Even within close friendship circles, lesbians don't often share detailed economic information with one another, for a variety of reasons.

The significance of these differing perceptions is that they translate into behaviors. For example, it affects how lesbians

---

* Results of the survey are available to lesbian separatists only, and the survey was administered with that understanding. I encourage readers to use any and/or all of the survey questions you find helpful in developing surveys of your own communities.

If you are a lesbian separatist and are not already aware of how to get the results of the survey, please network with other lesbian separatists until you find someone who has access to the results and get them from her. The results cannot be obtained from Third Side Press.

The survey has been completed; I am not soliciting responses to the survey (from any population) at this time.

Copyright © 1994 by Janet Miller

pay on sliding scales. At the local women's coffeehouse in
Chicago*—whose policy is to suggest a donation amount for
admission to events, with the idea that women will pay "more
if you can, less if you can't" and that no woman will be turned
away for lack of funds—all three of the lesbians previously
mentioned pay the "suggested" donation—not more, not less—
because all of them consider their economic situation to
be average. Another example is played out in personal
relationships. One lesbian might suggest to another an outing
that would involve spending $40.00 over the course of an
evening, without being aware that the other turns down the
invitation because she does not have enough income to be
able to spend that much money in a single evening. A third
consequence of these differing perceptions is that some
lesbians routinely throw away (or donate to a charity out of
convenience rather than support) material possessions they
don't want anymore, not realizing that other lesbians would
find those things very valuable.

▲ ▲ ▲

As I began to think about money, and how it influences our
community and our relationships to one another, I realized that
economic prosperity is not based on money alone. Not only can
differing levels of need influence how far a certain amount of
money can go (medical bills? children? cost of housing in New
York City vs. Peoria?), but many of the most critical things
people usually get with money can be and often are obtained
by other means.**

What are the most important needs (i.e. *survival* needs) we
get met with money? I settled on food, health care, and shelter.
I decided that access to the means to satisfy these survival needs
equals one's true economic status. This economic status may
not be the same as one's access to money, socioeconomic class,
or place in other measuring standards commonly used to

---

* Mountain Moving Coffeehouse for Womyn & Children
** See "Lesbian Economy: A First Step," pages 287-292 in this book,
  for some of my ideas on this subject.

conclude how well one is doing economically. The survey was designed to see how lesbians were doing in light of this more basic standard: access to food, health care, and shelter, regardless of how these necessities were obtained.

▲ ▲ ▲

The survey, which included formulation and input from many lesbian separatists of varying backgrounds, had several results. Reading the survey itself stimulates new ways of thinking about economic prosperity and scarcity. Many women who read it mention that reflecting on their own economic access in light of this different definition makes them more aware of ways that their survival needs were being (and could be) met without using money.

Separatists reading the results of the survey may re-evaluate their choices, and/or change their behaviors, about where they pay on sliding scales, what they throw away, etc. Other communities—lesbians, feminists, gays, or others—may decide to use this survey, as is, or as a starting point when designing their own surveys, to assess economics in their own communities.

The collated results may give information on the relations between need and economic access in the lesbian separatist community as a whole. Overall, is there enough access among members of this community to meet the needs of everyone in this community?

▲ ▲ ▲

Some lesbians have asked why I restricted the survey to lesbian *separatists* only. The lesbian separatist community is of a small enough size that I anticipated being able to compile the responses. While very interested in this subject from the view of the entire lesbian community, I am an individual, not an institution, and have only my personal resources, and those lent me by friends, available to use in collecting and collating the results. I would have been unable to handle a larger population without additional support. One advantage I had by making the survey available to lesbian separatists only during the collection period is that I didn't have to filter the respondees, as is necessary with other surveys. I knew that all the surveys returned to me were from lesbian separatists; I was therefore saved an entire section dedicated to determining the gender and sexual orientation of the respondent.

One drawback to surveying such a small population was that certain identifying factors, which are already known to heavily influence economic access, had to be left off to protect the respondent's privacy. Had the survey addressed a much larger population, questions would have been included to establish basic demographics such as age, race, educational level, kind of job (for those with job-related income), region of the country, and whether the respondent was from an urban, suburban, or rural environment.

THE SURVEY

HOUSING

1. You are homeless. You have no regular access to a place to sleep, or you sleep in shelters. (Y/N)

2. Your access to housing depends on someone else. Someone is putting you up or paying your rent for you, and if they stopped you would not have access to housing unless another person got it for you. (Y/N)

    If your housing depends on someone else, who is that person? (Give that person's relationship to you, not her or his name.)

3. Do you live in government-subsidized housing? (Y/N)

4. Do you live in any of the following?
    - ☐ mobile home, trailer, or car (because you are traveling)
    - ☐ mobile home, trailer, or car (because you live there)
    - ☐ hospital
    - ☐ psychiatric unit
    - ☐ prison
    - ☐ nursing home
    - ☐ college housing
    - ☐ other institution (please explain)

5. If you could put up some other dykes if you wanted to, please fill out the following.

Number of dykes I could put up	for this long
	a few days
	a few weeks
	a few months
	longer (how long?)

6. If you are providing housing (not the money to get housing, but housing itself) for others, how many others are you housing (not including you)?
   Who are they (relationship to you, not names)?

7. If you know people who would house you if you needed it, please fill out the following.

How long would they house you?	How many people would house you?	Who would house you? (relationship to you)
a few days		
a few weeks		
a few months		
longer (how long?)		

8. Would your way of getting housing have to change (get more roommates, move to a cheaper place, get a higher income, etc.) if your monthly housing cost went up what amount or percentage or more? (Y/N)

9. Is your access to housing affected by you or anyone in your household being differently-abled? (Y/N)
   If yes, please explain.

10. Does racism affect your access to housing? (Y/N)
    If yes, please explain.

11. Do you "pass," or pretend to have access to more housing than you have? (Y/N)
    If so, how do you do this?

12. Do you rent the place where you live? (Y/N)

   If yes, please complete the Renters section immediately following.

13. Do you own or co-own at least one housing space? (Y/N)

   If yes, please complete the Landholders section (after the Renters section).

RENTERS

14. You need to combine with other people to meet rent. Otherwise, you could not pay even the lowest rent in your area alone. (Y/N)

15. You combine with others to rent your housing by choice. If necessary, you could pay the lowest rent in your area alone. (Y/N)

16. You provide services to your landlord . . .

   instead of paying rent. (Y/N)
   for lower rent. (Y/N)

17. You pay the rent alone. No other people live with you, or if they do, they give no money or services toward the rent. (Y/N)

18. If you rent at least one housing space, please fill out the following for each below.

Kind of Housing (house, apartment, condo, yacht, etc.)	Kind of Use (primary home, vacation home, etc.)	Used right now? (Y/N)
1.		
2.		
3.		

LANDHOLDERS

19. If you own or co-own housing, please list the following for each one below.

Kind of Housing (house, condo, yacht, cabin, etc.)	Kind of Use (primary home, vacation home, rental unit, etc.)	Own or Co-own	Used right now? (Y/N)
1.			
2.			

20. You pay all the costs for housing that you own alone. No other people live on your property, or if they do, they contribute no money or services toward housing costs. (Y/N)

21. Does someone else pay part of your ownership housing costs with you? (Y/N)

   If yes, who is that person? (Give the person's relationship to you, not her or his name.)

22. Could you meet the payments on the housing you own/co-own if others (tenants, co-owners, etc.) didn't pay part of the costs with you? (Y/N)

23. Is the property you own falling into disrepair or becoming less livable because while you meet your mortgage, property tax, and insurance payments, you can't afford maintenance and repairs? (Y/N)

24. Are you currently behind on your mortgage payment? (Y/N)

25. Do you still owe money on your property?
   Property 1 (Y/N)
   Property 2 (Y/N)

HEALTH CARE

26. Do you live in the U.S.? (Y/N)

   If you do not live in the U.S. right now, feel free to ignore the rest of the Health Care questions. Turn over the survey to the blank side of the page and write about your health care access.

27. Are you a member of the armed services, and so are covered by the military medical care establishment? (Y/N)

28. Do you pay for all of your health care out of your own pocket? (Y/N)

   If yes, this is because . . .
      O I choose to.
      O I have to.

29. Do you provide free health care? (Y/N)

   If yes, what kind of health care do you provide, and to whom do you give it?

30. Do you have access to free health care? (Y/N)

    If yes, what kind of health care do you get free, and how do you get it?

31. Do you have enough money or insurance that you could try many different kinds of therapy or get many different doctors' opinions in solving a health problem? (Y/N)

32. Can you routinely afford to travel long distances to see health care experts? (Y/N)

    If yes, can you travel out of state? (Y/N) out of country? (Y/N)

33. Are you in prison, and therefore your only access to health care is through the penal system? (Y/N)

34. Have you skipped routine medical or dental checkups for any of the following reasons?
    ☐ because of the cost
    ☐ because the only health-care providers you have access to are
       ○ men
       ○ racist
       ○ sizeist
       ○ homophobic
       ○ sexist
       ○ other (please explain)
    ☐ other (please explain)

35. Have you not gotten medical care when you were sick or injured for any of the following reasons?
    ☐ because of the cost
    ☐ because the only health care providers you have access to are
       ○ men
       ○ racist
       ○ sizeist
       ○ homophobic
       ○ sexist
       ○ other (please explain)
    ☐ other (please explain)

36. How many of your teeth are missing?

37. Do you have permanent problems that could have been healed with good dental or health care? (Y/N/M)

    If yes, please describe the permanent problem.

38. If you answered yes to item 12, did you not get the care because

    ☐ you couldn't afford to.
    ☐ you had to spend the money on something else.
    ☐ while you were a child, no one in the family could afford doctors.
    ☐ other (please explain)

39. Do you have a current health problem that could be healed if you had access to good health care? (Y/N/M)

    If yes or maybe, please describe this current health problem.

40. Do you have a job that offers paid sick leave (not vacation)? (Y/N)

    If yes, can you use the sick leave for routine doctors' visits? (Y/N)

41. Is your access to health care affected by your being differently-abled? (Y/N)

    If yes, please explain.

42. Are you paying for the health care of other people or non-human animals? (Y/N)

    If yes . . .
    how many people?
    who are those people (in relation to you)?
    how many
    ___ pets/companions
    ___ guide dogs (seeing-eye or hearing)
    ___ farm animals
    ___ others

43. Do you ever exchange or barter for health care? (Y/N)

    If yes, please describe.

44. Do you "pass," or pretend to have more access to health care than you really have? (Y/N)

    If so, how do you do this?

45. Do you have any type of health insurance? (Y/N)

    If not, please skip to the next section, on Food.

If yes, how do you get your insurance? (Medicare, employer, family, etc.)

46. How much do you pay each month for this insurance?

47. Does your insurance assign you a doctor, without giving you control over which doctor you see for care? (Y/N)

48. Do you have some choice in which doctor you use, but must pick from a list of "approved" doctors? (Y/N)

49. Can you choose any doctor, but only get to spend a certain amount for a given service? (If the doctor charges more than the approved amount, you must pay the difference.) (Y/N)

50. Does your insurance allow you to choose any doctor, and cover expenses at a certain percentage no matter how much the doctor charges? (Y/N)

51. Does your insurance cover "well care"? (Y/N)
    If yes, how much (amount per visit, percentage, etc.) does it cover?

52. Does your insurance cover chiropractors? (Y/N)
    If not, can you obtain this care another way? (Y/N)

53. Does your insurance cover alternative health care? (Y/N)
    If not, can you obtain this care another way? (Y/N)

54. Does your insurance cover everything? (You have no expenses for covered services other than your monthly premiums.) (Y/N)

55. Does your insurance not cover certain health problems? (Y/N)

FOOD

1. Are you usually hungry? (Y/N)

2. Are you frequently hungry? (Y/N)

3. If you answered yes to (1) or (2), why are you hungry?
   - [ ] I don't have any way to get enough food.
   - [ ] Those I love encourage me to diet.
   - [ ] I myself choose to diet.
   - [ ] With limited access to food, I feed others before I feed myself.

☐ Other (please explain)

4. I have enough food to not be hungry, but can't get the kinds of foods or variety necessary to be healthy. (Y/N)

5. I have access to all the food I need to be satisfied and healthy. (Y/N)

6. I grow some of my own food. (Y/N)
   If yes, why?

7. I regularly receive some of my food from gifts. (Y/N)

8. Do you regularly steal food to eat? (Y/N)

9. Do you occasionally steal food to eat? (Y/N)

10. Do you steal food to sell? (Y/N)

11. Do you regularly barter (trade) your services or products for food? (Y/N)

12. Do you use coupons when you buy food? (Y/N)

13. Do you use food stamps to buy food? (Y/N)

14. Do you harvest wild-growing foods to eat? (Y/N)

15. Do you regularly get food from dumpsters or garbage cans to eat? (Y/N)

16. I have regular meals, but no control over what's in them because my food is controlled by: (Fill in the blank.)

17. Do you regularly get meals at soup kitchens? (Y/N)

18. Do you regularly eat in restaurants? (Y/N)
    If yes, why?
    Who pays for it?
    How many times per week?

19. If you could feed some other dykes if you wanted to, please fill out the following.

Number of dykes I could feed	length of time I could feed them
	a few days
	a few weeks
	a few months
	longer (how long?)

20. If you are feeding others, how many people are you feeding not including yourself?

Who are they (relationship to you, not names)?

21. If you needed it, do you know people who would feed you? (Y/N)

    If yes, please fill out the following.

How long would they feed you?	How many people would feed you?	Who would house you? (relationship to you)
a few days		
a few weeks		
a few months		
longer (how long?)		

22. Do you ever throw parties and provide all of the food? (Y/N)

23. Do you ever throw parties and hire a caterer to provide the food? (Y/N)

24. Do you employ someone to cook for you? (Y/N)
    If yes, is this
    - O their entire job (full time)
    - O one of their many duties (you still employ them full time)
    - O a part-time job for them

    Where do you get the money to pay for this?
    - O own money
    - O government
    - O other

25. Do you eat organically grown/natural foods?
    - ☐ always
    - ☐ sometimes
    - ☐ never

    If no, this is because
    - O I don't want to.
    - O I can't afford it.
    - O It's inconvenient.
    - O I don't have access.
    - O other (please explain)

26. Are you vegetarian or vegan? (Y/N)
    If yes, this is because

○ I choose this diet.
○ I cannot afford meat.
○ other (please explain)

27. Do you feed non-human animals? (Y/N)

If yes, do you feed
○ wild animals (birds, squirrels, etc.)
○ your pets/companions
○ guide dog (seeing-eye or hearing)
○ farm animals who provide food and/or labor for you
○ other (please explain)

28. Do you hide the fact that you are hungry from others? (Y/N)

If yes, this is because
○ you don't want others to know you don't have money for food
○ you are a fat sep and don't want those around you to put you down for eating
○ you eat foods that other people find "unacceptable" and don't want to deal with their disapproval
○ with only so much food to go around, you don't want the others who are getting the food to feel bad when they eat it
○ other (please explain)

MONEY

1. What was your total income last year from all sources before taking anything out?

2. How do you get your money? Please list all sources: job, loans, gifts, government, stealing, recycling, interest, investments, etc.

Source of money	How much do you get this way?	How often?

3. Did you file a tax return last year? (Y/N)

4. How many people do you fully support from your income, including you?

   Who are they (relationship to you, not names)?

5. Do you share your income with other people? (Y/N)

   If yes, fill out the following:

Who do you give money to? (their relationship to you)	How much do you give them?	How often do you give it?

6. Have you given money or goods to other people in the past year (not institutions, charities, or organizations)? (Y/N)

   If yes, fill out the following:

Who did you give to? (their relationship to you)	How much did you give them?	How often did you give it?

7. Do others give you money? (Y/N)

   If yes, please fill out the following.

Who gives you money?	How much do you get?	Is this regular (how often) or occasional?

8. Are there things you barter or exchange to get other than food, housing, or health care? (Y/N)

   If yes, what are they?

9. Are there things you get free other than food, housing, or health care? (Y/N)

   If yes, . . .

   what are they?

how do you get them free?

10. How much debt do you have?

_____ mortgage
_____ school loans
_____ credit cards
_____ car loan
_____ gambling debts
_____ other: _____
_____ other: _____

11. Do you expect to inherit money? (Y/N)
    If yes,

How much?	How soon?	From whom?

12. Do you choose not to use all of the access to money that you could? (Y/N)
    If yes, please check all that apply.
    ○ I work part time when I could work full time.
    ○ I have chosen a lower paying career, when I could have taken a higher paying one.
    ○ I have refused inherited or family-offered money.
    ○ I have given away inherited or family-given money.
    ○ I have restricted my career by not "passing" at work.
    ○ I refuse to work overtime.
    ○ other (please explain)

13. Do you pretend to have more or less money than you actually do? (Y/N)
    If so, how?

14. How much money do you have in the following:

_____ IRA
_____ 401K
_____ insurance policies
_____ trust funds
_____ other (please explain)

15. How much money do you have ready access to?
    _____ checking accounts
    _____ savings accounts
    _____ CDs
    _____ stocks/mutual funds
    _____ other (please explain)
16. What is your total equity in real estate?

GENERAL

1. What is your class?
   If this has changed, please explain.
2. You are . . .
   ☐ never het
   ☐ ex-het
3. How long have you self-identified as a lesbian *separatist*?
4. Where do you get your clothing?
   ☐ thrift store
   ☐ mail order
   ☐ borrow
   ☐ hand-me-downs
   ☐ make them
   ☐ hire others to make them
   ☐ buy new at a store
   ☐ steal
   ☐ other (please explain)

   Why do you get them this way?

MONEY AND THE SHAPE OF THINGS

MINNIE BRUCE PRATT

All this fall my lover was getting pushed out of the apartment she'd lived in for ten years. Not because she is a lesbian, not because I would come over to visit and the neighbors would get offended. No, in the District of Columbia there are, for the moment, a few minimal protections against discrimination on the basis of sexual orientation; legally, she could not have been thrown out of her apartment for being queer. But there was no law to protect her from the forces of capitalism at work in the market for property and land. Because of rising property values and taxes, her apartment building was being sold by its owner; rent control would no longer apply to the tenants; and Joan, who could not afford to buy, had to vacate for the new owner.

The neighborhood we lived in had long been a settled, Black, working-class area with only a few white folks, mostly septuagenarians who didn't flee after the uprisings of the 1960s. Lately, however, young white singles and couples, middle-class, white-collar, had begun to perceive the city as "safe" and "interesting," after eight years of restrictive Republican administration. They had begun to move onto Capitol Hill; property values had gone up; owners with limited incomes were struggling to meet tax payments. Suddenly, *For Sale* signs clanked and clanged on every street, new glossy oak doors appeared, and more bars on the windows, lots of fresh paint; the old-fashioned yards were dug up to be replanted in a day with hostas or pampas grass bought at the nursery, like no other plants seen on the block.

Copyright © 1991 by Minnie Bruce Pratt

All fall we worried about how to find another apartment
Joan could afford, with rent as low as hers had been under rent
control, and with room enough for her to live and run her
business in. I would walk back and forth between her place and
my apartment building and look bitterly, enviously, angrily at
the houses along the three blocks. Where I used to examine
people's yards with interest, to investigate whatever new leaf or
bloom had appeared, to appreciate the way brick details on the
old houses shifted into different angles with the changing sun,
now I found that the shape of everything had changed.

The world I walked in was more hollow. Sunlight fell on the
facades of the houses beautifully, and coldly. I was outside; and
inside were the people who were safe, who had money enough
to pay their rent, money enough to buy their houses. A huge
distance spread between me on the sidewalk, and the front of
the houses, and the people inside them, a menacing distance.

Though, of course, not everyone inside *could* pay their rent.
Usually around the second week of the month, after the
late-rent period had expired, I'd be walking or driving around
the neighborhood, and there'd be piles of furniture heaped up
like garbage on the sidewalks. Except the garbage was
someone's laboriously accumulated possessions, all of their
possessions: clothes, furniture, plastic dishes with a rosebud
design, a blue maternity smock, sagging mattresses, a shaky
fake-wood TV cart, a red velour chair. If people were lucky,
when they got back from work or wherever and found their life
spread out on the street, no one had taken anything. If they
were lucky.

But why was I being so upset? I still had my apartment, big
and cheap for the city, protected by rent control, heat included.
At least, I had it for the moment, after the two campaigns we
had fought as tenants to limit (though not eliminate) exorbitant
rent increases. Nevertheless, the sound of money rustled around
us all the time, like steam escaping from our radiators: how
long before the landlord would try again for his profits, the
ones allowed by law? The machine of profits clanked and
turned somewhere constantly in the background.

People were beginning to talk of the District as a city under
siege, because of drugs and resulting violence. But what about
the folks living in the street or shelters like displaced persons
because they couldn't pay their rent? Over the years, whole

neighborhoods had been uprooted and dispersed as part of "development," and the frail ties that had been established so tentatively between people who were not blood kin had been broken. Yet no one was talking about the despair behind the drugs, despair at being caught in the inexorable turning of higher rents, and fixed or no incomes, and no skills to get jobs or higher-paying jobs, and no place to go.

Though I still had my apartment, I realized *I* was feeling like someone who would have nowhere to go if Joan lost hers. I lived in three rooms on the fifth floor, a long way from the ground. But her apartment had a front yard with a huge, sweet-smelling abelia bush just like the one outside my back door at home in Alabama. I'd planted her front yard with daylilies dug up from home, and from a roadside in Georgia—orange, yellow, red. And in her enormous backyard were mulberry trees, hawthorne bushes, a crabapple, a native holly tree; and a shady little garden of coleus and caladiums, with a blue witches' ball on a pedestal, with redbirds, doves, blue jays, and the liquid syllables of wood thrushes, all the bird sounds from home.

When I thought about Joan's moving, I realized myself to be *in* the city in a way I had not before. She had been family only three blocks away, a presence that kept me from being alone in a town where I had no kin, and where no one but her and one other person had known me longer than four years. The yard outside her apartment had been like the dirt of home. When she moved, I wouldn't have a place I could go to dig and plant; I'd have no land, not even a tiny bit of land.

▲ ▲ ▲

Walking back and forth past the yards of others, I thought bitterly that at home I didn't envy people so much. I had less desire for *things* because things mattered less in the country than in the city; I could always go out my door and in five minutes be in the woods; I didn't need to own things, and there weren't these fences every two steps, everything marked off into little squares of ownership.

What I was remembering about home was my sense of freedom in walking after my father through the sweetbay thickets, poplar trees, sweetgums, and magnolias, on the land that he owned. He walked the land with an assurance he lacked in so many other ways; a confidence from his childhood, him walking the land his father owned up by River Bend; the confidence of the landowner, who knows no one can order him off the land. Or, at least the confidence of the white landowner in the South, who has never had someone try to frighten him off his land. I was remembering this, and forgetting that *his* land was fenced.

Now I wonder how much of my bitterness, my envy, walking in the city, was from my expectation that I would be the owner, I would own the land. Instead, I find myself an immigrant in the city, like so many others here, but different from them also: The Black folks from North and South Carolina, Virginia, the folks who came up the coast away from towns where no one would hire them, or there weren't enough jobs, or they would be hired for only the most menial jobs, cleaning white people's houses or stemming tobacco for the women, the sawmill or nothing for the men. The immigrants from Honduras, Guatemala, El Salvador, fleeing from the wars being fought in their homes over whether the land would be redistributed from the plantation owners to those folks who worked for them for starvation wages. The Koreans at the corner store, the Eritreans at the Seven-Eleven, all the other refugees and immigrants fleeing from war, oppression, poverty in their homes, come to "the capital of the free world," to a land made rich from their countries' despair. The people looking for some work, in construction, in a restaurant, maybe opening a store of their own, maybe living in a house no one can throw them out of.

And me coming up from the country, needing to live my life as a lesbian, looking for work where I wouldn't have to hide that life, a real possibility here in the city; for the first time living in a place that was not my land, not the land of my father. Someone else owned this land.

▲ ▲ ▲

Christmas Eve, about three years after I moved to the city, I heard a radio interview with a homeless man living in Lafayette

Park, across from the White House: Benjamin Franklin
Johnson, from Kentucky. Asked how he felt about so many
people walking through where he lived, he said: "At home,
when Bradley was alive—me and Bradley would go hunting.
We'd look and walk and listen, and if a twig snapped, it wasn't
us. Bradley Howard, my blood brother. Me and Bradley could
go in the woods, and Bradley did not talk." Showed a picture
of himself peering out from his plastic shelter, he laughed when
asked if folks at home would recognize him: "Not likely. I look
like I'm looking past things, not like I'm looking two steps
ahead. At home I was an independent person. Here I'm not in
control of my life." Midway through his talking I began to cry,
and cried wildly, inconsolably, for maybe an hour, the tears of
an exile. Yes, at home you could just walk out in the woods;
and in the pastures there were blackberries if you wanted to
dare the copperheads; and someone at home was always trying
to give you their extra squash or corn.

But here you had to have money to get food. In the Safeway,
I had stood looking at apples, and the woman next to me
rummaged in the pears, $1.99 a pound, late in the year. She
was scornful, snorting at the price. "At home," she said, "I
could just go out and pick as many of these as I wanted up off
the ground." The man with her got very still and quiet, and
said, "Yes, but you are not back home *now*."

I cried because, here, money seems like everything. I wasn't
out of control of my life like Mr. Johnson, but I was in the
presence of the inexorable necessity to have money.

Yet I was remembering my past, at home, as if money wasn't
a problem, and that wasn't true, that was not a true memory at
all, but a longing for something that really had never existed, or
had existed only for brief moments, like the afternoons I
walked in the woods behind my father. Yes, there was land, and
there were neighbors and friends, but, in the true memory:

My uncle, who as the only son had inherited the family
farmhouse my mother grew up in, had a garden, but we didn't.
For my father, white skin was not enough to hold onto the
family land, lost in economic crises during the 1920s and
1930s. Perhaps one of the crises, at least, was precipitated by
my grandfather's drinking; there were vague stories that he'd
get drunk and strip and run naked outside, going too far even
in a town where alcoholism was accepted as a fact of life, too

far even for someone who, like him, was probate judge of the county. (And how much did his drinking have to do with despair at what he was in that job?) He finally lost an election, and his job; perhaps that's when he had to sell the family land.

Another version was that my grandfather was staunchly anti-Klan in the 1920s when the Democratic party machinery was run by pro-Klan forces; that he refused to prosecute Black men who used guns to defend their land, houses, and families against white terrorists at the time; that he actually registered some Black men to vote. Perhaps he lost his job and the family land because of his skin, his disloyalty to white skin. In any case, my father spent his adult life traveling, living in cities, and in my home town, tiny, not like the city I live in now, but, nevertheless, a town where he yearned for the land, the country; and felt out of control of his life; and drank. He hated being an alcoholic. His drinking made him improvident and careless with money; he missed weeks of work often during my childhood; and probably kept his job because he was a white man from a good family, and what else could they do with him?

My mother worked all the time, all the time, during the day as a social worker, at night and on weekends with canning and cooking and sewing and knitting my clothes. She made all my clothes herself, because, I always assumed, that was the least expensive way to dress me. I worried, underneath, about money constantly. I can remember thinking, after Christmas Day one year, that my mother had spent too much money on presents for me, an only child, small presents of a few books, a doll, and some clothes.

I worried about money, yet I knew how secure we were compared to most others in the town, and out in the countryside; I saw the houses that poor white and Black folk lived in, when I drove my mother in the summer to see her clients. We had a bathroom, running water, a gas floor heater; I had my own room. But ours was a boxy little house with my twelve-foot-by-twelve-foot room at one end of a narrow hall, and at the other, my parents' equally small room. Next to my room was the cramped kitchen, with no door between it and a dining room with seldom-used matching table and chairs and an old upright piano. No door between there and the living room, shabby until after I went off to college and got married; I can remember my mother saving money in a glass jar for years to get a new couch. A very small house, in which every word said in one room could be heard in all the others; a house that, in another region, or in the city, would have been seen as a modest working-class home. But in my town it was a middle-class house, a very nice house, with mostly good furniture, a home that my mother made for us only through incessant work.

But I worried about money. On Sundays I would read the *Birmingham News*, and stare resentfully at the pictures of the debutantes, curled and frilled and white, who, in season, would go to swim parties, dance parties, roller-skating parties. I didn't resent the parties, which seemed to always have the same people at them, the same names mentioned over and over, and the same refreshments, pink-and-green mints and sugary cake. I think I resented those girls because they had all the money they needed; I thought they did not worry about money. And I did say to myself, even then: They are *ahead* of me. I'll never catch up. I'll never get to be easy about money the way these girls are.

A middle-class child anxious about money, with the terror of sliding back somewhere—where was it? A place where you "couldn't take care of yourself." A child with a resentment of the others ahead of her; no matter how hard she worked, she'd never catch up. A child one generation away from the family farm, whose father (so far as I can tell from the perspective of years later) held a job mostly on the strength of family, skin, and charm; whose mother held her job partly because she was a white woman from a respectable family, and partly through great tenacity and competence in her work.

A child whose parents managed enough money to shape her in crucial ways: braces for her buckteeth to make them straight and shining, so she wouldn't look poor and ugly; contact lenses for her terrible near-sightedness, so she'd be an attractive marriageable woman; nice new clothes twice a year, handmade, but at least not from chicken-feed sacks, like the clothes some cousins had to wear some years. And, finally, an education, the best in the state, at the state university. Never a discussion about sending her out of state, despite her exceptional grades; only the wealthiest families did this for their daughters, sent them to Radcliffe or Sweet Briar.

A middle-class child, with her own particular understanding of, and experience of, money, who years later still feels irritated

when a reviewer of her poetry persists in identifying her as
"working-class," presumably because she was from the Deep
South and wrote about dirt and trees. Was the irritation
because of the ignorance of a critic who would not see the
nuances of Southern reality, a reader who could not imagine a
rural small-town middle-class existence, though the poems gave
enough clues—mention of her silver napkin ring on the table,
the fact that a Black woman worked for the family? Or was her
irritation because she was afraid of sliding back, afraid her
poetry hadn't gotten her far enough up and out, away from her
precarious existence in that town?

A middle-class child angry and resentful about the
impossibility of catching up, who, as an adult, becomes angry
when another writer, also from the South, implies that their
lives have been quite similar. The child's rage because she
knows this woman was raised in a family where the mother
had "culture," the father a professional job, parents who read
and talked about ideas, a mother (she thought) who did not
have to sit at the sewing machine all night, a father who didn't
sit drunk watching the Friday night boxing matches. The rage
of the child knowing she'll never catch up to this woman who
started ahead of her.

Her rage at the way that money and the insecurities of class
position make her life into a place where she will always be
running to keep from losing ground, like some hidden treadmill
in an old Hollywood movie. Or like the assembly line she
worked on one summer in high school, earning money for
college, trapped on the line putting grippers on children's
sportswear, doing the same motions over and over, day after
day, working frantically so the garments wouldn't pile up by
her, so they would move smoothly down the line to the other
women. She swore then she'd never do that kind of work
again; that's why she was going to college.

The middle-class child who doesn't understand that no
matter what kind of work she ends up doing she will still be
caught in the flow of money in this country, in the world;
caught in the process of how money is made, and how money
is spent. The child who wants to be a professional somebody,
not a worker. The child who early has a huge rage for those
ahead of her. She imagines that they will become secure, will be
able to stop working to sit down by the pool sipping lemonade

while she still steps repetitively on the treadmill, the assembly line, the line that she, at the same time, denies she is part of.

As for the people behind her, the ones she sees working, working, but who have less than she does, for these she is allowed to feel pity. From her mother, and from her Christian religion, she has learned to have sympathetic feelings for those "less fortunate," and not judge a person's value by whether or not they have money. She is taught clearly: Money corrupts; it is not possible to be a good person with a lot of money; how you act is what determines goodness, not how much money you have. She is not allowed to despise those with less money than she, but she can feel sorry for them.

But if she feels sorry for them, that must mean she is better off, better *than* them in some way. Perhaps she thinks they suffer more than she does; there *is* a suffering that comes with no money; she's seen that clearly enough through her mother's eyes, and her mother's work. Perhaps she allows the people an existence only as poor suffering people, somewhere behind her, so that then she can continue to feel she is better, better off than them, better off than *somebody*.

She doesn't consider the contradiction between being taught to respect someone if they have no money, and being taught to feel sorry for them if they have no money, until many years later, after her girlhood. Nor does she, then, want to think of how, somewhere, there are people who think they are better than *she* is, better off, and that they, from their distance, sit pitying her. Yet, for years, whenever she travels outside her home, she dreads to meet, and prepares to meet, those people. She has no way of talking about the huge reservoir of fear, anger, resentment, dread, false pity, and guilt that she carries about money and people.

▲ ▲ ▲

This was the child I was growing up in the South just after the Great Depression and World War II, a South in which the Depression still existed. A child growing up less than ten years after Southern tenant farmers, Black and white, met to organize a radical union to protect themselves from farm mechanization, especially the cotton-picking machine, whose introduction threatened to wipe out even such a precarious hand-to-mouth living as they then led; there was a militant branch of the Southern Tenant Farmers Union in Tallapoosa County, three counties east of where I lived.* The principles of the union included land for the landless, full and decent employment, the holding in common of all natural resources and all scientific processes, and the liberation of all workers from enslavement to the machine.**

While the tenant farmers' organizing was being broken up by threats, physical violence, and lynchings arranged by the large landowners, the steel companies in Birmingham were forming a committee to keep labor organizers out of the mills. The owners had the organizers, many of whom were young men connected to the Communist party, beaten up, or arrested and held incommunicado in jail.*** When the mills closed during the Depression, Tennessee Coal and Iron allowed workers to stay in the company houses, but shut off the electricity, water and heat; Republic Steel drove people from the houses with armed guards and posted men to shoot people if they came back to their homes. Many folks began to live in the coke ovens, the brick beehive-shaped ovens where coal was turned into coke for smelting iron ore into steel. To get out of the rain and cold, people began living in the ovens like caves.****

When the cotton-picking machine was put into mass production by the Rust family of Memphis, and World War II started, and the steel mills went back into production, another migration of workers from the land to the city began, one of many such in the history of the U.S.+ Sometimes the migratory shift was huge, sometimes slight, like the one that happened in

---

    *   See Theodore Rosengarten's *All God's Dangers: The Life of Nate Shaw* (New York: Knopf, 1974).

  **   Anthony P. Dunbar, *Against the Grain: Southern Radicals and Prophets 1929-1959* (Charlottesville: University of Virginia Press, 1981).

***   Virginia Durr, *Outside the Magic Circle* (New York: Simon and Schuster, 1985), p. 110.

****   Durr, p. 79.

   +   W.J. Cash, *The Mind of the South* (New York: Vintage/Random House, 1941), p. 422.

my home county. The women who were working as housewives on farms that were five-to-ten miles outside my town—women used to working in the family garden, canning, sewing the family clothes, keeping chickens—became women working in the garment plant, clocking in and out every day, and at the end of the week being handed, for the first time in their lives, a pay envelope.

This particular shift came to my town in the 1950s when the garment plant, run by some people from up North, got built. At the time I thought they were locating in Centreville because it was such a nice place, a good location, and we were a pleasant people. I thought, really, that they were doing it for us, as an opportunity. Later I figured out it was a runaway factory from the North, brought down South where the owners could pay lower wages. I don't know what happened to the people who had worked in the plant before it came to our town, whether they lost their houses when they had no jobs, whether they ended up with nowhere to live.

When I worked at the garment plant, I was saving money for my college education, and I'm not sure I would have let myself care about those people if I had known. Because I needed the money: if I worked eight hours a day, five days a week on the assembly line, I could earn about $60 a week, $700 in a summer of work, a large part of my year's tuition.

To get a job in the plant, we had to pass a dexterity text, which was held in the county courthouse. Tables were set up in the courtroom itself, on the platform where the judge and jury usually sat. The day I took a test a Black woman was also taking it, an occurrence explicable only by the fact that the owners were from up North, since everything in my town was segregated—water fountains, schools, doctor's and dentist's waiting rooms, everything. We both worked away at putting pegs into holes, and I never thought about why we were taking this test watched by three white men in the courtroom; never thought about whether the site of the test had been chosen deliberately to intimidate Black women from coming to take the test; or whether this arrangement had been demanded by the white businessmen of the town in some compromise with the Northern owners, who, for reasons of their own, probably not having much to do with civil rights and more to do with keeping wages low, wanted to be sure they could hire Black women as well as white.

Both the Black woman and I were hired; we were part of two new assembly lines of women who had never done factory work before. We were very slow. Whenever the plants ran out of work, middle of the summer, one of the two new lines would get laid off. However, I don't remember being laid off myself; I'd get sent to work in the warehouse until my line got called back. I think management tried to keep the few college-bound kids working, since we were the children of the middle-class men who'd arranged for the plant to come to town. The women I worked with grumbled about the plant, yet were glad of the money, since the other jobs for women in town were white-collar: social worker, teacher, clerk at the shoestore or drugstore. When they got laid off, the women would stalk down the aisles between the lint-covered machines, through the air acrid with the smell of dyed cloth; the women would march toward the door, saying loudly they were going down to the unemployment office *right away*, going to go down to apply for their "pennies."

▲ ▲ ▲

The first time I lined up for unemployment was the day after I slept with my first woman lover. I was married and had no job, though I'd been trying to get one. After I told my husband that I was going ahead with my love affair, it became clear I'd better arrange to have some money of my own coming in, somehow. Since I wasn't doing the job of being his wife satisfactorily, I couldn't count on his money.

I didn't quite have my Ph.D. then; I had to finish writing my dissertation. But I had had years of graduate classes and was certainly qualified to teach at college level. This was the education that was supposed to make me independent, the education that was supposed to be the equivalent of having land of my own, something valuable and permanent to draw an income from, and, unlike land, something that would be mobile, flexible, something I could travel with, useful for a woman in the modern world.

But married, with two children and a husband when I began my life as a lesbian, I had not yet been able to get a university job. Not even after two years with scores of letters and resumés sent out, after interviews at several professional conferences with male interviewers asking me who would take care of my children, and staring at my legs, and admiring my pleasant voice, just what they needed around the department. Even though by then I had learned some feminist analysis from women in my graduate school who were involved with women's liberation, at the end of the two years I believed that I couldn't get a teaching job because something was wrong with me: I was being lazy and procrastinating too much about sending my letters out; I didn't have a good enough job interview, or have a good enough resumé; I wasn't working hard enough to finish my dissertation; if I had it finished, I would certainly get a job (but meanwhile, my male peers were being hired without having finished their degrees); I wasn't being aggressive enough about pursuing opportunities (but none of the professors in my field, all men, referred me to their connections at other schools).

Now it seems obvious: I simply wasn't acceptable in the upper ranks of teaching, a woman with two children in such apparent control of her husband that he intended to follow her to her new job. I was not the kind of woman to admit into the upper academic bracket, the place reserved for themselves by men who imagined that they had stepped out of the production line, and were standing on the side, observing and commenting ironically, amusedly, on the striving world, while others did the dirty work. College was the place for *ideas*, which they developed individually, gracefully, the beautiful golden apples of thought, grown in their secluded garden. Women didn't belong in the grove; women belonged somewhere else, at home doing the laundry, or at the lower levels, in the schools with the children, or with the lesser minds of junior colleges.

That was fifteen years ago, but when I was reading through my journals of that time in order to write this essay, only a few days ago, I realized: I was *not* the one who was wrong; I could not have worked harder; I was not lazy. I was denied work because I was a woman. The realization has taken me this long because, with some part of me, I still must have believed that ideas weren't like other kinds of work; that eventually the men would acknowledge and admit me because of my *mind*; that my education would make me independent of the fact that I was a woman. I must have believed that people with ability *always* get hired in this country to the job they deserve, and if we don't, why it must be our fault: we must be lazy and unqualified, just like all the people without jobs. I didn't get hired, therefore I believed that I was inferior.

I had not connected my life to the lives of the women I observed the summer I worked on the line: Only men were allowed at the cutting table, slashing out the patterns through brilliant thick layers of cloth, cutting out a hundred, a thousand shapes, the inalterable pieces that we women sewed into finished form, each woman performing one tiny isolated task, over and over. Women were never hired onto the cutting table, nor men onto the line, and, of course, the men were paid much more for their dangerous, important work, the making of the shapes. (But the men at the cutting table, white working-class men, did not decide or design the patterns they spent their days following. Others, higher, unseen, more distant, made those shapes.)

▲ ▲ ▲

The job I finally got, the one that enabled me to leave my husband and be financially independent, was at a historically Black four-year college. I was hired by a woman, the head of the English Department, who asked not a single question about my personal life. It was no accident that I was hired by this school, an institution that was part of a long tradition of Black families educating their daughters best as they could, in order to qualify them for jobs that would get them out of domestic positions in white households, or factory positions under white bosses. Dr. Elaine Newsome did not seem to think that there was a *thing* peculiar about my being a woman who needed to earn her own living.

But she wasn't in a position to promote me; in the end I suppose I was lucky to keep my job at all. When I came back in the fall of the fourth year I taught at the school, another English teacher gossiped to me that all the Black lesbians on campus, some at the very highest positions in the school administration, had been fired or demoted. I was already in the lowest teaching position that I could be; I was not fired, perhaps because I was white, since I certainly had been outspoken about my feminism, and my students had hinted that they knew I was a lesbian. I had not spoken about this to my colleagues, nor did I know as lesbians any of the women who were named; we were all hidden from each other, trying to survive.

The college was dependent on the state university system of North Carolina for money; on good relations with the hierarchy of the nearby military base to get nonscholarship white students; and on acceptance by the white businessmen in the area, one of the most conservative in the state, in order to place its students in jobs. The mostly Black men in the administration, struggling for the survival of the school, perhaps thought that they could not afford to have too many women in positions of power, especially women who weren't attached to any men, women who allied themselves with other women; these women could not be trusted at a high level with shaping the plan for the students, for the school. Always there was immense pressure coming down from the white authorities above to run the university like a cost-effective assembly line; or like a plantation, by growing ideas of only one kind, in orderly, endless rows, like cotton; pressure to produce students from our classes year in and out, in huge numbers, prolifically, like women producing babies.

Just the other day I got a flyer from the school; I saw that the white man who was hired after me, and promoted the year that I finished my degree but did *not* get promoted, is now head of the English Department. Once, when we were at our desks in the English faculty office, he spoke to me about the baby he and his wife were expecting. She would stay at home with the child, he said to me, and added violently: "She'll stay at home, not like the women *here* who just drop their children, and get up again and go back to work, like animals." He is now chair of the department, but, so far as I know, none of the Black lesbians I taught with are still employed by that school.

▲ ▲ ▲

I've been sitting up in the attic that's now my work place, doing my taxes this week. Since I moved to Washington and began to work as a lesbian and a writer, I've patched together an income from part-time teaching in women's studies, creative writing residencies, lecture fees and poetry readings, royalties, money back from my income taxes. I haven't stepped outside the economic system or off the line, but sometimes I feel like I'm hiding out in crevices and chinks in the system, the way raccoons and possums live in the middle of the city and no one ever knows or sees them.

This year my income was three thousand dollars over the official poverty line—or at least according to the D.C. government I'm in the bracket of the almost-poor. But I am not poor, I don't feel poor, and I certainly do not live in poverty in relation to poor folks who live in the District. I have a car, a Ph.D., middle-class skills, and arrangements for work that give me time to travel, meet people, do my own writing.

Partly I don't feel poor because I'm teaching some classes right now and know where my money will come from. When I have money in the bank it's easy to forget when I was so worried about my finances that I would spend only the change I had in the house on daily errands. It's easy to forget how I stood at the Seven-Eleven laboriously counting out pennies for a loaf of bread. But with just a little money in the bank, I recover my confidence quickly. I still carry the middle-class child around with me, the child who has never been hungry a day in her life, who knows she can still turn to her mother for help, the child who is the adult who glimpses, and then forgets, the stark fact of money and need for survival in the world.

Partly I don't feel even close to poor right now because of the house I'm living in, with Joan, a huge house with an attic for me, a basement for Joan's darkroom, a ground floor for her office space, a big kitchen and a back porch, a second floor with living space for us and for company. An enormous house, twice, maybe three times as big as the house I grew up in. The rent is low for its size, but we could never manage it individually. We're able to be here by sharing the rent, and because the man and woman who own it, a Black couple perhaps only a little older than we are, wanted tenants who would keep the yard up. When the landlord interviewed us, I knew the names of the bushes and shrubs the woman before us had planted, snow-on-the-mountain, crown-of-thorns, rose of Sharon. This, and the fact the owners were happy that we were not a couple with several children and many pets, got us the house.

Before we moved in, I worked three days transplanting bulbs and plants from Joan's yard, shifting the round yellow rocks that marked the flowerbed borders in the new yard, weeding, mulching, twelve-hour days for three days. At the end of the third day, my neighbor, Miz Harris, came out of her back door, beckoned me over, introduced herself. An African-American woman in her eighties, a hairdresser for years, she now gives a home in her big house to teenaged boys and young men who need a place to live. She looked at me, filthy with dirt, hands too muddy to shake hers, and nodded approvingly, and said, "You work hard. I like that," waving me through some test that I hadn't even known I was taking. She and most of the others on the block are working folk who own their houses; she approved when she sees me, a renter and a white person, on her knees, cleaning up the yard of a house I don't even own, a house, in fact, owned by Black people. Miz Harris' house and the one we're renting are as big as the nicest old homes where I grew up, but only white people lived in those houses.

A few days ago, Mr. Keyes, found for me by Miz Harris, came with his Rototiller and turned a patch of dirt at the back of the yard so we could plant tomatoes, squash, okra, beans. He was old enough to be my father, at least, and alternated between calling me *ma'm* and *baby*, sliding me back and forth between being a white woman, and being in the same affectionate category of young person as his grandbaby who had come to help him rake. A Black man who owns an acre and a half of ground somewhere in the District, he told me that morning he'd planted three rows of peas, in rows as long as "from here to that light pole over there." I was comforted by his presence, made at home by him calling me *baby*, and by the fact I'd be able to grow food in my backyard.

Today, looking out at the crabapple tree in rosy bloom— maybe there will be apples for jelly later—I think how being poor is about having possibility closed off to you; and how easy it is to forget this when one has the land or the money or the right clothes or the bus/train/plane fare in hand, or a high school or college diploma. How easy it is to forget that someone without those things cannot *choose* what someone else who has these things can. How glibly I have heard my students and other people say that women not like them could just choose to live differently; they imply that if "those women" don't so choose, why they must just be lazy, not willing to make an effort, something must be wrong with *them*.

The only reason that I can now choose to piece together my financially precarious but deeply satisfying way of making a living is because many women, those in the women's liberation movement, the civil rights movement, the gay and lesbian liberation movement, have made places within the economic system where I can do my work and be paid for it. I can work because folks established women's studies programs, first outside, then inside the universities and colleges; student groups put together cultural programs about women's and lesbian issues; women began feminist and lesbian publishing houses, magazines, newspapers; women started women's bookstores and traveling libraries that operated out of the trunk of someone's car; women in small communities formed production companies to bring visiting artists to town.

Because of their work, I now have a choice. I do not have to kill my feelings and go to work every day to produce some thing or some idea that has no meaning for me. Unlike so many of my students and my friends, I do not have to leave the land of myself, my lesbian self, my woman self, in order to do my work. I do not have to pretend to be someone not myself, to assimilate or disguise myself. Though sometimes I go into hostile places, I at least can do so as myself and survive.

But this place where I work and live, how different is it from the life of the academic men, deluded in thinking they were out of the way of the assembly line of the world? I think of the classes I am teaching in women's studies this semester, how the academic program for women is entrenched in the class hierarchy of the university. There is the salary difference between full-time tenure-track staff and part-time lecturers who may teach as many classes as full-time people for a tenth the money. There are the differences in space allocation, with full-time but lower-level workers placed in cubicles, and higher-ups, who may come in two or three days a week, occupying offices with doors that close. There are the attitudes about who is doing important work and who is not, about whose work can be interrupted at any time and whose cannot; assumptions about what kind of language is acceptable as intellectual and appropriate and what is not; about what should be taught in academic courses and what material isn't really literature or theory worth taking seriously. I ask myself as I work and teach, am I merely making a place to be complacent, thinking I've gotten off the assembly line? Or am I doing work to try to change the shape of things?

▲ ▲ ▲

When Joan and I moved into this house, we hired a moving company, which sent three men and a supervisor, a foreman, all Black men. The men labored for twelve hours, loading, unloading, up and down the elevator, and then up and down two flights of stairs, boxes, tables, the TV on their backs, repetitively, over and over, without a pause, except briefly for the supper that we brought in. I cringed with discomfort, with shame, as I watched them, which I had to, in order to direct where boxes and furniture went.

I could hardly bear to look at them. I remembered photographs of white men, bosses, overseers, or owners, sitting on their horses in the field, watching Black people work. I remembered my great-aunt, in her eighties, calling in the Black man who oversaw her dwindling farm, a short, stocky, very Black man of great dignity and presence, a laborer all his life; my great-aunt's daughter, who said she valued him, who said she felt affection for him, would laugh and call him her Short-Man, Shortie, calling him into their sitting room to account for work on their land, year after year.

I've known intellectually for a while that the world economy rests on the backs of people of color; but until the day we moved I had not had to watch that work up close in a long time, and perhaps never for so many hours at a time. I calculated: even if the company was paying the men $10 an hour (which was highly unlikely), they couldn't be making more than $120 for the day; even with the tip of $50 apiece which the foreman had made clear was expected, and which we paid, they wouldn't go away from this long day of literally back-breaking labor with more than about $170 each. On the day we moved in I had a letter waiting from a magazine, accepting a poem of mine with the payment of $150, by far the most money I'd ever been paid for a poem, a very little poem, fourteen lines, $10 a line; I'm not sure if I worked on it as long as twelve hours.

At the end of the day, when I paid the foreman the company fee and the men's tips, and he made out the receipt, I could see he could hardly write. He'd been a mover for seven years, since he got out of the Army, and was so skillful at his trade that he had walked through our houses in the morning and predicted down to the half-hour how long it would take to move us out and into a house he'd never even seen, only heard described. But he said he didn't want to do this his whole life; he hoped his luck would change. I paid him and said goodbye; the men were tired, exhausted, irritably urging him to come on and go home, their muscles tightening up and getting sore already from the day's work.

I kept thinking about how much money the company made that day, how much we'd paid, how little the men got, how I wanted to be paying *them* more money, which I had only because my mother had sent me money. And no matter how large my tip had been, I alone would never have been able to give enough, the money alone would not have been enough, because they still would have had to get up the next day and bend their backs to the same labor.

▲ ▲ ▲

A couple of weeks ago Joan and I took a weekend vacation, just the two of us for the first time in a year and a half. We drove down to the beach where it rained and rained, and ended up on Friday night, inside, playing bingo at the Chincoteague Fire Department. Across from us were four women, white women who reminded me of the women I'd worked with at the garment plant. There were very friendly and explained the arcane language of bingo to us: what a postage-stamp game was, a crazy seven, a diamond game, a blackout. They laughed and rattled their big magic markers like dice, daubing neon purple, red, blue spots on the numbers in their green paper squares. Only one of them won, and at the end of the night we saw that she divided up her cash between herself and the other three. One of the women, seemingly the oldest, said that they were sisters, at least, three of them were, and the fourth one, that one that had won, who was younger and more blonde, well, she was a neighbor and an honorary sister. The two oldest worked at the bike rental place, a tiny, cramped wood lean-to next to the pizza place on the boulevard. They came every other Friday, all together, to bingo; and they always split their winnings, no matter how little or how much they won, no matter what their luck. They always shared, the oldest one said smiling, as the youngest parceled out the eight dollars she'd won among the other women.

What do we have yet to learn about sharing our money? How do we figure out the way to do more than share our windfall, the rare winnings? How do we do more than sit and wait for people's luck to change? And how do we learn to change the shape of things so that money is not what determines how people live, or if they die, or whether we live our life out bent to someone else's use, instead of in meaningful work and in joy?

WHITE PROMOTION, BLACK SURVIVAL

GLORIA I. JOSEPH

White skin is to racism,
As the penis is to sexism,
As class, profit, and corruption are to capitalism.

Three women are standing before a covered mirror. At a given signal the cover will be removed and the following question will be put to them:

Mirror, mirror, on the wall,
what is the greatest oppressor of us all?

The mirror is unveiled and all three see their reflections bouncing back.

Woman number one sees her Blackness. "It is my Blackness that is most dominant. That is what makes for my oppression. And who oppresses Blacks? Whites. So it is White racism that is the greatest oppressor. Yes, racism oppresses!" So thinks woman number one.

Women number two says, "I see myself as female, and as such, dominated and controlled by men. Men and their sexism oppress women, so sexism is the greatest oppressor of us all."

Woman number three observes her reflection and sees her gender, race, and class. "My femaleness, my color, and my class are sources of exploitation. Who is exploiting me? The question deserves serious consideration. An immediate response will not do."

The mirror reflects images, but cannot show the experiences which have shaped the perceptions of these three women. The

Copyright © 1994 by Gloria I. Joseph

49

racism, classism, and sexism associated with each woman's experience of being Black and female in the United States are the critical measurements of their oppression.

Many factors contribute to the institutionalization of racism, classism, and sexism. These include what kinds of work are available and to whom the wages are paid; the meaning of volunteer labor; assumptions about the family; mutual dependence in marriage; access to education; images of women and men, Blacks and Whites, in the media; availability of health care; the distribution of wealth; laws and law enforcement. All of these and much more define how privilege, exploitation, and powerlessness are distributed among women and men, Blacks and Whites. Underlying all of this is the profit motive, which perpetuates racism, sexism, and classism.

The debate about whether race or sex is the major source of oppression has separated Black and White women in both current and past liberation struggles. The analogy that leads off this article indicates that both White skin and the penis, as "biological determinants," are false measures of superiority and, like most false things, are maintained and supported by systems that are corrupt, unjust, and fused with ignorance and prejudice. Women, all women, must look for the root causes of their oppressions. As a first step, they must take a good look at themselves and discover where their present attitudes came from, as well as where they now stand on certain issues. Then, and only then, can they begin to make a concentrated and effective effort toward change.

Who Said
It Was Simple

There are so many roots to the tree of anger
that sometimes the branches shatter
before they fall

Sitting in Nedicks
the women rally before they march
discussing the problematic girls
they hire to make them free

An almost white counterman passes a waiting brother
    to serve them first
and the ladies neither notice nor reject
the slighter pleasures of their slavery.
But I who am bound by my mirrors
as well as my bed
see causes in color
as well as sex

and sit here wondering
which me will survive
all these liberations.

—*Audre Lorde*

In 1981, *Common Differences: Conflicts in Black and White
Feminist Perspectives* by Gloria I. Joseph and Jill Lewis was
published. It was an unprecedented and unparalleled
examination and analysis of an alarming schism in the Women's
Movement: *the differences between Black and White women's
perceptions, attitudes, and concerns on key issues.* The authors,
speaking from their Black and White perspectives, expressed the
cultures and histories out of which grew the political
differences. In the opening chapter, coauthor Gloria I. Joseph
examined the different attitudes and responses expressed by
Black women concerning their ideas about the women's
liberation movement. A nationwide questionnaire was
administered to Black women who represent varied historical
and social experiences. One of the questions asked was
"How would you define the women's movement in the
United States today?" A representative sampling of their
responses in 1981 follows.

JANET : *age 42, three children, married, born and raised in the
Southeast, college professor, upper middle-income level.* "It
seems to me that we can see a general awakening or sensitivity
to the issues of women's inequality—ranging all the way from
the Madison Avenue corporate world's hustle of one more
genuine people's concern, to various expressions of political
activism. But I'm not sure there is a women's movement in the
sense of a sustained, organized, and in some sense mass-based

program directed toward gender equality. What we clearly have
are many groups, factions, interests, ideological persuasions
regarding the woman question. Which is the women's
movement, or are they all: equal rights advocates, National
Organization for Women members, militant separatists,
lesbians, Coalition of Labor Union Women, Women for Racial
and Economic Equality, National Council of Negro Women?"

DOROTHY : *age 27, no children, unmarried, lesbian, raised in
the Midwest, college teacher, income $12,000.* "The White
women's liberation movement is basically middle class. Very
few of these women suffer from the extreme economic
exploitation that most Third World women are subject to
day-to-day. The economic and political and social realities of
the Third World woman's life are not an intellectual
persecution. It is not a psychological outburst. It is tangible,
present in every endeavor we choose to undertake. The
problems are realities of day-to-day living which affect the
well-being of all Third World people. A common bond cannot
exist between White women and Third World women if there is
no realization on the part of the White groups that they are
fighting racism and capitalism. The realization must come that
their condition stems from a debilitating economic and social
system and not from the exploitation of their bodies. There is
no logical comparison between the oppression of Third World
women on welfare and the suppression of the suburban wife
and her protest about housework. This is exemplified in the
situation of the welfare mother who does not know where the
next meal is coming from and the suburbanite who complains
about preparing and serving meals."

HULDA : *age 24, no children, single, college graduate,
temporarily unemployed, part-time waitress, born and raised in
Washington, D.C., low income bracket.* "I see the women's
movement in the United States today as a struggle for (1)
self-identity, (2) uplift in social strata, and (3) a unification of
females to fight and ultimately change the sexist and racist laws
that run this country. As a member of NOW, I feel that Black
women should be an active part of a movement that is fighting
for women's rights. Who else is doing that for us?"

BARBARA : *age 37, no children, married, divorced, born and raised in the Midwest, income $15,000, professional counselor.* "I see it as cyclical in the sense that almost 100 years ago the women's suffrage movement was started. Now, let's see, about this women's movement, as a Black woman I don't know which issue comes first. Third World women view the feminist movement with suspicion and mistrust because it is primarily a White women's effort. The feminist issues are not relevant to the needs of Third World people in general or Third World women in particular. Feminist issues revolve around sexism and it's a laudable cause. However, they do not confront the effects that racism or economic exploitation have on the Third World communities throughout the world. As a Black woman who is concerned with the impact of the feminist movement in American society, it is obvious to me that feminists have not analyzed any of the historic conditions of Black people or Black women and consequently have ignored a genuine ally in terms of the struggle for equality in all walks of life. Black women, on the whole, recognize that Black men are not as 'sensitive' to the needs of Black women and their quest for justice or their fight against discrimination. However, we are cognizant of the 'divisive' tactics which alienate Black people from the continuous struggle against our existence, and that includes the feminist movement. Black women perceive that the feminist will want to alienate themselves from men, and Black women will not participate in that effort."

KATE : *age 19, single, no children, first-year community college student, working-class parents, born and raised in suburb of New York City.* "I don't want no part of those women libbers. I don't know what they're about and neither do they."

ANN : *age 45, eleven children, separated, born and raised in Mississippi, income minimal, low socioeconomic level.* "They just a bunch a women that don't know what they want. One while it's this and the next it's that. It's a whole lot of gibberish about nothing. If they so tired of staying at home, let them change places with me for a while and see how tired they get."

MARY : *age 25, high school graduate, working as a cleaning (domestic) aide in Washington, D.C., income poverty level.* "I know nothin about the women's movement."

CARRIE : *age 65, no children, married twice, living with husband, born in Janica, West Indies, raised in the Bronx, income $9,000.* "Women's liberation? Not for me! A women should get equal pay if she is equally qualified as a man, but a woman is supposed to be a woman. She must not let herself be pushed around, but she must be feminine. Where most colored people are concerned, it should be fifty-fifty. Both have to share the responsibility equally. They both have to go out there and do the do. These women liberationists just want to get in the same position as men so they can do the same incorrect things like men. It's wrong for Black women to get in the women's movement. A relationship will only work if there is care and trust."

EVELYN : *age 53, divorced, seven children (one adopted), husband deceased, worked as domestic, waitress, shipyard worker, cigar-factory worker, postal clerk, born and raised in the South, lower income bracket.* "I'm old-fashioned enough to want a man to carry my heavy load and open doors, but a woman should have control over her own body. I couldn't even get a diaphragm without my husband's consent. I like the way women are demanding more for their bodies and for better jobs. The man has nothing to do but listen. Things will change."

Those verbatim responses struck a familiar chord in the orchestra of Black expression. An analysis of the responses showed several distinctive categories. Overall it clearly showed that Black women—from all strata of life—considered the movement to be one that was defined by White women and one that gave little or no recognition to the cultural and historical realities of Black women's lives. To many women the feelings of exclusion, coupled with the dissatisfaction and disillusionment that they held for the movement, relegated it to a nonentity. It simply did not exist as far as they were concerned.

The meaning of feminism and how sexuality is expressed and appreciated became a clarion call of cultural differences between Black and White women. It was in this area that ignorance on the part of both Black and White women about one another's cultural differences made its most distinctive mark. The responses indicated that many Black women felt that the liberation movement was designed to separate them from their Black men. The collective consciousness of Blacks and the socialization process that Black girls/women experience differs profoundly from that of Whites. The history of slavery and its effects on the sexual socialization of Black males and females must be taken into account in any sexual liberation theory. The women's liberation movement did not do this.

It is critical to observe the contradiction that exists in the words of the Black women with regard to their simultaneous "rejection and acceptance" of feminism. Carrie's comments clearly expressed this confusion. She flatly rejects the movement. "Women's liberation? Not for me!" In the same breath, she gives recognition and acceptance to basic tenets and principles of feminist theory. This particular phenomenon repeated itself through the analysis of the questionnaire. The Black women did not espouse feminism—many of them outright rejected it—but they govern themselves, family, and friends very much in accordance with the goals of feminism.

In particular, the Black women recognized the economic exploitation of themselves and of Third World communities. Dorothy explicitly states that very few of the middle-class White women suffer from the extreme economic exploitation that most Third World women are subject to on a daily basis. When Ann says that if White middle-class women are "so tired of staying home," let them change places with her, she is referring to the laborious, monotonous, low-paying, backbreaking, menial labor to which she and her Southern sisters are subject. Those jobs include plucking chickens, janitorial work, and assembly-line work in pickle factories and slaughterhouses.

The exploitation of Third World communities is particularly evident in the garment and electronics industries. American manufacturers import the raw materials and export products virtually exempt from tariffs and other trade restrictions. Within the free-trade zones, they can pack up and disappear

overnight, moving from Mississippi to the Phillipines, if
threatened by strikes or other labor unrest. Women between
the ages of 16 and 25 bear the brunt of this type of
exploitation. They are first to be hired because employers
see them as vulnerable in the sense that they have limited
education, are usually passive, and are not politically astute
to the ways of big business.*

Carrie speaks of equal pay for equally qualified persons
regardless of race or sex. She also speaks about relationships
between Black men and women being based on care, on trust,
and on a fifty-fifty basis. What has not been openly discussed
in feminist literature is the fact that the inequality of African-
American life is conflated with Black men's inequality. A crucial
determinant of Black life today is not simply Black men's
marginalization from work but the social transformation of
Black women's labor. However, Black male joblessness alone
does not account for the tremendous disadvantage of the Black
poor. Race/gender segmentation and low wages as reflected in
the positioning of African-American women are conceptually
central to African-American class inequality today. Women's
work in the USA is gender/race-divided . Disproportionate
numbers of Black women are at the bottom of this division
of labor.**

One of the consequences of economic restructuring in the
USA is that about two thirds of all working persons are
engaged in services. A good number of these are
African-American women performing work as nurses' aides,
old-age assistants and in fast food outlets and cafeterias. Highly
skilled labor is largely technical labor and unskilled labor is
largely manual and clerical labor. In most places in the USA,
both Black and White women do the same work, but Black
women are more likely to be paid less, unemployed, and
supervised; and White women are more likely to do the
supervising.*

---

* See Rose M. Brewer, "Theorizing Race, Class, and Gender," in
  *Theorizing Black Feminisims: The Visionary Pragmatism of Black
  Women*, Stanlie M. James and Abena P.A. Busia, Eds., pp. 13-27.
  London and New York: Routledge, 1993.
** Ibid.

Despite the lact of acceptance of the (White) women's liberation movement, all respondent's criticisms, acceptances, qualifications, rejections, and/or dismissals were systematically related directly to the women's movement. Therein lies the major difference between the 1981 and the 1994 responses!

Thirteen years later, the sexual, racial, political, and economic climates worldwide have had a tremendous effect on the personal/political lives of all people. An attempt to update the chapter, "White Promotion/Black Survival," provided a clear indication of how social movements have been affected by the national and international political upheavals. It was not possible to simply modify or analyze the new data through the 1981 lens. In order to determine the extent of changes in Black women's attitudes toward the women's movement, the same lead question, "How would you define the women's movement in the United States today?" was asked. Some of the original respondants (the first five, Janet, Dorothy, Hulda, Barbara, and Kate) were located, and new ones (Crystal, Toni, Irma, and Pam) closely matching the backgrounds of the original respondents were included. Verbatim responses to the 1994 questionnaire follow.

JANET: *age 55, tenured college professor.* "I would describe the women's movement today as global, more dispersed, more multidimensional, less dominated by a particular perspective. Unfortunately the perception about the women's movement among most African Americans, I think, is that it's irrelevant with respect to the problems we face—drugs, crime, racism. I think the women's movement has altered in significant ways gender politics, made more important improvements in the lives of women as a group, BUT has failed to transform the lives of poor women, particularly those of color. After 30 years, the women's movement needs to broaden its scope, redefine what women's issues are, and arrive at strategies which would make feminism more palatable to broader segments of female populations."

DOROTHY : *age 40, college professor.* "The women's movement for all intents and purposes does not exist. The White women's movement, which in most cases the women's movement has always been, is now relegated to reactionary moves related to who will control women's bodies (reproductive rights, abortion, etc.). The consistent struggle for survival in a hostile environement that continues to cut short their lives and the lives of their children goes on among women of color, relatively unnoticed by the marjoity of White men and women who continue to operate as if women of color were invisible."

HULDA : *age 37, working as a chef/cook in a restaurant in D.C., lower middle income bracket.* "You know, I quit NOW about seven years ago and for good measures. During the Anita Hill/Uncle Tom Clarence trials, the women's movement was very up-front, vocal, and active. As a result of this trial, which had everyone glued to their televisions and showed the brutal treatment Anita Hill received at the hands of the racist, white, conservative pigs in the Senate, many women were enraged and turned out in great numbers to support their sisters whom they encouraged to run for Senate seats. Since that time, I am sure they are still actively and quietly working to support various issues—but they are not making headlines. And since I am not a member of any feminist group—no more, had enough of their talking about but doing nothing to help poor Black women—my knowledge would be based solely on the unreliable press. I've got to help myself make a living."

BARBARA : *age 50, remarried, social worker, counselor.* "In the past 10 years, the women's movement has made noteworthy strides and progress, and this is especially true for Caucasian women. This is evident in the appointment of two women in the U.S. Supreme Court, the recent plan to have a women's team for the U.S. American (Davis) sailboat Cup, Janet Reno U.S. Attorney General, and the number of women in Cabinet positions (also all the controversy regarding the role of Hillary Clinton as First Lady).
   "This progress cannot be said to be true for African Americans. The main issue for us is not to allow or exacerbate a schism in the African American community between men and women. To do so would give the White males a kind of power through the 'divide and conquer' theory. The gains for African-American women have really been a shift. Rather than walking

behind our African American men, we now walk beside them and sometimes our strides put us ahead.

"The gains made in the White women's movement—and by the way, they copied from the Civil Rights Movement—have been orchestrated by White men who made the choice of relinquishing and sharing bits of power first to White women and second to the Black women in preference to the African American male. This has resulted in the African American woman emerging with some gains and being put in a dilemma or pursuing, attaining, and fulfilling our talents, abilities, and interests, and still not being a pawn to the white-male-dominated culture that 'gave' us these gains.

"In spite of all this baggage, African American women, as has been our tradition, continue to show enduring strength, intelligence, and untold abilities as witnessed by Carol Mosely Braun, first Black woman Senator; Toni Morrison, Nobel Prize for Literature; Jackie Joyner Kersee, Olympic medalist; Maxine Waters; and countless others who remain behind the scenes as threats to the 'good old boys power structure.'"

KATE: *age 52, completed college, working at a major department store in the sales/accounting department.* "Due to the increase of hate related racial crimes and health issues (i.e, gay bashing, Rodney King beating, and second-hand smoke vs. cancer), I feel the emphasis is no longer on the women's movement. Black people are more concerned with their lives and health—like AIDS, drugs, Black and Puerto Rican gangs killing other Black and Puerto Rican gang members. We don't have no time for White women's problems."

CRYSTAL : *age 35, housewife, works part time with day care.* "I don't deal with the movement as a whole. I've broken it down into smaller units that have a direct effect on Black people. Also, I'm working with primarily Black people and belong to some women's organizations. Despite all the rhetoric (20 years of it) of the women's movement the racism is still there. We have to deal with our problems ourselves."

IRMA : *age 27, lesbian, manages a bookstore.* "The issue of race and class has not been properly addressed. The emphasis on

trying to get what the White boys have is inappropriate. Until
men take the responsibility for rape and battering, we are
essentially maids doing the clean-up jobs. A few examples of
men taking their responsibilities exist, but for the most part
men are not doing this. Lesbians, well there is not much of a
difference between the straights and lesbians in terms of dealing
with the issue of race and class. Among lesbians, there is more
intermixing and interpersonal relations along race and class
lines. Colonization exists worldwide and the root cause of
colonization has its base in race and class. White women must
recongize that they are part of the colonizing force and then,
and only then, can they make the necessary changes."

PAM : *age 24, grad school, majoring in film making, native New
Yorker.* "Today the 'women's movement' exists as an adhoc
coalition of individuals, groups, and constituency-based
institutions that work and mobilize around a great number of
issues. The movement as it existed in the 70s and 80s had a
positive influence on the empowerment of Black women. These
days it is easy to spot contradictory symbols of Black women's
efforts to achieve liberation, particularly the eroticization of
Black women within pop culture. Within our Black
communities, we are acknowledging genocidal policies directed
against people of African descent. Issues such as self-image
formation, the spread of AIDS among Black heterosexuals,
access to safe abortions, teenage pregnancies, rising cancer rates
are problems that males and females must face. But though our
sights are set on the blossoms of Black female affirmation, our
roots are besieged by poverty and violence. While a new digital
information highway is being activated, too many of our
(mostly women-headed households) use the pay phone on the
corner. The circle of empowerment is not in place."

The responses from Black women to the 1994 questionnaire
routinely showed a shift from viewing the women's movement
as a social movement designed to help women become liberated
from sexual oppression, to focusing on issues directly related to
their personal well-being and the survival of Black people.
    The 1994 responses, similar to those of 1981, spoke of the
economic realities of Black women's lives. Janet says, "the
movement has failed to transform the lives of poor women,

particularly those of color." Dorothy speaks of the consistent struggle for survival in a hostile environment that cuts short the lives of women of color and their children. Kate and Pam discuss how Black women and their children are besieged by poverty; they express concern for the health and lives of Black families. All of these concerns are directly related to the realities of their lives. Improvement in economic conditions will lead to an improvement in the quality of life. The fulfillment of basic needs—housing, health care, decent meals—is basic to survival. The service work mentioned earlier falls disproportionately on Black women and other women of color. Wages are very low; the average salary is less than $12,000 per year. This is certainly not enough for a head of household to support a family. Black women's placement in poorly paid jobs; Black men's increasing marginalization from work altogether; and little state social support for men, women, and children points toward the increased impoverishment of the Black family.*

Barbara is very specific in her comments about White promotion and Black survival. The movement has been successful in furthering the achievements of a recognizable number of White women, she claims, but not those of Black women. She ends her piece on a highly positive note for Black women, but the facts do not reveal an encouraging picture. For example, in the USA in 1970, one percent of Black women were engineers, and by 1980 only seven percent were.** Ninety-five percent of all corporate executives are still White and male, and that has not changed since 1979, when it fell from somewhere close to 100 percent.***

---

* See Rose M. Brewer, "Theorizing Race, Class, and Gender," in *Theorizing Black Feminisims: The Visionary Pragmatism of Black Women*, Stanlie M. James and Abena P.A. Busia, Eds., pp. 13-27. London and New York: Routledge, 1993.

** See Theresa Amott and Judith Matthaei, *Race, Gender, and Work*. Boston: Sound End Press, 1991).

*** See references at end of Patricia J. Williams, "Disorder in the House: The New World Order and the Socioeconomic Status of Women," in *Theorizing Black Feminisims: The Visionary Pragmatism of Black Women*, Stanlie M. James and Abena P.A. Busia, Eds., p. 119 (London and New York: Routledge, 1993) to Mann, "The Shatterproof Ceiling," *The Washington Post* (17 August 1990: D3, col 5).

In 1981, the major tenets of the women's movement were a growing part of Black women's counsciousness. A significant level of scholarly interest existed among Black women in academia. Definitions of feminism and questions about who is a feminist and what makes a feminist were popular topics at conferences, panels, and debates. A burgeoning of Black women's organizations and groups addressed issues espoused by feminst leaders. And many grassroots organizations fueled by the vigor and zest of the movement were encouraged to pursue their causes with more fervor and diligence.

All this is not to say that the vast majority of Black women wholeheartedly embraced the movement, or vigorously jumped on the bandwagon. They showed varying degrees of distrust, skepticism, and ignorance. The movement was praised, denounced, condemned, supported, criticized, and misinterpreted. Nonetheless, it WAS a big, popular controversial topic of discussion among Black women.

Today we see a marked difference in Black women's attitudes toward the movement. It cannot be said that there is an outright, blanket rejection of the movement. What was revealed was a focusing of energies and interests on issues pertinent and relevant to their daily lives as Black citizens living in an increasingly hostile and insensitive social and political environment.

The frequent responses that the movement was "irrelevant," "non-existing," expressions of "not concerned" about the movement and "we have to deal with our own problems ourselves," make a clear statement: For all of the hard, earnest, and courageous work of feminists, the movement has not served as a vehicle capable of recognizing and acknowledging the critical needs of Black women nor as one able to provide remedies or solutions.

Nonetheless, all of the work done by feminists over the past 20 years—raising issues of poverty, abuse, violence, rape, battering, wage equality, abortion rights—must be credited. The movement suffered a great setback during the conservative right-wing Reagan/Bush regimes. Over the years, critics and the media have tried to dismiss or trivialize it. These weapons against the movement are serious impediments and contributed to the existing problematic state of the movement. However, I believe the most serious reason for its faltering and weakened state is the protracted, insidious racism on the part of White feminists and their refusal, based on ignorance and arrogance, to acknowledge this internecine flaw. Racism still remains as one of America's most serious social problems, and the Women's Movement has neglected to consider it as a key factor in feminist ideology and theory. The Women's Movement focused almost exclusively on the lives of White women.

Even when the White feminists considered Black women, they lacked the capacity to conceptualize and analyze Black women's history, culture, and daily experiences. The inclusion of Afro-American, Asian, Hispanic, and Native American women on an equal status with White women would have rectified the Movement's greatest weakness—the failure to see that the intersection of race and class and gender is crucial to all feminist scholarship and theory.

The respondents to the 1994 questionnaire state that problems of crime, drugs, teen-age pregnancy, AIDS, excessive homicide rates among young Black males, and inadequate health care are critical issues that demand their attention and energy. It is not about rejecting or deliberately denouncing the Women's Movement. Rather it is about concentrating on a political agenda that addresses these problems realistically and strategizing a realistic plan of action. The Republicans won't do it! So the weight is on the Blacks.

White feminists have not seriously tackled the issues of race and class as they have championed the fight for rights and reproductive freedom for African-Amerian women within their historical struggle against racism, sexism, and poverty. Ever since Black women were stolen from Africa and shipped to American soil they have been involved in the struggle for reproductive rights. It is not new to them. Today African American women obtain 24 percent of the abortions in the U.S.A., more then 500,000 annually. Black activists/scholars like Loretta J. Ross are in the forefront of the pro-choice, pro-life struggle for Black women. It is incumbent upon feminists whether addressing drugs, AIDS, crime, homophobia or teen-age pregnancies to place these phenomena within the historical context of race, class, and sexual oppressions.

In 1981, many of the Black women interviewed in *Common Differences* were very much aware of the neglect of race and class in feminist ideology. At that time, there was a willingness

to allow feminists time to recognize and attend to this serious
shortcoming. Some twenty years later, Black women are no
longer waiting. Sisters are doing it for themselves! This is
particularly evident in the academe. Black feminist scholarship
is growing steadily, gaining strength and capturing new
audiences. Black women are defining themselves as a group and
working to conceptualize Black women's lives in all spheres.
Black feminist thought lays the theoretical groundwork for this
to be accomplished.

The concept of Black feminist thought did not spontaneously
blossom on the scene. In the 1970s and 1980s, there were
Black women scholars who defined themselves as Black
feminists to distinguish themselves from White feminists. This
distinction was articulated as being a woman equally concerned
with fighting racial and class oppressions as well as sexual
oppression.

The March 10, 1994, publication of *The Chronicle of
Higher Education* contains an article, "The Rise of Black
Feminist Thought" by Karen J. Winkler. She does an excellent
job of updating the growth of Black feminist thought, and
Black feminist presence in publishing. She discusses the steady
stream of publications on the subject, starting with the 1982
publication of *All the Women Are White, All the Blacks Are
Men, But Some of Us Are Brave*. She also mentions the
founding of Kitchen Table: Women of Color Press, which is
devoted to Black feminist writing and SAGE: A Scholarly
Journal on Black Women. *Black Feminist Thought* by Patricia
Hill Collins (Unwin Hyman, Inc.) and *Theorizing Black
Feminisms* (Routledge), edited by Stanlie M. James and Abena
P.A. Abusa, were published in 1990, and in the summer of
1994, the inaugural issue of *The Womanist*, a publication
devoted to Black feminist thought, was issued. Two young
assistant professors from the University of Georgia, Layli
Phillips and Barbara McCaskill, are the creators behind
this effort.

The schism that existed in 1981—the differences between
Black and White women's perspectives, attitudes, and concerns
on key issues—still exists today. What is dramatically different
is that Black women are no longer relying on White feminists to
define them in terms of findings based on White women's
history, culture, and research. The gap between Black and

White can be bridged or at least lessened. The difficulty of the task largely depends on how readily White women divorce themselves from their cultural imperialism and intellectual arrogance.

Today, a younger generation of Black feminists is asking more self-reflective and self-critical questions about the Black church, homophobia in Black communities, and Black sexuality. These questions are directly related to the critical issues expressed by the respondees in the questionnaire. It is incumbent upon this younger generation of Black feminist theorists to seriously and systematically address questions concerning the economics of the Black family, concentrating on the intersections of race and gender. Welfare rights, health care, and world tariffs and free trade zones are all related to the economic status of an individual and family. It is important that the theories and information resulting from their research be pertinent, meaningful, and accessible to all Blacks; and be presented in a manner unencumbered by excessive academic vernacular.

It is the summer of 1994. The Women's Liberation Movement is not dead. A serious liberation movement does not die until all the victims are liberated. The second wave of the Women's Movement may be referred to as dead, dormant, irrelevant, or a waste of time, but as long as one individual or one collective is aware of their victimization and strategizes rebellions, the struggle lives on!

IF WOMEN COUNTED

A REVIEW

DEBORAH R. LEWIS

What Barbara Walker's *The Skeptical Feminist* and Mary Daly's *Gyn/Ecology* do to religion and metaphilosophy, Marilyn Waring's *If Women Counted* (Harper San Francisco, 1988) does to economics. She lays a photograph, with all its darkroom tampering, next to the real world, demonstrating what we need to know: numbers, like photographs, can lie and are frequently manipulated to do just that.

First, she outlines a basic underpinning of traditional economics: the traditional work of women—including childcare, care of the sick and elderly, subsistence farming/gardening, food gathering, food preparation, property maintenance, and making textiles and clothes—is traditionally treated as a fact of biological determinism and usually goes uncompensated. Because such work is unpaid, the United Nations System of National Accounts (UNSNA) neglects to calculate a value for billions of woman-hours worked annually. The exclusion, Waring shows, is hardly oversight. It is in the interest of the system to exclude women: if women are counted as productive, then women must be considered in policymakers' decisions and economic allocations.

In many countries, laws and "customs" treat women as the personal property of fathers and husbands, and the reason for Waring's book becomes apparent:

> It is my confirmed belief that this system acts to sustain, in the ideology of patriarchy, the universal enslavement of

Copyright © 1994 by Deborah R. Lewis

women and Mother Nature in their productive and
reproductive activities.

> If I am wrong, then the system, when turned on its
> head to include a recognition of *all* economic activity,
> will be operative. . . . [I]f the system at that point
> disintegrates, then it is invalid. (p. 44)

From this comment, which appears at the end of the first
chapter, to the end of the book, Waring proceeds to rip apart
the traditional economic system, leaving it in tatters. Her list of
the exploited includes women, children, and the planet itself.
Analyzing the way the UNSNA's numbers respond to war and
toxic substance clean-up, Waring comes to the conclusion that
what the system values is death. Traditional modern economics
was put into motion by John Maynard Keynes, who intended
the system to help Britain figure out how to pay for its portion
of World War II. The whole of the structure was based on
"how to pay for the war," not to "account for death, poverty,
homelessness, refugee populations, ruined food sources, the
enormous waste in investment in armaments, and an
increasingly fragile and exploited environment" (p. 165).

Waring writes about the values centered around reproduction:

> Women give birth. Women deliver human life to the
> world. Sometimes they are sold to men that they might
> bear children, and sons in particular, and they can be left
> or divorced if they fail in this. These are not market
> transactions—they are the economics of reproduction.
> (p.187)

She begins with surrogate mothers in the United States. If a
prospective surrogate mother doesn't conceive after six months
of twice-monthly artificial insemination, she is removed from
the program and the prospective father begins the process again
with another woman. The rejected woman receives no
compensation, expect fees and medical expenses. "What does it
cost you," Waring quotes the director of one such company,
"unless you start putting a value on your time?" (p. 166).
Furthermore, if the surrogate mother miscarries before the fifth
month of pregnancy, she receives nothing except her medical
expenses. After the fifth month, if she miscarries, she is paid
medical expenses, plus 10 percent of the fee. The doctors and

lawyers get their cuts regardless, but the woman's services are free.

> Louise Brown, the world's first test-tube baby, cost more than . . . $1,820,000 to "produce." It was never suggested that too much had been paid to any of the medical practitioners to produce this child.

> The new reproductive processes are sold by the patriarchy . . . as being a wonderful answer for the problem of infertile couples. . . . [W]omen who do accept payment for surrogacy are seen as greedy, calculating, and heartless women extorting undeserved money from a poor desperate infertile couple. (p.191)

In wrongful birth court cases (in which the woman believed herself to have been sterilized but conceived), damages tend to be diminished because it is believed that "sentimental value" and the "obvious joys of motherhood" ought to be considered as some sort of compensation. The time and monetary cost of raising a child tend not to be considered.

Waring writes about what she calls "reproduction of the relations of production," explained as follows:

> In the traditional labor force theory, this concept leads to the exploitation of women's productive work (lower pay, lower status, fewer benefits, less job security). In the household, this is the reproduction of enslavement. (p. 188)

If property and/or business titles are in the husband's name, regardless of how much work the woman may have put into the property or the business, she is unlikely to receive any claim to productive property or real estate if the couple divorces. Meanwhile, child custody cases, when parents do not agree, easily turn into financial blackmail, as women who have worked unpaid generally do not have money for large court battles. Some fathers raise fears of a custody battle to lower financial settlements and child support payments.

Waring refers to those people who are not part of the economics of reproduction as existing outside the reproduction boundary. She identifies such people as prepubescent people and old people, celibate people, people perceived as threatening (because of their poverty/enslavement, capacity for revolt,

and/or their number), heterosexual women who demand
reproductive freedom through abortion and/or contraception,
and same sex lovers, especially lesbians. Lesbians are the most
offensive to the status quo, because a lesbian is

> perceived as having placed herself deliberately outside the
> reproduction boundary, with two additional offences
> [sic]: she has done so during an age-overlap with fertility
> years (unlike children or elders), *and* she has separated
> sexuality from conception *permanently*, thus bringing
> down the whole house of cards. Finally, it is just possible
> that she may have seen through the whole process of the
> reproduction of enslavement, which is threatening to the
> masters and threatening to the enslaved, for the mirror
> she holds up to their lives may reveal too clearly for the
> powerless the extent of their co-option. (p. 206)

Feminists have previously discussed lesbianism from various
political angles, but when Waring puts it in the economic
context it feels like something new. In the lesbian world, there
are women who are lesbians for reasons beyond same-sex
attraction. One hears of women who live a lesbian lifestyle for
political reasons, and now Waring opens the door for
"economic lesbians." These are women who, regardless of
sexual orientation, choose to reject the male model of
economics and especially choose to control their own bodies
and their own money.

Waring goes on to show that when governments cut healthcare services, the burden there also shifts back to women, who
traditionally care for their families and for other people, either
in the extended family or as friends and neighbors. The services
women provide when they care for others are not considered
part of the economy.

Women and children are the first to experience the pain of a
recession. Females are the first to be pulled from schools for
tasks that need to be done at home, despite the fact that the
education of the mother improves nutrition, health, and fertility
of her family.

Waring recognizes that politics and economics are closely
linked. She quotes Republican U.S. Representative Dannemeyer,
arguing that abortion ought to be banned not simply on moral
grounds, but economic ones as well:

If we are going to pay off the debt, somebody has got to
be born to pay the taxes to pay it off. Now since 1973,
the decline in the birth rate per fertile female has reached
the point, where, as a civilization we run the serious risk
of disappearing from the planet.

Waring spends some time discussing the evolution of
housework in the modern era. Regardless of whether or not
men have actually learned to help around the house, there is
still no doubt that women work harder than men. In fact,
Denise and William Bilby, sociologists at University of
California—Santa Barbara, studied the work women and
men do on the job and at home:

Their findings were (1) that women work harder than
men at home and at their jobs; (2) that women give more
time and attention to their jobs than men, despite the fact
that women also spend more than twice as much time on
household tasks; and (3) that more women than men
reported having jobs that require a great deal of physical
or mental effort and at which they do even more than is
asked of them. The result is, of course, that women get
very tired and cut back on sleep and leisure time to get
everything done. (p. 240)

Waring insists that this must change:

The reasons for calling for change vary, but the sense of
urgency for change is shared. Physicist Fritjof Capra
writes: "The social and economic anomalies that can no
longer address global inflation and unemployment,
maldistribution of wealth, and energy shortages, among
others are now painfully visible to everyone. The failure
of the economic profession to come to terms with these
problems is recognised [sic] by an increasingly sceptical
public, by scientists from other disciplines, and by
economists themselves. It is within the scope of economic
theories to include qualitative distinctions which are
crucial to the understanding of our lives and the planet."

Among the qualitative distinctions Waring makes, beyond the
day-to-day living conditions of individual women, is the
observation that economists can impute monetary values for
pollution several ways: they can figure the actual cost of

pollution control; they can estimate hypothetical costs of achieving certain standards of air, water, and soil purity; or they can estimate the cost in damages consequent to pollution. She divides resources by their renewability:

1. Renewable over time (forests)
2. Degraded by pollution or mismanagement (air, water, soil)
3. Immediately renewable (radio waves)

Throughout, she maintains that the planet ought to be valued in its own right, and the sense is that the values she wants economists to impute are to keep the planet visible in policy-making decisions. If this is done, fresh water should be abundant and forests and wildlife shouldn't become extinct. Waring points out that with careful management, the planet might be better able to support us and, more importantly, to carry on despite our presence.

Marilyn Waring, discontent with merely pointing out the failings of the world economic system, concludes by outlining some solutions. She recommends using the model invented by Hilkka Pietila, a Finnish feminist. At the center of this economic model, she places the Free Economy, which includes unpaid work done for the well-being of families, etc. Radiating out in concentric circles are the Protected Sector, which includes the home market and public services, and the Fettered Economy, which includes large-scale production and is fettered to the world economy. Money, according to Pietila, is not the sole criterion that could be used to assess work—it could also be measured by volume in terms of the number of workers or work time absorbed or in physical units "done" or in number of people cared for.

I would like to have seen the book include Waring's analysis of feminist businesses, other businesses owned and operated by women, and environmentally-sensitive businesses. She doesn't discuss these things in *If Women Counted*. However, Waring accomplishes a lot in 326 pages. From Gloria Steinem's excellent introduction through the very last page, *If Women Counted* manages to keep amazingly sharp focus in light of the massive amount of information Waring describes and analyzes. The system of economics Waring proposes is simpler than traditional economic models because there aren't any complexities or contradictions regarding what is and what is not counted. Everything counts, everyone counts. Destruction is negative. It makes sense.

PSYCHIC ECONOMICS

MARY KAY BLAKELY

I used to be an unbeliever. I questioned the integrity of an
economic system that valued women's work only half as much
as men's. I was—and this seems almost preposterous to admit
now—dissatisfied with the lot of women.

Before I reached enlightenment, I suffered from a common
form of math anxiety caused by statistics from the Department
of Labor. I was easily susceptible to depression whenever the
words "supply and demand" came up in conversation. I kept
getting lost in the void of the earnings gap. Years of
investigation about women revealed many things to me, but
didn't make sense of those numbers: Women earn 59 percent of
what men earn. Until last week, I was like a haunted
woman—devils of injustice chasing me, demons of inequity
plaguing me.

My conversation happened unexpectedly, during a business
meeting with a highly placed administrator. I had
noticed—because skeptics habitually pay attention to damning
facts—that women employed in this prestigious institution were
being paid much less money than the men. Like most
unbelievers I was there to complain about the inequity. That's
the major problem with those who don't have the gift of faith
in our economic system. They have their visions trained on the
temporal facts of their lives.

The discussion began predictably enough. With benign
paternal tolerance, he reviewed the intricate principles of
economics, the baffling nuances of budgets, the confounding
factors behind the salary schedules. With the monosyllabic

Copyright © 1993 by Mary Kay Blakely   73

vocabulary educators use to address slow learners, he explained
the familiar platitudes.

He invoked the dogma of salary surveys—the objective
instruments used to determine what "the market will bear."
They prove beyond a shadow of a doubt, that women workers
are "a dime a dozen." That's reality, he reported almost
regretfully, that's how life is outside of Eden. Practitioners of
sound business—the members of the faith, so to speak—can in
good conscience pay them no more. If he didn't adhere to the
precepts of salary surveys, it would cause economic chaos.
Other women, in other institutions, would begin to think they
were worth more too. The brethren in other administrations
would expel him from the faith.

"You have to think about what the job is worth, and not the
person in it," he cautioned me. It always gets you into trouble,
thinking about what a person is worth. He warned me against
engaging in the fallacy of "comparing apples and oranges," a
comparison odious to members of the faith. It is only the
unbelievers, the kumquats, who try to argue for the fruits of
their labors. Mixing the categories would produce
uncontrollable hybrids on the salary scale. Men are men and
women are women and their paychecks are just further
evidence of their vast biological differences, the powerful
influence of the X and Y chromosomes.

I confess, I had heard these tenets of the faith many times
before. It was the kind of conversation that might inspire the
vision of a lawsuit. So it wasn't with an open heart that I asked
the question one more time. How could he accept women's
invaluable contributions to the success of his institution,
witness their obvious dedication, and withhold their just
rewards?

He paused, regarding me carefully, deliberating, apparently,
on whether I was prepared to hear the truth, to embrace the
amazing mystery of women's wages. Then slowly, respectfully,
he revealed the fantastic reason.

Women came seeking positions with an intense longing for
work, but with a paucity of credentials and experience. They
were filled with gratitude when they were offered a job. They
worked in a pleasant environment, doing meaningful work, and
had the privilege of writing the name of the prestigious
institution on their resumes. They received such an

extraordinary sense of well-being, it would be almost a violation of female sensibilities to compensate them with cold, hard cash. Instead, they received something much more valuable; they earned a "psychic income."

I heard my voice becoming hysterical. Hysteria is not at all uncommon during conversions. I was loud—perhaps I was even shouting—when I asked him how much of his income was "psychic." Like many doubters, I didn't immediately see the light. I thought one of us was mad.

Not an hour later, enlightenment came. I was in a car dealership, chatting with the amiable mechanic who had repaired my transmission. He seemed to enjoy his job, especially when he handed me the bill. I gasped, knowing that the balance in my checkbook wouldn't cover the charge. Then I remembered my "psychic income" and that people who love their work, who are dedicated to it, are better paid with congratulations and a pat on the back. I told him what a wonderful job he did, how much I appreciated it. And then wrote a "psychic check."

Suddenly I was filled with the spirit. A happiness, a release flooded over me. I realized that every act of spending my psychic income was an act of faith. I had so much catching up to do. I worked steadily to increase my state of grace. Immediately, I applied for a loan at the employee credit union at the prestigious institution, authorizing payments through "psychic payroll deductions." I used my "psychic credit cards" to charge two pairs of spiritual Adidas for my kids, whose real toes were poking through their real tennis shoes.

I was filled with a fervor to spread the Word. At a rally of working women, I brought them the message of "psychic incomes," and many converts came into the fold.

Nurses, who had an extraordinary love for their work, felt "psychic bonuses" coming to them. Their sense of self-esteem expanded miraculously, and they no longer bowed down to the false gods in the hospitals.

Clerical workers grasped the theory of "psychic work for psychic pay" and began typing only intangible letters, filling transcendental folders, and making celestial phone calls.

Prior to their conversions, working mothers thought they had to do all their housework, because their earnings were only half their husbands' salaries. But when they learned how to bank on their "psychic incomes," they never cooked dinner again. They served their families supernatural pot roasts.

Of course, everyone will not accept the gift of the Word. There are those who will try to persecute us for practicing our faith. We must learn to smile serenely at the unfortunate creditors who lack the vision. We must have a charitable attitude toward the bill collectors whose interests are rooted in temporal assets. Beware of the pharisees who pay spiritual salaries but still demand physical work.

And judge not the angry women who file the interminable lawsuits, who still rail against the status quo. Their daily struggle to exist prevents them from accepting the good news. Remember that there, but for the gift of "psychic economics," go we.

OUR WORDS IN OUR HANDS

A BRIEF HISTORY OF WOMEN'S PRESSES AND BOOKSTORES

CAROL SEAJAY

The roots of feminist bookstores go back to the very beginnings of this wave of the feminist movement. In the late 1960s, women were beginning to talk to each other about our lives. Oftentimes, when we described our most horrible moments or revealed our most shameful secrets we discovered that other women had had similar experiences. That *many* women had had those kinds of experiences. Something went "click" and the personal became political. The more we talked, the more we had to say. In those days, it was called "consciousness raising."

We were discovering that women were discriminated against in employment, that women in general made only 59% of what men made, and that Black and Hispanic women made even less. It was exciting to discover that women were the majority of the population (53%). "Equal pay for equal work" was a radical concept. Abortion, in the moments before this burst of feminism, was a secret, private matter never mentioned in public. To be in the streets chanting "Our Bodies, Ourselves, Our Right to Decide!" and "Free Abortion on Demand!" was unheard of, outrageous, and exhilarating.

The early part of this wave of the women's movement developed a new way to think about women and invented a *feminist* literature of women. We had to. Looking back, it's hard to imagine a world with so little information about women in it.

Reprinted by permission of *Ms.* magazine © 1992

The women's liberation movement became a print movement out of necessity. Little of what we needed to know was available in any written form. When we did get coverage in mainstream publications, our ideas were distorted and trivialized. It became increasingly clear that if we wanted our ideas in print we would have to put them there ourselves. Women wrote their ideas down, typed them onto stencils, and printed them up as pamphlets on mimeograph machines. Articles like " The Myth of the Vaginal Orgasm," "The Woman-Identified Woman," "The Politics of Housework," and "Why I Want a Wife," were passed from hand to hand. Women took over the anti-war underground newspaper *Rat* (*LibeRATion News*) and organized special women's and women's liberation issues of all kinds and then started our own newspapers and magazines with names like *The Furies, No More Fun and Games, The Kalamazoo Woman, So's Your Old Lady*, and *Mom—Guess What!* and consciousness-altering contents. *It Ain't Me Babe, Ain't I A Woman, Up from Under, Women: A Journal of Liberation,* and *off our backs* all burst into print within three months of one another at the beginning of 1970 in communities as far flung as Berkeley, Iowa City, New York City, Baltimore, and Washington, DC. Every town that didn't have a newspaper seemed to have a women's liberation newsletter.

But deciding to have a newspaper, writing the contents and headlines, ordering typesetting, learning to paste-up the newspapers and raising all the money for it all wasn't enough. All too often male printers and male-controlled printing presses refused to print our work, declaring our articles to be obscene. Printers decided that the photographs illustrating *Ain't I A Woman's* articles explaining how to do your own vaginal exam and reporting on the women's self-help movement were obscene and refused to print them. Mainstream printers refused to print an issue of *off our backs* that included a parody on feminine hygeine products that featured two men running through a meadow as the backdrop for an "ad" for similar male products with names like "Meat and Potatoes" and "Locker Room" in phallic shaped containers. To get that issue into print, the women who published it had to take *off our backs* to a pornography printer. Allegedly women-controlled printing presses weren't always free to print feminist work, either, if they were dependent on male approval for funding: the United Way threatened the funding of a Michigan YWCA when letters in the local women's liberation newsletter (printed on the Y facilities in conjunction with the women's center located in the Y) shifted from complaining about lesbian oppression to advocating lesbian pride.

Freedom of the press, we learned by the early 70s, belonged to those who owned printing presses. So we established our own so that no man could ever again tell women what was true, what was relevant to our lives, or what we could publish and read. Printing presses like the Iowa City Women's Press and Diana Press were a direct outgrowth of women's anger that men had refused to print work like *Ain't I A Woman* and *off our backs*. To further that autonomy, we established our own typesetting shops, binderies to bind the books the presses printed, bookstores to put them into women's hands, and our own wholesale distributors— KNOW, Common Woman Distribution, Amazon Reality, Old Lady Blue Jeans, Diaspora Distribution, and Women in Distribution (WIND). It was a wonderfully exhilarating time. Women were doing everything we'd ever been told we couldn't do: opening auto repair shops, starting abortion clinics (legal and otherwise), moving furniture for one another, starting construction companies.

▲ ▲ ▲

Many of the bookstores in the early 1970s were the result of a burst of energy in a circle of women who worked together on other projects. If the idea of the moment was to start a women's bookstore, two or five or twenty women would join together and start one. Most of the stores were collectively run in styles as diverse as the women's communities that started them. Many, if not most, of the women who felt the need for a bookstore strongly enough to get involved, raise funds, build bookcases, and do volunteer shifts week after week after week were lesbians. For all women working in women's bookstores, their weekly shifts were an important part of their social and community networks. Some of these bookstores lasted only a few months. Others, including Everywoman's Bookstore, Fan the Flames, Mother Kali's, Sisterhood, The Thirtyfirst Street

Women's Bookstore, the Vancouver Women's Bookstore, and The Toronto Women's bookstore, are still serving women's need for information today.

Often, even when women deliberately opened bookstores in storefronts, it was difficult to tell the difference between a women's bookstore and a women's center. There were always places for women to sit; the coffee pot was always on. There were usually more plants and bulletin boards than books. The women who worked in the bookstore provided information and meeting space and were as likely to answer questions or to aid a battered woman as they were to sell books. Many women who wanted the help or information that a women's center could offer had been so intimidated by the media's portrayal of bra-burning, man-hating feminists that they were afraid to go into women's centers. Socialized to shop, they found women's bookstores to be a safer entryway into feminism. A woman could look at the books until she found the courage to ask the questions she needed to ask.

There was one important difference between women's centers and women's bookstores: selling the books paid the rent. During the years when women's centers lost funding and/or were "deprioritized" for space, the financially independent women's bookstores stood firm. In those wonderfully anarchistic days, little attention was given to details of ownership, structure, long-term goals or financial planning. Creating equality-based, nonhierarchical organizations where each woman would be respected for her unique gifts was deemed far more important than setting up procedures to deal with such unlikely eventualities as conflict, collective members who failed to keep commitments, or (what unthinkable lack of faith in women!) embezzlement. Traditional business practices— the domain of the patriarchy—were automatically suspect. Most stores survived—and thrived—on constant fundraising, donated labor, and donated supplies (often "liberated" from patriarchal institutions). Collective members often wrote personal checks for books or magazines they wanted to see in the bookstore if the bookstore couldn't afford to buy them. "Long-term financial planning" had more to do with raising money or saving it out of sales to pay the rent than anything else.

Social, educational, and consciousness-raising events—
women's coffeehouses, dances, and other programs that also
raised funds—were integral parts of the political and economic
make-up of most stores. These bookstores, like today's feminist
bookstores, had tremendous impact on their communities.
Women from all walks of life and experiences found
community and resources as well as books and ideas. Some
women walked many times around the block before they found
courage to enter. Once they made it through the doorway, they
took what they found and changed their lives—left abusive
relationships, found new self-images, came out, found
sisterhood and community. Many went on to become activists
whose work has changed all of our lives. At least one
enormously effective comedian—Roseanne Arnold—got the
boost she needed working in a large collective bookstore, The
Woman to Woman Feminist Bookcenter, where the women
understood and supported her humor.*

The development of the women-in-print movement was a
part of the drive for women's independence. Its growth has
been phenomenal. There was a time at the beginning of the
women's movement when a committed feminist could store
everything in print about the women's liberation movement in a
few file folders on her desk. Now there are *140* women's
bookstores scattered across the U.S. and Canada. The larger
stores stock 15,000 to 18,000 titles. None of them are large
enough to stock everything about women, but most have more
books than any one woman could read over the course of her
lifetime.

The survival rates for feminist stores are surprisingly high
despite all the obstacles we've faced. Of the 60 women's
liberation bookstores in the U.S. and Canada in 1978, almost a
third of them (19) are still open sixteen years later. Of the 73
feminist bookstores that were listed in the September 1983
issue of *Ms*, 39 (54%) are still serving their communities eleven
years later. These are excellent survival rates for any small

---

*   Woman to Woman closed in 1982. Denver women now shop at The
      Book Garden.

businesses—nevermind undercapitalized, politically based bookstores.

Many of the earliest feminist bookstores closed for various reasons—constant turnover among volunteers, loss of skills when staff turnover occurred more rapidly than skills could be passed on. Some collectives developed structures to deal with conflicts and thrived, but others were closed by unresolved and unresolvable conflicts. Declining national economic conditions meant that more women had to work full time and had less time to do volunteer work. Women's continued lack of access to capital continue to plague the current generation of bookstores.

▲ ▲ ▲

The first generations of women's bookstores explained (again and again and again) the economics of scale that made feminist-press published books more expensive than books churned out in larger quantities by better-capitalized mainstream presses. These booksellers pointed out the new feminist published books as they arrived and taught generations of women to value and cherish feminist press books, and to support feminist presses (and bookstores!) whenever humanly possible.

Financially speaking, *none* of the first generations of bookstores or publishers should have survived: there simply weren't enough books for feminist bookstores to sell to stay afloat, nor enough bookstores to sell enough books to make feminist publishing financially viable. But women kept opening feminist bookstores and feminist publishing companies just the same, and kept them open as long as they were able, until the time came when there *were* enough outlets to make feminist publishing viable and enough books to support feminist bookstores. All of these early bookstores and publishers—whether they survived or not—paved the way for the successful stores and publishers we have today. Women who run feminist bookstores today—and all of the women who shop in them—benefit from the extraordinary vision, commitment, ingenuity, and hard work of the feminist booksellers and publishers who came before. Their work and vision is a gift to the generations of feminists, women's bookstores, and publishers who were to come.

Over the years, feminist booksellers have developed a number of ways to work together and to provide mutual support. Feminist booksellers representing 18 of the estimated 25–30 feminist bookstores in the country gathered together for the first time in 1976 at the first national Women In Print conference. We found that we had so much to say to each other—so much information to share and so many skills to teach and learn from each other—that we established a newsletter for feminist bookstores as a way to share information. Over the years the "newsletter" has grown into a 120+ page magazine, *Feminist Bookstore News*, that is published bi-monthly. It features information about new and forthcoming titles, profiles of feminist bookstores, news of both the feminist and mainstream book trade, and information about bookselling skills. Subscriptions were (and still are) on a sliding scale, with larger bookstores contributing more to help finance subscriptions for small and/or financially troubled stores.

A Feminist Bookstore Network has evolved to give us a visible public body and to facilitate joint projects, such as a series of ads reminding women to support feminist bookstores. Feminist bookstores meet every year for two days of workshops and discussion before the American Booksellers Association Convention. Booksellers who can afford the trip attend the International Feminist Bookfairs (most recently in the Netherlands in 1992 and in Australia in 1994) to share skills and information with feminist booksellers and publishers around the world.

▲ ▲ ▲

Initially feminist bookstores were able to start with very little capital. A Woman's Place Bookstore in Oakland, California started with $400 in cash and a $400 credit line at a local distributor in 1972. By using all of the proceeds from book sales to expand stock, it became one of the largest feminist bookstores in the country during its heyday. (Two of the women who started A Woman's Place now run Mama Bears Bookstore & Coffeehouse in the same community.) A Room of

One's Own, a collectively run bookstore that is still thriving, started in 1974 with $5,000 in donations and loans raised by the Madison (Wisconsin) women's community. New Words in Boston and Womanbooks in NYC started at about the same time with about $8,000– $10,000 each. Diligent work turned these stores into some of the largest and best stocked feminist bookstores in the country. The six largest feminist bookstores in the country were able to turn these kinds of investments into bookstores that grossed $300,000 to $400,000 a year by 1981. As bookstores grew larger and more complex, booksellers learned to value bookselling skills along with political priorities and to excel at both. Virtually all feminist bookstores were (and still are) undercapitalized. Skill and hard work compensate for the lack of financial resources.

▲ ▲ ▲

By the mid-1980s, fewer of the new bookstores were being started by collectives and more were opened by triads, partners and/or lovers, and sole proprietors who, in addition to providing a community with literature, wanted to create a satisfying livelihood for themselves. Volunteer labor was in increasingly short supply, and more and more of the stores were staffed by paid workers. There were many more books and fewer coffeepots (booksellers having learned how many books can be damaged with a single spilled cup of coffee), and ever more nonsexist, antiracist children's books, reflecting the baby booms in both the lesbian and heterosexual communities. Overstuffed couches gave way to the additional bookcases needed to display all the new books. Sidelines such as cards, calendars, music and woman-oriented jewelry continued to provide images not available elsewhere in our culture as well as to supplement bookstore incomes. Potted ferns were no longer essential, but virtually every feminist bookstore had large sections of books by/about women of color, not so much out of an obligation to "political correctness" as out of a passion for validating women's lives and experiences. If the straight world has yet to learn to cherish lesbian literature, at least feminist bookstore customers of all races have come to cherish Black, Native-American, Asian-American, Latina, and Chicana

women's literatures. Stores that are thriving have broad-based
stock, reflecting the needs of the class/age/race/sexuality/politics
and priorities of the *diversity* of women that use the stores.
Women's bookstores are still the first place women turn to find
community resources of all kinds.

▲ ▲ ▲

   The amount of money needed to start a successful store in
the 1990s varies with location and other resources. Essentially,
a store must have enough stock so that sales of books (and
other items) can generate enough income to replace the books
sold, buy new stock, and cover all of the overhead expenses
and pay whatever salaries are needed. A bookstore owner with
a partner willing and able to cover most of her living expenses
for the first two or three years will need much less money than
women who must be self-supporting.
   The general expectation in the book business is that
bookstores can expect to "turn" a wisely chosen inventory 3½
to 4 times a year. Booksellers pay between 60 and 65%
(including postage) for each book, leaving 35 to 40% of sales
to cover expenses. Thus a bookstore that anticipates
$70,000/year in overhead (expenses + salary + inventory
growth + inflation) needs to sell $200,000 in books to generate
enough money to meet those expenses. To achieve that level of
sales, a bookstore needs a $50,000 inventory (which costs
about $30,000 at wholesale) in stock at all times. While many
stores start with smaller inventories, turn their stock over more
quickly initially, and invest every cent in inventory expansion, a
store that is just undercapitalized for its expenses can hang on
for two or even three years, but it creates a stress that is hard
on its community and is very hard on the booksellers. In
addition, a new store needs to have an inventory that compares
favorably with other sources of books within driving distance.
And booksellers must be wise enough to keep newly published
books coming into the store, so as to *always* have something
new and interesting to offer their most regular customers.
   While the women's movement has made great strides in
many areas in the past 20 years, access to capital isn't one of
them. There's a glass ceiling in lending as surely as there is in

corporate promotions. Lack of access to enough capital to allow a bookstore to prosper has probably killed more bookstores than any other single problem. As the size of inventory needed to open women's bookstores has increased, the number of women from groups with the least access to capital able to open bookstores has declined. Money to start feminist bookstores generally comes from personal savings, cashed-out retirement programs, loans, and other private sources. There are no public funds available for starting bookstores.*

Bookselling in the 90s is a complex—though eminently learnable—skill. An apprenticeship in a bookstore small enough that all the aspects of bookselling are visible is invaluable. Lacking experience and capital, vision, idealism and commitment have turned many women into feminist booksellers with thriving community centers/bookstores regardless of the odds against them. There's nothing like telling a feminist that she can't do something to guarantee that she will.

For an up-to-date list of feminist bookstores, addresses, and telephone numbers, in the U.S. and Canada, send a SASE and $1 to Feminist Bookstore News, PO Box 882554, San Francisco CA 94188.

---

*   In 1994, the Small Business Administration's "Opinion Molder Rule," which prohibited the SBA from lending money to businesses that might influence public opinion—such as publishers or bookstores, was repealed. In theory, SBA loans should now be available to people who want to start bookstores.

TAKING A SLIDE

NETT HART

Every now and then someone asks, "What happened to the
sliding-fee scale?" Every once in a while a feminist group
produces a feminist event on a sliding-fee scale or a feminist
practitioner offers such a scale for her services. Almost never do
we see an event or service produced by a not explicitly feminist
organization—even when the performer and/or the intended
audience is feminist—offer a sliding scale. It's a feminist
idea/ideal that never caught on, not even in our own
communities. Why?

The politics behind it are never reproached. Vast disparities
in resources are themselves an inequity that creates and
perpetuates oppression. In our analysis of sexism, few doubt
that if all women had the financial autonomy of white men
many oppressions would be dismantled. Money and power are
inextricably linked. Power cannot become power-of-the-people
without sharing resources.

Few women have enough power or money, yet we cannot
dismiss the failure of the sliding-fee scale, or the economic
parity it represents, by citing this deficiency of sexism. In our
community, some women have the resources previously
accorded only to white men, and some are the inheritors of
family wealth. Some women have this hard-earned earning
power thanks to their abilities, feminism, and a larger pool of

A shorter version of this paper appeared in Feminist Bookstore News
(May/June 1992). *I'd like to thank Terri Carver, my production
partner, for the measure of how far we've come thinking about money
over coffee.*

Copyright © 1992 by Nett Hart

impoverished women. If no women had money, feminist/lesbian events at prices that represent a day's work or more to some members of our community would not be produced.

It's not just that the sliding scale is disappearing. It doesn't work. Seldom is the scale realistic. The resource discrepancies in our community cannot be accounted for in a $5 to $15 slide. Even in these very modified slides it is difficult to cover production expenses if the mathematical average of the slide is the actual cost. That's because the average of fees collected is usually close to the minimum. At one conference I organized, we displayed a large sign, "IT'S NOT A SALE . . . IT'S SLIDING SCALE" because many people do notunderstand how the scale works. This is at least partly because of the reluctance in our culture as a whole, and in the downwardly mobile feminist culture in particular, to discuss the down and dirty of money. Many women don't know what their ability to pay really is and how it stacks up in relation to the ability to pay of other members of the community. At the conference, we provided further information about the statistical average income for women in our region and what the actual costs of the conference were. We realized that often women feel broke, when in fact they have resources, just because they do not have the cash in hand. Because we wanted women to take seriously the scale, if they were willing, we were willing to take a postdated check for part of the conference fee, to offer women who could not pay their fair share that particular day to do so over the following two weeks. This approach was hugely successful. A lot of provocative discussion ensued, and we the organizers were careful not to extract by fear or shame what a woman was unwilling to pay, but to ask for a fair contribution to offset the costs of the event by which all of the attending women benefitted.

One of the things I hear most often about the sliding-fee scale when it is offered is that women who would pay at the upper end of the scale say they cannot "afford" to go to such events. This statement lacks awarenesss that the woman who pays $5 and lives on $200 a month is paying a lot more than the woman who pays $50 and lives on $3000 a month, a not uncommon figure in our communities. So accustomed are we to getting a good price, shopping sales, and not overpaying for services that we cannot think well of ourselves if we pay $30 for an event that another woman enters for $10. This is a remnant of women feeling that they are taken advantage of in the world of finance and having a gut-level distrust of anyone who wants to part us from our money. Granted, in these economic times, we're all feeling the crunch, but feeling a squeeze on your disposable income is not poverty.

I don't know of any feminist bookstore or publisher that sells books sliding fee, and I'm not suggesting it, because those who could pay "more if..." would simply buy cheaper at the chains. The failure of the feminist community to develop economic alternatives is evident in the disappearance of lending libraries. At a time when there are enough of "our" books to fill whole walls in some feminists' homes and offices, when a very small percentage of "our" books ever see public and school library shelves, where are women who really cannot afford these books going to gain access to them? If we are serious about building a diverse culture, we need to make available the resources of this culture to all women and make the means of production available to all as well. A few feminist bookstores carry used books that sell for reduced prices. That certainly helps. Feminist publishers are frequently asked to donate books (and the cost of shipping) to women's centers, archives, and studies, many of which are housed in institutions with more resources than the donating publishers. But lots of our books are not getting to the women with fewer resources.

Many feminist bookstores and production companies have gone to a membership base. My local store began a membership program ten years ago with lifetime memberships for $100 and annual memberships for $15 and $25. All levels of membership receive a 10% discount on merchandise; some for that year, some forever. Most of us in the community were not able to support our bookstore with a lifetime membership; of those of us who could afford to buy a membership at all, many opted for an annual fee (the lowest of which is now $25 per year). If we consider that the women who paid for lifetime memberships were those members of the community who were most able to pay $100 at one time from some kind of disposable income, then we see that in these ten years their 10% discount has cost them $100 and the 10% discount of the middle supporters has cost $203 as the annual fee rose. Poor women who cannot pay for a membership but support the bookstore with their purchases receive no discount and may actually contribute more to the store's income than the membership-based sales. Yet our community still rewards those women who are able to "support" the institutions with large one-time contributions.

When we are talking about creating economic parity for the artifacts of our culture, we have to take into account that many of the things we buy are available through other venues that do not even pretend to support feminist economic agendas. And many feminists buy these books and specialty items from sources other than the feminist bookstores, forgetting that most of our books and other merchandise were not available before the feminist bookstores and feminist and Lesbian publishers existed. Merchandise that is bought elsewhere is a sale that is not going to the community. When merchandise is available only from the feminist outlets such as bookstores, festivals, and conferences, this is so because the publisher or craftswoman puts a priority on politics to build an economic and cultural alternative. That many women produced these books and music and crafts before they were finacially viable means that the producers created a sliding fee scale of their own and kept the resources of our culture more available to a larger part of our community. Now that these are profitable, the mainstream is interested because it talks money.

Events that used to be produced with a sliding-scale entrance price eroded into a fixed price, often moderate but high for some members of the community, with the "substitute" option being a "work exchange." If someone wanted to go to the social event, her first choice probably would not have been to work the event instead, but for some women it is the only way to attend at all. For producers working hard without a lot of sweat support from the community and no shared financial "risk," the work exchange option offers a means of having co-workers at a price that the producers can afford—nothing. But for women who are poor, everything takes more effort and most poor women are tired. So that this is a gesture of accommodation is lost when it does nothing to address the inequities of ability to pay and requires of some members of the participatory community that they work not only a first and second shift but a third as well, hiding from community consciousness that the fact that having less money is not related to doing less or being less but simply having less.

In another example, a Lesbian community festival was
financed by contributions of Lesbian craftswomen for a raffle.
This is a common practice. It offers exposure to craftswomen
of music, books, periodicals, and other kinds of crafts and a
chance to support the community event. It does not take into
account that many craftswomen live a subsistence lifestyle and
are asked over and over again to make donations and that they
usually do so because as a whole they support our culture. I
challenged the ethics of the raffle because I believe that the
culture we are creating is not about having winners and losers.
Competition for scarce resources is one of the first things that I
think has to go. Instead the organizers decided to hold a silent
auction, but they realized that poor Lesbians could not
participate. I think that raffles in which the measure of your
chances to win are determined by the ability to buy more
tickets are just as classist but not as apparently so. Here we
have the challenge: to create community events in which any
member of the community can participate and still be able
to pay the production costs. Cultural workers of many
communities are financially marginal, but in a community
that strives for social justice and economic justice, support for
culture is the responsiblity of everyone.

When Audre Lorde asked at the NWSA conference in 1988,
"What kind of a movement does it take $50 to join?" there was
silence. Now we must ask what kind of movement will we have
if events and music and literature and art and theory are out
of the financial reach of the most marginalized, the most
politicized, members of our community? What will we gain
and how will we know it?

Money represents one of the oppressions that constitute
patriarchy. In every way what money buys is insularity:
insulation from hunger, insulation from the elements, insulation
from street crime/police brutalization/landlords, insulation
from worry, insulation from untreated health needs, insulation
from other people's condescension. The life of insulation does
not equip anyone for political analysis. I am not arguing for
deprivation. I am saying that insularity is also insularity from
the needs of members of our community and insulation from
the momentum for change. How can we rally behind the
cartoon character of Hothead Paisan, homocidial Lesbian
terrorist when she takes out man after man, yet not financially

support the struggle for a fair trial of Lee Wuornos when she is accused of the same thing? The struggle for justice in our community is a real issue with real consequences for women we dare not forget. The translation of this concern into cash needs to be done according to ability to pay, using a self-evaluated sliding scale, because the vulnerabilities of any women in this system are our own. In sharing the protection from unfair treatment that money can buy, we share the resources we each can claim.

There has been a lot of talk recently about feminist organizations not only surviving (goddess know we've lost too many of them!) but thriving. What is the nature of this thriving and by what standards? How do structures for longevity fit with a revolutionary agenda? It is my understanding that we created feminist and Lesbian organizations as ways to promote an alternative social structure and basis and that they were not meant to become part of the patriarchy under which we still are not respected. If tough economic times for 95% of us can stall our movement, do we believe that economic parity will revive, if and when "the economy" changes? If we are unwilling to commit to economic reform in the short term, how can we remember to do so in the long term? We all did more on less before.

Can we use the principles of good management inherited from the patriarchy and still be about radical change? Is the sliding scale an acknowledgement that there will always be disparities in the ability to pay, or is it a challenge to end the disparities in access that money causes? The sliding scale as a solution to an acknowleged discrepancy rather than as a strategy for change simply holds in place an injustice. In any radical feminist agenda, the sliding scale must become a part of the strategy to end economic oppression. When we take seriously the slide, we begin to address the real issues of money, class, and access in our communities, and we are better able to challenge the necessity of those particular structures of oppression. By insisting on authentic sliding scale access to events in our communities, we begin to understand the needed changes and become better allies to one another across economic tiers. In my five-year plan, the answer to where I want to "be" is not "-pressed"— oppressed, depressed, repressed. Can you dig it?

PROPOSAL FOR A REALISTIC SLIDING FEE SCHEDULE FOR A FIVE-DAY CONFERENCE:

1% of annual income from all sources

+

Amount you spend on eating out, entertainment, comforts, and treats in an average week

+

Add $10-$50 for each of these you have:

▲ health insurance
▲ a car worth more than $5000
▲ education beyond high school
▲ credit cards
▲ loans available from family or friends
▲ retirement plans or annuities
▲ workers compensation insurance
▲ your own home
▲ additional recreational, rental or investment property
▲ savings account
▲ investments, stocks, bonds
▲ inheritance or anticipated inheritance

Deduct $20-$70 for each of these that apply to you:

▲ chronic illness
▲ disability
▲ unusual travel expenses due to distance not convenience
▲ special dietary needs requiring you to supply your own food
▲ primary financial support for partner, friend or child
▲ wages for a PCA to enable you to attend conference

=

Total Participatory Fee

FEMINIST FUND RAISING PHOBIA

KAREN RUDOLPH

Money is the number one source of arguments in families and organizations. We seldom resolve how to make it or spend it. Self-esteem, survival, pleasure, pressure and political power are all connected to money (look at the success of millionaire Ross Perot in the 1992 presidential election). Despite our progressive politics, the feminist community is not immune to all the mixed-up feelings that revolve around money in this society, nor are we immune to greed or envy.

In the United States, people with money are seen as smart, hardworking, and successful. People without money are seen as dumb and lazy. As feminists we know that isn't correct, so some of us just turn this proposition on its head. We see rich women as corrupt, exploiting oppressors and poor women as heroic role models. Rich women are defined as anyone who has more money than me. I personally manage simultaneously to feel like a loser for not having enough money and guilty for having too much.

Underneath our politics we have layers of emotions about money. Money is dirty, the root of all evil. There is never enough money. Being competent about money is unfeminine and upper class. Making money is a betrayal of our parents if they were poor, selling out like our parents if they were rich. I have been in feminist meetings where women literally cried and yelled until the wee hours of the morning about money.

In our organizations we come from different class and family backgrounds. To further complicate things, some middle-class

Copyright © 1992 by Karen Rudolph

women are now poor and some working-class women are now
middle class. We fear and suspect each other's backgrounds.
You have to really know and trust someone to trust them with
money.

I know a woman from a wealthy background who chooses
to work part-time for low wages. She never donates any money
to any organization. She thinks that feminist projects should
only be run by volunteers. She feels that asking anyone for
more than $20 is outrageous, because it makes poor women
feel excluded. To raise funds, she favors holding small concerts
and charging $5 per ticket (more if you can less if you can't).
She is complimented for being sensitive to poor women.

I know a woman from a poor background who is now
making $50,000 a year with full benefits. She thinks that it's
time for feminists to raise some serious money to make some
real changes in society. She donates at least 10 percent of her
income to progressive causes. She wants to raise $10,000 to
support women union organizers in South Africa. She plans to
establish an honor roll and an engraved plaque to acknowledge
women who have donated $1,000 or more. I've heard her
called an elitist.

I have worked with countless women who refused to take
any responsibility for raising money. They think they aren't any
good at it and that some other women should do it. Yet they
see it as their duty to veto any fundraising scheme that doesn't
perfectly express their politics.

In many feminist organizations, fundraising is considered a
side issue. We attempt to live in a world of pure political
theorizing. We demand diversity and accessibility but we won't
raise the money to pay for the wages, plane tickets, and
wheelchair ramps. We demand that money be spent on our
important issues without looking at the whole budget. We
expect only a handful of women to be responsible for the
money but we allow anyone to criticize their work.

Women in feminist organizations who are knowledgeable
about budgets and accounting are often considered to be
boring, sell-out, male thinkers. Instead of learning skills from
them, we toss the bank books in their laps and run away. We
are relieved that someone else will think about that distasteful
money while we concentrate on creating a feminist utopia. We

demand to learn nontraditional skills yet we still approve of, and accept, being incompetent with money.

Raising money is hard work, physically, intellectually, and emotionally. There is a lot of competition for that charitable and political dollar. I was brought up to believe in self-reliance and to feel shame at the thought of asking for money. I find it difficult to request a donation. What if they don't have the money and I embarrass them? What if they think it's a stupid cause and that, therefore, I'm stupid? What if they say no? What if they think I'm being pushy?

I have to really believe in a cause to go through all that to raise money. It is easier to sit in meetings and endlessly discuss "the issues" than to face my financial emotions. I would rather blame someone else for my discomfort.

An organization has three parts: its goals, the work to institute those goals, and the fundraising to support that work. We demand that the work and fundraising exactly mirror our goals and ideals. This is important and admirable but sometimes we forget that these goals are not current reality. Our fundraising cannot be absolutely politically pure because we live in a capitalist society.

Not everyone can afford to attend banquets, concerts, or dances. Not everyone can afford a T-shirt, poster, pin, or book bag. Not everyone can afford to make a donation or to bid on an auction item. All of these discriminate against someone, leave someone out. Does this mean that we can't use these things to raise money for our organizations? Do we help poor women by raising the money to include them? Can we do both?

Most of us have extra money that is not absolutely necessary for our survival. We decide what it is enjoyable to buy: dinner out, a movie, a book, jewelry, clothes, gifts for friends. No one wants you to donate your rent money to feminist causes. Fundraisers are asking you to make choices about your extra money. When I donate money to a feminist cause, I feel wonderful. I know that my energy is helping to make a difference. I am delighted that there are organizations doing work that I believe in. But they need to remind me that they exist and that my money is necessary. Sometimes I need a little extra incentive.

People are encouraged to give money with the rewards of public recognition, special invitations, and benefits. People are encouraged to give money with the promise of fun activities with interesting people. People are inspired to give money when they see that other people are also giving money. People are inspired to give money when they receive attention and acknowledgement.

The perfect fundraiser would be one in which every woman would automatically give her fair and just share, without being asked. Everyone would receive the same, public recognition and gratitude. In a perfect world, enough money would be available to fully fund all our projects, and to include everyone in everything. In a perfect world, no one's money or skills would give them any power or control.

But we haven't won the revolution yet, and we must work in this imperfect society. All effective fundraisers have negative implications. Our job is to create the best fundraiser possible. We use imperfect means to reach a valuable end. We need to enthusiastically support the fundraisers in our communities. We have frightened away too many supporters with our constant criticism. Look around at all the feminists who just aren't involved anymore. Look at how many feminist organizations no longer exist because there wasn't enough money.

If I give money to the Girl Scouts, I receive a thank-you note acknowledging my gift. If I give money to a feminist organization, I'm barely acknowledged (and I have even been trashed). I have read feminist articles claiming that it is wrong to acknowledge privileged women for their donations, that it's their "duty" to give money to us—they shouldn't have to be thanked. With these attitudes, few of our projects will be funded.

Even if we never say the word "money," it is part of every political discussion and decision. Money is people's energy and resources in paper form. Understanding money is a real and necessary part of every political movement. We can refuse to talk about money but we still need it to reach our goals. Fundraising phobia does not further social or economic justice.

LESBIAN LAND PATTERNS

IN WHICH SOME POOR LESBIANS CONSIDER
THOUGHTS ABOUT WHO MAY OWN LAND AND
THOSE WHO MAY NOT, AND HOW TO OVERCOME
SOME LAND-OWNING BARRIERS

PELICAN LEE AND REBECCA HENDERSON

We are sitting at our kitchen table writing down the thoughts from the night. It is tricky to go to sleep if you have both just read an exciting article about Dyke Economics by Kiwani in *MAIZE* (issue 34). We waited though, for the light of day to get our minds together on this. Kiwani speaks many things that have been on our minds for a long time. May her words continue to be heard.

We too have been poor and economically marginal all our lives, and have dreamed the dream of rural land-based lesbian community. Pelican lived in a few of the first attempts at this in the 1970s in Oregon. Rebecca grew up in a rural Quaker farming community. For some years we were able to rent rurally near women's land. We planted perennials even though we knew, as renters, we might have to leave before we were ready. We considered major building projects so the place would better suit our needs, but rejected them, knowing we'd eventually have to leave. We hoped people in houses nearby would move and we could arrange for our lesbian friends to move in, so we could have more lesbian community. Then the landlord's needs dictated that we had to leave our beautiful country home. Economics forced us to relocate into town. At our kitchen table we look out our window at a shed we built in the small yard to hold our country dyke stuff, the shovels,

Copyright © 1993 by Pelican Lee and Rebecca Henderson

rakes, pots, peat, nails, and tools. Now we are displaced country lesbians, still carrying and nurturing the dream of land-based lesbian community.

During the last three years we were involved in organizing the New Mexico Women's Land Trust to save Arf Women's Land. We looked beyond too, to the ways the land trust could serve more lesbians seeking to live in lesbian land communities. One thing we found was the great, great interest in this. So many shared what little they had to help save Arf. One day we received a single dollar bill in an envelope with no return address. Little contributions from lesbians in poor circumstances did as much for our morale as the large contributions did for the project. *Both* were essential.

In the patriarchal world, we get disconnected from each other. Everyone is trying to keep what they have. The attitude is KEEP. But whenever we've been where circumstances are hard and money is scarce the attitude is SHARE. Such a paradox! Sharing comes, we think, not just from an altruism, but from necessity. "I'll need help later so I'll help you now," or "You helped me last spring, I'll help you this fall." When there is a community, and people are together over long time, the exchange doesn't have to be instantaneous (trade or barter). Sharing happens over changing years and changing circumstances. And for community to grow we need places and/or proximity to each other. To quote Kiwani, "Land-base allows for a fundamental security, a place to grow from in strength that remains in the womyn's world."

In our land trust work we gained insights about ownership. When someone "owns" something they get the impression that can "keep it" or "sell it." But in fact and in practice, all that we have has been given to us by others, by family, by the earth, by Spirit, by the magical gift of having a body and mind that works. Our rightful part is not in keeping these gifts, but in being caretakers of them.

Sometimes the word "stewardship" is used when we want to use a word other than "ownership." But that word comes from Europe where the rich noble had a "steward" who looked after all his affairs, a high class servant who had delegated authority to preserve his master's estate. The concept is patriarchal, representing someone who tells everyone else what to do and collects income from the poor on the estate. This represents the worst type of "ownership." The word *caretaker* is a word that fits women's situation better. It represents our inclination to pass what we are taking care of along to another.

How often it is up to us to take care of others, of things, of our own selves. When we take care of gifts we've been given we pass them on to others in as good or better shape than we found them. When we take care of things, we love and cherish them, adding our energy to their essences. When we take care of others we help, nourish and comfort them to their benefit and ours. And when we take care of ourselves we strengthen and comfort our bodies and spirits and tend to the gifts we've received.

When we think of being caretakers of land or of community space, we can avoid the KEEP versus SHARE mentality if we hold clear to the idea that we are caretakers, not owners. If there are others around us, and others to follow in our places, we have a better sense of *who* we caretaking for. That's why land-based communities are important.

From European history come stories of the peasants being forced from the land by the loss of the commons with the rise of capitalism and industrialism. When the commons—the community land—was divided, partitioned, and fenced into private property, people lost their means of having crops and animals. People were herded into cities to feed the industrial machine. Europeans became landless. The chain of abuse continued as capitalism, industrialism, and "propertyism" were brought to this continent. And how many of us had grandmothers and great-grandmothers who watched their children be forced to leave the land for jobs in the cities? We are the next generation of the landless. Our task is to create land for women without repeating the patterns of abusive ownership. We need to think of ourselves as caretakers, rather than private property owners, sharing responsibility for the land.

Creating land-based communities based on caretaking land for lesbians may be one of the most important things lesbians are doing. We need to learn the skills of caretaking. We need to build the commons again. We need the security of not just land in private ownership, but also of land in common ownership. We need *places* where we can live together for long times. To quote Kiwani again, "We need to agree to live as though all are entitled to shelter, food, safety, in harmony with all creation.

We need to share our resources and make our womynsworld more accessible to all sisters." We need places to do this.

There are many variations of wimmin's land, from private ownership to open wimmin's lands. The creation of open wimmin's lands had been a community effort to create the commons—community owned land—and to address economic differences among lesbians. These lands are open to any woman to come to for camping, and living on when there is housing available. Presently there is Arf Women's Land in New Mexico, where one still needs to come up with $80 a month to be there, and Owl Farm and Cabbage Lane in Oregon, lands already paid for, so without a financial requirement. There could be other open wimmin's lands in the East that we don't know about. Arf's 11 houses have been full even through the tough winters for three years now. From what we hear, Owl Farm periodically has had openings, and Cabbage Lane right now is in need of women to come live there.

But it is not enough to throw together vastly different poor lesbians onto a few scattered pieces of land. Poor lesbians have many different visions and need for some control over their lives, and don't need the everyday insecurity of having to live with every woman who arrives at open wimmin's land. Having money enables lesbians to exclude those they don't want to live with. Poor lesbians today have only a few pieces of land available to them on which they have to live with women vastly different from themselves, or not be on wimmin's land at all.

On the other hand, we hear of lesbian couples who have both land and have a vision of community for their land. Other lesbians come to be part of the community, but eventually leave with hopes dashed. The land-owning lesbians too become weary of the revolving door, the comings and goings. Might this be happening because the vision is held by the lesbians who bought the land, and those who come later must either fit someone else's vision or leave? We poor lesbians have visions and dreams that we don't want to leave behind in order to fit someone else's vision so that we can be on land. It seems we will never have the economic resources to manifest our visions, not even if many poor lesbians band together.

Some lesbians talk of dividing land, saying this part is for disabled lesbians, this for poor lesbians, this for rich lesbians to build their own homes on, this section is for lesbians of color,

this section is for separatists, that one for meat-eaters. But
segregation is not what a lot of us have in mind, and neither is
stratification based on either economics or age.

Another option for poor lesbians is to wait for the right
vision to come along which is backed up by start-up capital.
That was the base of most of the heterosexual communities of
the mid-1800s and today. In most of these cases, there was a
benevolent capitalist in the background who financed the
project. The model is not applicable to our situations as
lesbians with very diverse visions and spiritual grounds, and
diverse economic states. The earlier communities often too, had
a creed or set of beliefs that one needed to hold in order to
join. We know from our experience that creeds tend to divide,
and shared values can change with circumstances and time.

If our primary hope is to share what we have, rather than
keep what we have, there is a possibility that we can avoid the
old abusive patterns of community land ownership. Perhaps we
should first build our centers of the community, the commons,
and then through that, work out the diverse patterns of
dwellings surrounding these centers. Some may want to live
near the commons, some may live in nearby clusters or affinity
groups. Some may live on adjacent owned or rented land, some
might be far-flung neighbors. All these can be arranged by
choice and opportunity as need arises. As we build the
commons we can better find out how to share our skills and
gifts with each other. When we can create a place where it is
possible to share all of our skills, not just those related to
money, we can get away from the current limitations we have
that are based on patriarchal attitudes toward land and money.

ALL WE HAVE IS EACH OTHER*

PHYLLIS CHESLER

In only 25 years, a visionary feminism has managed to seriously challenge, if not transform, world consciousness. Nevertheless, I am saddened and sobered by the realization that no more than a handful of feminists have been liberated from the lives of grinding poverty, illness, overwork, and endless worry that continue to afflict most women and men in America.

I have seen the best minds of my feminist generation go *mad* with battle fatigue, get sick, give up, disappear, kill themselves, die—often alone, and in terrible isolation—as if we were already invisible: to each other and to ourselves, our role as pioneers and immigrants diminished, forgotten.

Immigrants always form infrastructure or self-help groups and tithe themselves accordingly. We are the immigrants who, in the late 1960s and early 1970s, left the Old Patriarchal Country to clear a path in History for the generations to come. It's too late for us to turn back, and we've still got miles to go before we sleep in our own feminist country.

There are few feminist networks in place whose mandate it is to assist feminists (or female adults) when they lose their jobs, fall ill, stay ill, face death, and are without patriarchal family resources, supportive mates, or other safety nets.

Surrounded by epidemics, I ask, Where are our feminist credit unions and emergency funds? (Remember those failed

* This essay appeared in shortened form as "In My View" in *On the Issues: The Progressive Women's Quarterly*, vol 25, Winter 1992, p 59.

Copyright © 1993 by Phyllis Chesler

attempts in the mid-1970s?) Our feminist soup kitchen, Meals on Wheels, land trusts, and old age homes? (Remember those fiascoes?) Our breast cancer fundraising campaigns, our hospices, our burial societies? (Feminists are just *starting* to get serious about breast cancer and about women with AIDS).

They do not yet exist. Instead, feminists say "I didn't tell anyone I was sick because I didn't want my employers *or my enemies* to know." Or "I didn't ask anyone for help." Pride maybe, but also fear. People tend to avoid you when you're in trouble. One survivor of breast cancer told me that in the mid-1980s, her newly formed cancer support group disbanded when its first member died. A formerly disabled lesbian feminist said, "Sick men know how to get others to take care of them. Sick women don't know how to ask for help and can't get it when they do. Maybe gay men are also learning how to take care of others. Gay men took care of me when I was sick, not other lesbian feminists." A chronically disabled woman said, "Only a few friends visited me more than once. Most had a hard time with the fact that a strong woman could become so sick, and an even harder time fitting me into schedules already overcrowded with other caretaking responsibilities."[*]

Some feminists blame those whose immune systems cannot absorb any more environmental toxins—or toxic amounts of hostility. Some of us still say "It's her own fault she has no health insurance,[**] no nursing care, no job, no mate. She should have planned better or compromised harder." Or we say, "But isn't she really a little (or a lot) crazy?"

In 1982, Elizabeth Fisher, Founder of *Aphra* magazine and author of *Women's Creation: Sexual Evolution and the Shaping of Society*, and in 1987, my dear friend Ellen Franfurt, author of *Vaginal Politics*, killed themselves. Not just because they were depressed, on drugs, discarded at midlife, or without hope that things would get better (although some of this was so), but

---

[*] So many women either opposed or were so uncomfortable with my identifying them by name that I chose not to do so.

[**] In May 1992, the Older Womens League released a report that showed that due to low-paying and part-time work, American women between the ages of 40 and 60 are far more likely than their male contemporaries to lack health insurance.

also because they were tired of fighting so hard for so long for a place in the sun (a Manhattan loft, a decent-enough book contract), tired of being hated so much and of never having enough money. They despaired of both man's and woman's inhumanity to woman.

So many of us have died, mainly of breast cancer. To name only a few: June Arnold, Park Bowman, Jane Chambers, Barbara Deming, Mary-Helen Mautner, Barbara Myerhoff, Lil Moed, Pat Parker, Barbara Rosenblum, Isacca Siegel, Sunny Wainwright, Audre Lorde.

We have no quilt, and no memorial.

So many of us have wrestled with and survived breast cancer. So many of us are struggling with long-time disabilities, reeling from lyme disease, and from Chronic Fatigue Immune Dysfunction Syndrome (CFIDS), myself included.[*]

Some of us have been blessed by feminist caretaking. I think of how magnificently Sandra Butler cared for—and orchestrated community support for—her cancer-stricken lover/partner Barbara Rosenblum (an account is contained in their book *Cancer in Two Voices*); I think of how tenderly, how enduringly Jesse Lemisch has cared for his CFIDS-racked wife, my beloved comrade, Naomi Weisstein; I think of how many lesbian-feminists cared for and sent white light to Barbara Deming, Jane Chambers, and Audre Lorde.

But these are splendid exceptions, lucky, individual solutions, even trends, not yet sturdy, immigrant infrastructure.

I recently attended a rent party for Ti-Grace Atkinson, author of *Amazon Odyssey*. Ti-Grace's health was seriously impaired by exposure to low-dose radiation. (Her father was the head of the Atomic Energy Commission's Plutonium By-Products Division at Washington States Hanford Reservation.) She says "First, I had a hysterectomy. Now, I have

---

[*] Some survivors of breast cancer are Phyllis Birkby, Blanche Wiesen Cook, Jan Crawford, Edith Konecky, Phyllis Kriegel, Eleanor Pam, Gloria Steinem—these names come immediately to mind. Some survivors of long-time disabilities are Flo Kennedy, Bea Kreloff, Bettye Lane, Judy O'Neil, Betty Powell; of lyme disease—Beverly Lowy, Max Dashu; of CFIDS—myself, Susan Griffin, Joan Nestle, Aviva Rahmani, Arlene Raven, Naomi Weisstein—to name only those I know.

no thyroid left. I take tons of thyroid medication, some of which has made me sick and unable to work."

The rent party was a determined, even inspired, grassroots effort that yielded more good will than cash; however, such events are too labor-intensive, too hard to repeat on a monthly basis for every pioneer feminist, whether or not she's written a book, who's in an illness-related economic crisis.

Ti-Grace at least has an apartment. Other feminist pioneers are—or are about to become—homeless. For example, a legendary anti-pornography activist has been forced to warehouse her files and move in with a friend. The coauthor of a lesbian feminist classic, a well-known feminist comedienne, an abortion rights activist—and countless other pioneers all sway unsteadily on the brink of joblessness and homelessness. The coauthor of a much-loved book on feminist spirituality became homeless last year; she left New York for a warmer climate to be homeless in. Shulamith Firestone, author of *The Dialectics of Sex* and a welfare recipient, had to battle hard to hang onto her rent-controlled apartment in between visits to Belleview in the late 1980s.

The fact that none of these women have written second books impoverishes us all.

Two of my dear friends, both major feminist leaders, have kept writing, despite a variety of health problems, but like so many great writers, both dead and alive, simply cannot earn a living by the pen.* Neither is independently wealthy, has a tenured position, or a pension; they remain dreadfully, bravely poor, unable to act on their own grand visions without unimaginable personal sacrifice and constant worry.

I am not blaming any of us for not having done more; we did the best we could, and we did a lot. But in all our imaginings, we failed to imagine that we ourselves would grow weary or fall ill and have no real, specific family to take us in and tide us over until we could get back on our feet.

Some of us acted as if we didn't think we'd *need* families again. Perhaps our collective experience of transcendence blinded us to our ordinary needs. But most of us were longing

---

* A writer's average annual income is about $5,000.00.

for "communitas." We talked about sisterhood and community, tribes and alternate families—but only in the abstract, as we rushed from one dazzling spectacle to another.

I know: the republic ought to provide employment, health insurance, and medical care for all its citizens, but it doesn't; and we have fallen on hard times, along with everyone else. All we have is each other: our sisters, ourselves.

PART 2

FEEDING AND WATERING: GROWING OUR OWN BUSINESSES

I like to think of the 1970s as the fresh spring of the woman-centered economy: when every idea was green and wet and new, when women were all colors but all young, all raised in homes where they were told anything is possible. Then there was the fresh storm energy of anger, as women first uncovered how unfairly they were being treated, how unreasonable the blockades that kept women from owning property, fighting fires, flying airplanes.

The woman-centered economy grew like babies grow, incredibly quickly, and one day without even knowing they had done it our foremothers were able to take a long breath. By then our businesses were children: growing more slowly, asking more questions. The 1980s, then, were the ugly teenage years, filled with self doubt and the dreadful realization that some of the feminist sisters who had shared our experiences were women we not only disagreed with but whom we couldn't trust. I like to think that now that more than 20 years have passed, we are striding into adulthood. We're still constantly changing, but not at the pace we once were.

The women writing in this section have been a part of the women's community for a widely varying number of years, from those who have been dedicated to the community since the 1970s to those just introduced to feminism in the 1990s. Their access to and attitudes toward money also vary widely.

WHY WE GROW OUR OWN BUSINESSES

Although many women are committed to the women's
community, few are interested in running our organizations
and businesses. As several women writing in this section
point out, there are many factors that push a woman to start
a woman-centered business, such as these:

▲ Personal desire to stop putting energy into men
▲ Personal desire to do things our own ways
▲ Personal desire to make a difference in the world
▲ Personal desire to produce products that aren't readily
  available in the mainstream
▲ Personal pride in our skills

No one can be goaded into running a business or starting an
organization unless she is personally motivated. Politics alone
do not a business make.

A reason given by many women for not starting a business is
that they lack the money to do so. Certainly "undercapitaliza-
tion" (as they call it in mainstream business books) is a
problem for most small businesses, including woman-centered
ones. But as many women in this section point out, it takes a
lot more than money to grow a business. The organizations
represented in this section are often the product of several
womens' vision and dedication (and money too).

Many women talk about starting their own businesses when
they are most fed up with the mainstream economy—whether
it's a job where they are being harrassed or a product they need
and can't find. Anger is an important component to many
feminist concerns, in that anger encouarages people to act. In
the woman-centered economy, however, anger at the
mainstream is often transformed into a willingness to learn
what we can and unlearn what we have to. Anger may spur
women to action, but commitment keeps a business going.

ALMOST ANY BUSINESS CAN BE A WOMAN-CENTERED BUSINESS

One of the aspects of the woman-centered economy that makes
it hard to define is that almost any business can be a

woman-centered business. To my way of thinking, however, no factor determines whether a business is woman-centered more than marketing. A woman-centered business is a woman-run business whose market clearly includes or focuses on feminists and/or lesbians. Unfortunately (for the businesses), we are not an easy market to define or reach.

Some of the factors that make us difficult to reach as a market are these:

▲   Homophobia, both external and internal
▲   A wide range of personal economic realities
▲   A wide range of physical locations
▲   A wide range of expectations and needs
▲   Competition from the mainstream
▲   Personal distaste for being manipulated as a market
▲   Political conviction not to be reduced to being a market

Despite this, there are several ways that we are easy to access as a market, via

▲   Women's music festivals
▲   Feminist publishing & bookstores
▲   Women's bars and coffeehouses

In this section, women who run women's music festivals, bookstores, publishing companies, and bars, as well as other feminist venues, discuss the conflict that arises when women who don't want to be a market realize that they have become one, and how we can acknowledge marketing as part of feminism without losing feminism in the process.

WHERE THE MONEY COMES FROM

For the most part, the money in the woman-centered economy comes from women's disposable (excess) income. Several of the businesses represented in this section sell products women can do without if they don't have the money. The good thing about businesses that run on excess income is that they can often be run in excess time; women work part time in the mainstream to earn the money that they live on, and work the rest of the time at their woman-centered business. The bad thing is that these businesses tend to be more marginal, smaller, and less

permanent than mainstream businesses. In some cases, the
businesses are completely invisible to the mainstream, run by
women who don't pay taxes, don't advertise, by women who
have given themselves names rather than use the patriarchal
names on their social security cards.

Another point made in discussions with women who run
woman-centered businesses is that the more invested a woman
is in the community, the more likely she is to spend her money
with other woman-centered businesses. Women who are part of
the community spend in the community, which means some
women can start new businesses, festivals, and support groups.

Women who run businesses in our community are fond of
pointing out that buying from woman-centered businesses is a
way of giving to the community, because other women need to
survive in business in order to give to the community. Without
organizations that need money, we wouldn't have much of a
community to draw on. As Theresa Corrigan puts it in her
article in this section, we (woman-centered businesses) are not
in business to make money, but we need money in order to stay
in business.

GREAT EXPECTATIONS

Women business owners are aware that other women have
higher expectations for woman-centered businesses than they
have for mainstream businesses. Probably this is due to higher
expectations of ourselves: we like to think that the face we
bring to the women's community is not only our prettiest face,
but our most virtuous face as well. Our community is often our
last bastion of idealism; women who are completely cynical
about their jobs, their neighbors, and their families are still able
to be idealistic about Michigan,* for example. Unfortunately,
this can also turn into unrealistic expectations. Women who
earn $50,000 a year working for a mainstream company can
criticize other women who make $30,000 a year on women's

---

* "Michigan" is the community colloquialism that refers to the
Michigan Womyn's Music Festival.

music; women who think nothing of spending $30 a seat to see a mainstream artist will criticize a $15 or $20 a seat price of a women's music event as being inaccessibly high.

Other consequences of unrealistic expectations are doom and sunshine. Some women are inclined to assume a woman-centered organization, like a lesbian relationship, is more likely to fail. Others are too ready to think that our organizations will live forever, and so they take their existence for granted.

The role of internal politics is discussed by several of the authors in this section. Because woman-centered businesses are run as much from the heart as from the balance sheet, politics play an important and often positive role, encouraging us to see things from more perspectives.

BIG BUSINESS

LESBIANS DEAL WITH PERSONAL PROFITS AND COLLECTIVE ACTION

ANN HARRISON

When Provincetown businesswoman Martha Nelson opened her
second lesbian-and-gay gift shop in Northampton back in 1991,
she wasn't counting on becoming a national celebrity. Then she
appeared on the now-famous 20/20 segment on Northampton
(called "Women Who Love Women"), and her store began
receiving thousands of calls from lesbians across the country.
Nelson's store, Pride and Joy, has become information central
for a flood of lesbians who arrive in Northampton seeking jobs,
housing, therapists, and a social life.

As a lesbian entrepreneur, Nelson feels it's her responsibility
to help other gay women establish themselves in a supportive
environment. But she says her high-profile role as a business
owner has also generated some resentment from other lesbian
women. "Over time, I've had people perceive that I am affluent,
and that that is *not* okay," says Nelson. "The feeling is that if
you have money, you have in some way bought into the
patriarchal system, or exploited someone, or inherited it from
some man."

Established lesbian business owners around the state agree
that their perceived prosperity has sometimes made them
suspect in the eyes of their own community. Despite some
lesbians' desire for ideological unity, these businesswomen say,
the community is not yet comfortable talking about economic
success. Money, they say, is a much greater taboo than sex. But
as they acquire more expertise in their respective fields, these

Copyright © 1994 by Ann Harrison   117 women are in a position to serve as powerful mentors to other lesbians who want to put their dreams in motion. They also have some valuable advice about surviving the hard knocks along the way.

▲ ▲ ▲

Boomer Kennedy, owner of Chicago Auto, in Cambridgeport, has trained four lesbian apprentice mechanics in her shop. Her business, which was the first lesbian-owned garage in the Boston area, now grosses more than a quarter-million dollars a year and employs five people. But when she first graduated from a mechanics' training program and began looking for employment, she was asked to take a job as a secretary and offered pitifully low wages to work in other shops. When told that she didn't have the experience to start her own garage, she ignored the advice and applied the business skills she had learned as the owner of a small manufacturing company. "I would say opening your own business is easier than everyone thinks," Kennedy says. "There is just a psychological leap that you need to take."

When she first opened her garage, Kennedy depended on word of mouth within Boston's large feminist, lesbian, and gay community to attract customers. She estimates that 40 percent of her business still comes from lesbians and gay men. Although she's held fundraisers for AIDS support groups and for the plaintiff of a lesbian sexual-harassment case, Kennedy says her primary contribution to the community is being an honest person and projecting a positive image for lesbians. She says she has always been out to her landlords, neighbors, and business associates—yet she doesn't consider Chicago Auto a "lesbian business."

"In 1984, I had to make a fast decision: did I open my shop as a lesbian or did I open it as a person who wanted to be a mechanic?" says Kennedy. "the truth is, I was a businessperson first, and I never projected a big lesbian identity—although I made damn sure that I was never, ever, pushed back or closeted."

Kennedy says that in the past ten years, she's seen an evolution in the way her lesbian customers do business. At first,

she had difficulty getting women to accept the fact that they
had to pay for repair services. For example, shortly after she
opened her shop, in the mid 1980s, she had a customer who
had recently returned from an overseas women's conference.
The woman tried to argue that her lesbian activism entitled her
to a $90 discount on her car repair bill and was indignant
when Kennedy turned her down. Kennedy has also declined
offers to barter with women for automotive services, and will
not "process" with other lesbians who want to "share" their
car-repair experience with her.

"The community gets the feeling that businesses that are
lesbian-owned are owned by the *entire* gay community, and
therefore controlled by the gay community. And therefore your
politics have to be right," she says. Kennedy notes that there
was a time when lesbians had an aversion to making money
because it was associated with patriarchal values. But, unlike
Nelson, she believes this perspective has shifted in Boston, as
lesbians acknowledge their own diversity.

According to Kennedy, lesbians thought they had to be as
similar to one another as possible so that they could
overcome—as a group—the oppression they experienced. But as
more lesbians feel free to express their individuality, dress
provocatively, and shed what Kennedy calls the "lesbian
uniform," a broader culture is emerging. "There is nothing
about being gay that has anything to do with your politics or
how you behave sexually," she says. "In truth, there is nothing
we have in common with each other except our sexual
preference."

▲ ▲ ▲

This is not to say that lesbian and gay business owners don't
feel a need to act collectively. In Boston, they share expertise
through the Greater Boston Business Council (GBBC), which
now has 700 members. GBBC president Karen Lucas is the
owner of Whistle Stop Signs, in Melrose. She says that though
the corporate world has targeted the gay dollar as an attractive
demographic market, it's important for lesbian businesspeople
to network and circulate their money within their own
community. Lucas says that GBBC helps lesbians and gay men

share business services, and its members offer advice on such issues as how to deal with harassment in the workplace.

Lucas, who estimates that 75 percent of her business comes from gays and lesbians, says GBBC members prefer doing business with fellow members because they are more sensitive to one another's needs. She notes that when she and her partner purchased a house together, she found a lesbian lawyer (through GBBC) who knew how to draft the necessary wills and legal transactions without having to research the issue. "I didn't have to pay her to learn how to treat me," she says.

When Lucas signed on to her partner's health plan, she also went looking for a dentist who wouldn't treat the arrangement like is was anything out of the ordinary. "You just want to be normal and come in and say 'this is my partner' and sit down. You don't want it to be a big deal," Lucas says.

▲ ▲ ▲

Providing basic services to the lesbian community was a strong incentive to Nelson, who says she opened Prides, her original gift shop in Provincetown, as a way to provide lesbian- and gay-oriented gifts that were unavailable anywhere else. Unfortunately, she says, many straight people assume that a shop such as hers specializes in pornography. Nelson is beginning to carry more sexually-oriented merchandise, but she's still trying to challenge the image of lesbian-and gay-owned businesses as being somehow second-class, or degrading to customers.

"I was tired of going to some dark place with the shades drawn and sticky floors," Nelson says. "We have to create our own sense of dignity. The hetero world is not going to give it to us."

GBBC members also see themselves as promoting self-image for lesbians and gays. Lucas says the organization wants to provide role models to gay youth in particular. Toward this end, the GBBC has started a scholarship fund for gay teens, and there is also some discussion about starting a summer-jobs program through the Boston mayor's office. "These kids are our future and we want to be there as role models and be there to support them," Lucas explains.

▲ ▲ ▲

Perhaps the truest test of professional networking occurs when a business gets into trouble and its owners need support. Last month, the organizers of the three-day weekend Northampton Lesbian Festival racked up a $27,000 debt when the event drew a fraction of the expected attendants. The festival was planned by WOW Productions, and coowners Diane Morgan and Zizi Ansell watched with alarm as constant rain kept women away. By Saturday night, knowing they were in deep financial peril, Ansell and Morgan gathered a brain trust of lesbian festival promoters and entrepreneurs—including Michele Crone, producer of RhythmFest, and Janet Grubbs, producer of the Virginia Women's Music Festival. The group generated ideas for averting financial disaster.

"We were so tired and strung out from the stress of knowing that this was coming. It was so helpful to have people who were rested, who could think clearly, who could give a perspective," says Morgan.

By acknowledging their need for immediate assistance, Morgan and Ansell were able to draw on the skills of experienced lesbian businesswomen. Crone walked on stage that Saturday night, told the audience about the financial loss, and asked for donations. Morgan reports that the audience chipped in $2500 that evening; then $1500 was later raised through a sidewalk sale, $250 through anonymous donations, and $4000 through interest-free loans. She adds that though she and Ansell have witnessed infighting among lesbians recently, they still have faith that there is a commitment to helping the community survive.

"It's been pretty difficult to live through the past couple of years, but it's like the old family scene," Morgan says. "We might fight at the dinner table all the time, but if anything happens we get together and pull through."

Donations and loans started to come in, but Morgan was still apprehensive about covering checks that had already been written. She says financial and moral support from the lesbian community helped cushion the reception she got from the Springfield Institute for Savings, where her business banks. Morgan says the branch manager declined to discuss a short-term loan with her, refused to bend on the policy of offering no overdraft protections to businesses, and wouldn't even notify her in the event that a check was being drawn from the account. "It was basically her opportunity to let a dyke fly in the wind," Morgan says.

The future of the festival is uncertain, and its organizers are exhausted from having to locate festivals at a new site every year for the past five years—a situation Morgan blames largely on homophobia. Although a few spaces were simply too small for the festival, managers of some facilities were uncomfortable with the presence of several thousand lesbians, Morgan says. During the fourth festival, at the Swift River Inn, in Cummington, inn managers forbade promoters to mention the festival location in interviews with the national press. But Morgan says that she and Ansell are now taking the time to refine their strategy and digest the lesson.

Morgan says the lesbian community has high standards for lesbian-owned businesses. The community wants its businesses to reflect its core values of social responsibility, but this often leads to conflicting views of how this should be carried out. For her business, Morgan says, this ethic includes a commitment to preserving the land where the festival takes place, to making the event accessible to disabled and low-income people, and to including those with a range of ideological perspectives.

"There is an expectation that what we are attempting to create is a microcosm of a perfect world," Morgan explains. "We need to be patient with each other as we try to nail down the logistics of what that means."

▲ ▲ ▲

Lesbian business owners in Northampton, Boston, and Provincetown generally display an eagerness to serve as business mentors. They say it's a myth that they are too busy to share advice, and they suggest that any woman who is considering opening her own business spend a couple of months working for someone she admires who runs a similar enterprise. This strategy gives aspiring lesbian entrepreneurs an opportunity to see if the work suits them before they make an investment.

Provincetown entrepreneur Marie O'Shea is discovering that assistance from other lesbians can also translate into working capital. O'Shea, a former chef with a degree in hotel management from Cornell University, opened the Purple Cactus burrito bar with a partner two years ago. She says lesbians have been walking into her business offering to invest in a second Purple Cactus in Somerville, or in Boston or Maine. O'Shea plans to open another branch in Boston and is currently scouting locations.

O'Shea makes a point of crediting her workers as a key part of her success and says she is committed to treating her staff with respect. This is not necessarily an extension of her life as a lesbian, say O'Shea, it's just her personal ethic as a businessperson. "You walk into most of the restaurants in Provincetown and you get an attitude fast," she says. "[The staff] treat you like a shithead because they feel awful about working there. There are treated badly by the business owners, and you can see how they emulate the managers." Of Provincetown, she says, "It's a gay town. Just because it's a gay business doesn't mean it's a good business." In fact, O'Shea says, the key to her continued success and future expansion rests on her ability to communicate effectively with her employees. This isn't *lesbian* management—just sound management.

▲ ▲ ▲

Even though there is capital out there for up-and-coming lesbian businesswomen, there is still a certain amount of fear associated with being out in the business world. Lucas recalls that when a camera crew from the Channel 5 program Chronicle arrived to tape a GBBC networking party, a cameraman joked that he hadn't seen so many backs since taping a Mafia funeral.

"People fear," says Lucas. "They don't want to be on TV as gay or lesbian anything—because they fear retribution or they are not out or they don't want to be fired from their jobs. We want to create a safe place where they can be gay and lesbian businesspeople and don't have to be out to anyone else."

Lucas also notes that lesbian businesswomen in general are not as comfortable with networking as men who grew up with the old-boy system. "With women, it takes them a half an hour to get the card out of their pockets, as if they are afraid they are insulting you by handing you a business card," Lucas says.

Although women now make up only 30 percent of the organization's membership, she says, the GBBC is actively seeking more women members. She also notes that salaries of lesbian and straight businesswomen are still a fraction of their male counterparts'. But in Boston there is an established community of prosperous older lesbians. "I think there is a myth out there that lesbians are poor," says Lucas. "There are a lot of poor lesbians, but I don't think they're all poor."

Sincere there are fewer lesbian business owners in Provincetown, women are also a minority in the Provincetown Business Guild. In Northampton, however, lesbians make up 90 percent of the Northampton Area Lesbian and Gay Business Guild, where Nelson now serves as president. O'Shea says she would like to see a lesbian business guild in Provincetown, but notes that it would be a challenging undertaking. "You have a group of people with all different notions of what success is and what they want out of P-Town," says O'Shea. "It's tough to find a group of women with a common set of goals."

Some lesbians who have accumulated years of experience in the business world say women still have a lot to learn about economic cooperation. Gabriel Brooke, who has owned Gabriel's Bed and Breakfast, in Provincetown, since 1979, says she wants to put her business skills to work to teach woman how to manage financial clout effectively. "All we were taught is how to dress up and look good for the boys and be in competition with one another. When we get into a position of power, either economically or politically, I think sometimes we misuse that power and we feel suspicious of one another," says Brooke.

Brooke, who learned her business skills from Christina Davidson, founder of a Provincetown kite store, says most of the opposition that she has faced as a lesbian entrepreneur has come not from men but from other lesbian women in similar businesses. She says that, after years at the bottom of the economic ladder, women have developed a "scarcity mentality," which leads them to believe that they and other women don't deserve to get ahead. Brooke says she agrees with Nelson that the lesbian community is prone to a degree of self-oppression, or "horizontal hostility," which keeps women from celebrating and supporting economic abundance. "We can't strike outside of ourselves, so we strike across at each other," Brooke says.

Brooke insists that as more lesbians begin to generate a greater economic base, they need to take a hard look at their larger goals. The challenge, she says, is not simply to chase after money and power for their own sake but to temper them with a spiritual perspective that benefits the entire community.

Ansell, of WOW Productions, agrees that as the lesbian community moves forward in the material world, it needs to pay attention to its spiritual health. Despite her own financial setback, she believes that lesbian festivals and other collective gatherings should encourage lesbians to look more deeply at their values and plot a course for their cooperative future. "You can buy a condo or a car, you can buy a diamond ring—but unless you have some sense of spiritual community, it means shit," says Ansell. "What does success really mean?"

Brooke points out that though there are many lesbian business owners in Provincetown, the tourist culture, which centers on entertainment and recreations, has not translated into a unified sense of community for the women who live there. Her bed-and-breakfast, which employs 10 people, is not profitable, she says. But, according to Brooke, it serves as a micro-community for the women who run it and the guests they receive. "I feel strongly about supporting any kind of vision that women have, and that includes women who want to come to town and start exactly the same kind of business that I have," says Brooke.

After cultivating careers as a professional business consultant, computer trainer, photographer, and manager for Georgia Ragsdale and other entertainers, Brooke now wants to expand an ongoing series of workshops launched by her bed-and-breakfast. She says she wants to use her business as a launch pad to encourage greater discussion of lesbian arts, spirituality, politics, and health care. Upcoming workshop leaders include Kate Millett, author of *Sexual Politics*; Kay Gardner, an internationally known composer; and Charlotte Kasl, author of *Women, Sex and Addiction*. Though the workshops may help pay her mortgage, Brooke says, she is also exploring the feasibility of opening a nonprofit women's educational center in Provincetown. "Ultimately the strongest political statement any of us can make is through personal transformation," says

Brooke. "It's one thing to go out and make a lot of money and be really strong in the community. But if you don't understand why we're doing what we're doing, then we've lost the message."

MY MONEY, MY SELF

CAPITALISM, LESBIANISM, AND THE MYTHS OF SUCCESS

LAURA L. POST

Women have long struggled economically, due to the constraints of sexism, racism, ageism, and physicalism in our materialistic culture. Separatism, self-employment, downward mobility, and "new girls' networking" have all been discussed and attempted as methods of addressing the economic pressures placed on our lives. There is no single response that works for everyone, and I don't pretend that my experiences parallel everyone else's. Nonetheless, I hope they evoke thoughtful responses and, perhaps, at the individual level, new possibilities.

INTRODUCTION TO ME

I am a white, Jewish lesbian who grew up in an upper-middle-class home. I attended a state medical school and decided to become a psychiatrist. I chose a job, which I still hold, as Medical Director for the largest lesbian/gay mental health and services agency in San Francisco. Although the responsibilities of this job are similar to those of many psychiatric positions, I earn much less than my psychiatric peers, which I see as the cost of doing a job, which I enjoy, within the lesbian/gay community. Initially, I investigated positions within women's/lesbian mental health clinics, of which there are several in the San Francisco Bay Area. At that time, no agency had the funding available for a psychiatrist. It is difficult to know

Copyright © 1993 by Laura Post

whether this lack of funds is due to an anti-psychiatry bias on the part of the therapists and counselors who run these agencies, or simply a reflection of the limited number of healthcare dollars available to feminists.

CAPITALIST CHOICES IN MEDICINE

Part of what convinced me that psychiatry was right for me was the notion, common to many feminists functioning within the patriarchy, that I could tolerate the abuses and oppression in order to eventually be able to effect change within the system. Beating them at their own game required both some stealth about my ideals while acquiring the power (in order to be allowed to continue) and maintaining allegiance to those ideals despite external forces pushing me to compromise them. In other words, the trick was not to become coopted by the process. My goal was an idealized mix of a high disposable income, the free time in which to dispose of it, and fame. I soon learned that making higher-ups uncomfortable won't get you the space or funding or approval to do that research project on lesbians of color, or to open that clinic for lesbian incest survivors, or to start that group about lesbian sexuality. I had thought that these rules wouldn't operate in a humanistic field such as medicine. But they do.

For a lesbian to survive psychiatry training, several approaches exist: (1) to be closeted, (2) to excel all-around academically, (3) to develop expertise in a non-sexual (read: "non-threatening") arena, (4) to take on the public persona as the program's lesbian. Due to my wish to engage the lesbian population, options 1 and 3 didn't work for me. To stay sane and sober, my commitment to personal health over workaholic service, option 2 didn't work either. I joyfully chose option 4; however, in doing so I surrendered in the competition with my psychiatric peers for the most significant prizes: a respected academic career, mainstream recognition, and maximum financial rewards.

In addition to being a gainfully employed psychiatric physician, I am also a self-employed artist within the women's community. This began while I was in medical school and going through my psychiatric residencies. I won an award of several hundred dollars, which gave me the means to fulfill a dream I

had had since I came out—to produce a concert of women's
music. This led to interviewing performers for at first local and
within the year national publications. My involvement within
the community provided a welcome counterbalance to the
hierarchal hospital I worked in and made me want to direct
more of my energy to it. Unfortunately, despite careful planning
and thorough promotion, I lost money on every production I
put on. The economic realities of the women's community
didn't change my ideals.

MAKING THE DOUBLE LIFE WORK

I currently divide my time between 20 hours per week as a
psychiatrist and a more variable allotment of 25–30 hours per
week for my writing (I no longer produce). My psychiatric
salary is $35,000 annually, and is accompanied by health
insurance; as a writer, I earn no more than $200 monthly,
which is taxed at self-employment rates, and which brings no
benefits. I realize that I am lucky in having the amount of
unscheduled time that I do, and that many white-collar workers
are not able to enjoy a creative outlet as I do.

Having acknowledged my fortune in having one career that
supports another, I want to describe some of the financial and
moral difficulties involved in being an artist "part time." During
my writing time, I cope with fluctuating creative energies,
uncertain contracts for work, unpredictable public responses,
and poor reimbursements (most of the time). As with medicine
(or any discipline), compromises must be made between
freedoms and funding; unfortunately, it often happens that
having the freedom to write or produce something lesbian
means forgoing major sources of funding. As a writer, I also
face the obstacles of geographically distant editors, rapidly
changing information interfering with accurate news reports,
maintaining confidentiality, ambivalent or self-protective
interview subjects, and firm deadlines.

I believe that our society does not recognize the benefits of
creative minds, either in terms of truth, beauty, and change, or
even on the personal level of stress relief and ego reinforcement.
Much of the artistic process is maligned as wasteful and useless.
Therefore, as artists we are not remunerated commensurate
with our contribution to pleasure or innovation. A couple can

easily spend $20 to see a misogynistic and violent movie without thinking about it, even though they won't spend the same money to see a community theater production or purchase a handmade book.

It is, thus, morally, not financially, that I am driven to pursue payment. The feminist cultural network values artists far more than the rest of society does. Unfortunately, because women earn only 63¢ for every man's dollar, our community has little money to spare. Most of my pieces to women's/lesbian presses are freebies, while I demand payment for many of my efforts that find their way into the gay men's press. Men's publications, however, are often reluctant to publish pieces specifically for lesbians, believing as they do that AIDS issues, personals, camp, dish, and sexy pictures bring in the readers and ad dollars— again the conflict between choice and money.

I am convinced that my life has been enhanced by having two overlapping careers. With one foot in a "mainstream" profession and the other foot in an "alternative" profession, I am exposed to differing ideas about what these professions are and what they mean. Often I am able to alter what people who are more firmly rooted in only one world think of people on the "other side." For example, when a scientific article of mine is published in a medical or psychiatric journal, doctors are exposed to feminist and lesbian assumptions and language. Projects that focus on lesbians in a positive way force audiences to rethink at a very fundamental level their beliefs about lesbians. Hopefully, new understanding and insight result.

Less dramatically, when I work with clients, students, and peers, I make it clear that as a psychiatrist, I believe that all people are unique and to be treated equally, that unexamined bias and pejorative terminology are unacceptable. I am able to dispel negative stereotypes of psychiatry and Western medicine.

HOW MONEY FITS IN

As a creative writer, I am free to express many things I cannot express as a psychiatrist, including anger at the government, anger at the abuses perpetrated through the closed-mindedness of organized psychiatry and similar disciplines, and anger at individuals who have made a client's—or my own—life difficult. Artists speak society's voices of unselfconscious reason and protest. Women's presses perpetuate our vital and challenging culture and encourage change in the society at large. Therefore, I understand why those who have the most money in our society choose to restrict monetary reward to disruptive forces, such as women's writing.

I believe we need to improve cash flow into and around the lesbian community through education and communication. We need to convince wealthy lesbians that underfunded lesbian causes are worthy of their consideration and contributions. We need to reach beyond lesbians as well. Applying assertively for local financial support and developing mainstream media allies are as important to maintaining our community as doing private fundraising.

We need to develop awareness of our own personal issues, obstacles, and goals; and to share those goals with others who can help us carry them out. We need to convey to other lesbians as well as to people different from ourselves who we are and what we want. We need to believe in our skills and have faith while we try to persuade others of our worth and promise. I believe that, for us as individuals and as a community, knowledge is power and that honest, clear, direct communication is our most valuable tool. The interrelationships between money, power, words, and attitudes are complex and constantly changing. Perhaps, someday, I won't have to make the choices I now do about whether to write for money or for lesbian/feminist publications. Perhaps, in a less homophobic world, there will not be so many compromises. I envision a women's music correspondent for *Rolling Stone* and a lesbian issues column in *Glamour*. I like to imagine being well-paid as a writer and doing volunteer psychiatry for several hours per week.

For now, I will continue to write exactly what I mean and to encourage others to do the same.

BUSINESS WITHIN WOMEN'S CULTURE

MARY BYRNE

This is an edited transcript of an interview by Loraine Edwalds with Mary Byrne of Indianapolis, Indiana. Mary Byrne has made her living in various capacities, many of them directly involving the lesbian community: From 1978 through 1984, she owned a lesbian bar where she was one of the first lesbian music producers in the Midwest. She was managing editor of a lesbian magazine called *IKYK* (or *I Know You Know)* from 1984 through 1986. She has been the producer of the National Women's Music Festival (at Indiana University in Bloomington, Indiana) for 11 years. For 7 years while producing the NWMF, Mary worked as a realtor, often working with women who had felt it impossible to buy their own homes, helping them take a positive step to financial security and independence. She also gives workshops and seminars on how to produce successful concerts and fundraisers and is a consultant with women wishing to start their own businesses.

Did you start out running a mainstream business and then switch focus to the women's community?

I got out of college with an M.A. in psychology and got a job as a counselor with a small, alternative social service agency working with predelinquent teens. After I had been there about a year, I became the director of the agency. I left that job after a couple years because I had no idea what I was doing as far as the financial aspects of the agency were concerned. I could run the program and felt good about what we were actually doing, but I didn't understand how to go about making the agency financially secure by budgeting for the future. What's crazy is that what I did next was to open my own business! So, I truly learned business by the seat of my pants.

Copyright © 1995 by Mary Byrne

133

I've never really worked in a "business-business" in the mainstream. The closest to that was when I worked for *I Know You Know*, a lesbian magazine.

What happened with that?

The women who started *I Know You Know* owned an advertising agency and that advertising agency went bankrupt.

They were a regular ad agency getting business from the whole world?

Right. They just did the magazine on the side. They hired me to be managing editor, and one woman who worked in advertising sales for their company also helped me get advertising for the magazine. Their typesetter did our typesetting along with everybody else's. It could have been a very good thing; they just were not businesswomen. In fact, it's awesome that they lasted as long as they did.

They were artists, not businesswomen.

Yes. I was coming out of running the bar, and I'd been doing cash flows for five years, and cash projections, and that sort of thing, but they didn't have any idea what that was. That's a major thing with women in business, whether it's women in mainstream businesses, or women in women's businesses: you have to know how to run a business. You have to know what a profit and loss sheet is, and how to do a cash flow projection.

I think that because you get into the women's community partly because you want to do more for women, you're not really approaching it as a business, and you only find out it's a business afterward.

That's correct. When you stop to think that 80 percent of businesses are going to fail in five years anyway, I don't see that failure is a problem particularly with women. As a matter of fact, I sold my bar in four-and-a-half years.

I was twenty-seven years old when I got that bar, and it took me a year before I could figure out how to balance my balance sheet. At that point, I had to go all the way back from Day One, and do all my income and all my expenses and do all of my bank statements again, and balance it all the way through that year. So I do think the knowledge I've gained might make a difference now. But the bottom line is, it's your motive and why you want to get into some business, I think, that makes the difference in whether it succeeds or fails, rather than working with men or working with women.

The advantage is that with women you're committed.

Yes. And that's a big advantage. Before I got into the bar, Esther Fuller was my financial consultant. She said that you've got to know *why* you want to do whatever it is that you want to do. Bottom line. And, because you're going to live this dream, you're going to spend all of your time, you're going to spend all of your energy, you're going to spend all of your money with this dream, you'd better want to do it.

So, working with women, and having that as my primary motive, was the reason I wanted to get into that particular business.

As far as our own economy right now, I think maybe some women go into it thinking that they're going to make money.

Well, I think that everyone gets into it thinking that they will make money. No one would start a business knowing they were going to lose money.

Right. It's just they don't think they're going to make a lot of money. When you started the bar you thought you were going to make SOME money. You didn't think you were going to be rich.

Yes. I thought that I would be financially okay.

And you were wrong.

Ended up that way. Another major reason for getting out of the bar was time. Because the bar literally was open from 10:30 in the morning until 3:00 in the morning, I worked a lot of hours. And that's just there at the bar, that's not doing any of the buying, that's not doing any of the bookwork, that's not doing anything else. Luckily, the bar had to be closed in Indiana on Sundays. But that's when I did all my bookwork and lined things up, and . . .

*And you wanted to do even more with the bar. You started to
have musical acts come and you intended for all of you to
make money.*

Right. I had very clear philosophical expectations. Goals.
One, I wanted to have a space that reinforced women's positive
self-concept. This was the middle seventies, late seventies, and
all this political stuff was going on. I was involved with NOW,
we were working for the ERA, we were speaking out against
Anita Bryant, and we were getting real political on lesbian stuff.
This was really good stuff, meeting lots of really wonderful new
women who were feminist, who were politically astute. And
then, the only place where we could go in Indianapolis was
some dirty, dingy, dark hole-in-the-wall that had a couple of
pool tables and that refused to fix the john doors. You walked
in and you felt like, god, this is the only place where I can go?
To be okay with myself? And you weren't okay there. It was
like you didn't want anyone to know you were there. So, I
wanted a place where all these neat people that I was meeting
could go. That was one thing. And emotionally I was getting
hooked on women's music. I wanted to have a place where we
could do productions and bring musicians in. So those are the
two reasons I started the bar. Financially, my goal was that I
wanted to make a living.

So how did you start?

Esther's number one suggestion was to get a job in a business
doing as close to what I wanted to do as possible. At the time I
wanted to open a coffeehouse, so I got a job in a manager-
trainee position for a Waffle House. And I learned all about
the restaurant business, I learned all about hiring, and I really
learned about cash flows and inventory control and that kind
of stuff there. At that time, there were probably half a dozen
straight coffeehouses in town. And within that six months, I
think all of them went out of business.

But I was glad that that had happened at that time, because
here these people were looking at the population as a whole,
and they couldn't run a coffeehouse with music. And here I'm
not just talking about lesbians but I'm talking about feminist
lesbians, so how in the hell am I going to make a coffeehouse
work? So I think, okay, I'll get a liquor license. I went to

bartending school, learned how to be a bartender, and I got a job as a bartender for four or five months.

So you were really systematic about it.

I was. Esther said you have to be the expert. You have to hire a bartender and train that bartender how you want them to bartend. You can't assume they know how. You can't assume anything. You have to know how to waitress, how to bartend, you have to do your own ordering, you have to be the expert. So, I got to be the expert.

But then you did have to close the bar because it didn't make money. Did you fault the women's community for that, or did you feel like, oh, there just isn't enough community in this town?

It absolutely worked philosophically. And culturally, and socially. My bartenders, waitresses, and I made a great effort to meet new people; if we didn't know people who walked in, we'd introduce ourselves, get them to introduce themselves, get to know who they were. We made them feel at home, feel comfortable. I considered that that bar was my living room. If these new friends I just met, say they were teachers, and there was a teacher over here, I would introduce them. We started helping people make connections.

Culturally, in four and a half years we did something more than 150 concerts, or musical events or productions. We had plays there, we had open mikes, we had local people play, we had major concerts. I had everyone from Margie Adam to Mary Watkins to June Millington to Meg Christian, Holly Near. And then we had people who were kind of up-and-coming who nobody knew, who would be able to come through and have some sort of a place to play. So that was great.

But financially . . .

The most I got paid at that time was $15,000 a year. Didn't make very good tips. But the worst part was that I was regularly working between 60 and 80 hours a week. I put in up to 100 a week, at times. And, when you're not making much money, you can't hire people to work for you and take some of the slack off. Now, in a bar, when you have limited seating, it's not like a restaurant where you can turn tables over. You have a limited number of seats, and for you to make money, the people sitting in those seats have to spend money.

And not all women are big spenders.

We had as many non-alcoholic drinks as we had alcoholic. A very, very good friend of mine who worked for me got into AA at the time. So it made sense. Well, I'm sorry, but how many cans of Pepsi does a person drink in a night? You can have a person come in who drinks beer and they may have four or five beers that night, over the course of the evening. But they're not going to have more than maybe two cans of pop. And people don't want to pay over a buck for a can of pop. The moral dilemma is that you need to encourage people to drink more than they need to drink in a bar business for you to make money.

Now, there are other ways—you can charge cover. But if nobody else in town is charging a cover on a Wednesday night, you don't charge a cover, because the women will go to some other place. That's one thing. The other thing is that feminist lesbians do not consistently go out. They may go out once or twice a month. They may go to a concert once in a while. But to go party—you know, we're talking about mature adult feminist lesbians. We're not talking about twenty-four-year-old kids. How often do they hit the bars? And if they hit the bars, how many beers or drinks do they drink?

So part of the problem was that it was indeed a bar.

That's right. I had set up a business that didn't promote drinking, that promoted people to come into my living room and sit and talk and listen. We also didn't sell beverages during concerts. They played; we didn't sell. Intermission, yeah; afterwards, yeah. So we have a bar full of people, finally, and we're not selling them drinks during the show. But that was part of the way that I wanted this thing to run.

It wasn't something you felt was forced on you by other people.

No, no, it was respect. It's the way I could respect the women who were the musicians up front. We also asked people not to smoke. Hah! How many times have you gone in a bar and found out you couldn't smoke? Now, you could after the concert was over, but you couldn't before. There was about a three-hour period. During intermission, everybody would go outside. They were really wonderful about it, but they weren't willing to pay more for that. I had a real hard time charging money for the atmosphere. I knew they could go down to The Ten, which was another bar in town, and get a beer for a buck and a quarter. They would pay a buck and a half for that beer, but they wouldn't pay a buck seventy-five. Putting the kind of constraints that my political ideology had on my business was difficult.

So your politics did, in a way, contribute to your having to sell the business.

Yes. In a bar, like a restaurant, you either have to turn over tables, or the people sitting at the table have to keep spending money. You have a limited number of seats in a bar, and the women sitting in those seats have to continue to spend money, as in drink. So, in order for you to make a go in the bar business, you really have to promote the people coming in to drink more than they should. It ended up being a Catch-22: I wanted a safe and healthy place for women to be, and yet I needed to pay my bills.

Were there any other personal prices you have had to pay?

Yeah. One relationship down the tubes. . . . I'll tell you, one of the negative ramifications of owning that bar—and this is specific to a bar—is that I got to the point where my social interactions with 98 percent of my friends came in three-minute intervals at the bar. I'm behind the bar, and I'm talking with somebody, and then, bingo, I see that I have to run over there and do something, and I'm gone. So, when I got out of the bar business, I joined a therapy group to learn how to interact with people again. Because, I'll tell you, I was scared to death. I'm still much more comfortable throwing the party than going to one where I don't have a job to do. So I joined a group because I didn't have any kind of social skills at that point.

Maybe you had overdeveloped social skills.

No, I had overdeveloped responsibility, ingrained responsibility, in seeing what needed to be done, or how to

facilitate other people enjoying themselves. I found that to
enjoy myself was totally uncomfortable.

*Part of the problem is that people treat you differently when
they're used to seeing you as the responsible person, the one in
charge.*

That's true! And it's not just with work things, it's with
interpersonal stuff, too. It just makes me angry that they won't
approach me and say hello. But I'll hear back from other
people that I must be mad at somebody. Come on, get off of it.
People just don't take responsibility for what they'd like to see
happen. If they want to talk to me, walk up and say hello! I
feel like I'm a very approachable person.

*A similar problem happened with our organizations. Certainly
you run into it with the National Women's Music Festival.
People want you to somehow intuit what they want, but they
don't want to have to deal with it themselves.*

Oh, yeah. Well, see, I have a great line for National.
Somebody will come up and they'll say, why don't you do this
or why don't you include that, and I say, excellent idea! Are
you going to volunteer for it next year? Would you like to
coordinate that area? That either shuts them up or puts them
on the spot.

Sometimes it gets done. The play [a production of *Dos
Lesbos*] is an excellent example of that. These women came to
me right after the 1990 festival saying, "We'd like to produce
this play, how do we go about it?" I said, "Write me up a
proposal, and give me an idea of what your budget is." And
they did! They did! And if anybody will do that, they'll get that
goddamn money. Because if you're serious enough to put a
proposal in writing, to think it through, to do enough
homework that you know approximately what kind of money
you're gonna need, I will give you the money, because I know,
if you're diligent enough at that point, you're gonna get the job
done.

Of course, they totally overspent their budget, but it was
okay. And the response was absolutely phenomenal.

What about the issue of women who do become involved and active, but who turn out to be irresponsible?

I'll tell you, with the festival, that came to a head in 1988, because two women were fiscally irresponsible, one to a criminal degree as far as I was concerned. The problem was that, except for 1982, I did not handle the checkbook. I had a fiscal officer who without documentation or receipts issued reimbursement checks to the tune of $3,000–$3,500 to one staff member. After that happened, I took over the checkbook.

I also watch people's expenses a whole lot. If I can see that somebody's got $200 in their budget for phone for the whole year and by January they're almost to that, I call them up and say, "you've got ten more dollars for phone now. You can either start swallowing that yourself, or you can not spend it on guest fees." So I've got the checkbook; I write the reimbursement checks.

So you watch your people through the budget.

Everyone who has the power to spend any money gets a budget, which basically means that I write about 50 budgets. So, basically all coordinators have some sort of budget, and they know their limits. And that may just be money for posterboard, or it may be phone calls or it may be guest speaker fees or travel money. So with the Writers Conference, for example, there is a line item for fees, for travel, for room and board, and then for miscellaneous—phone, postage, copying, supplies. Say all that adds up to $2500. I really don't care how the area coordinator spends that money. I mean I do to some degree, but my bottom line is that she can't spend more than $2500. If I've outlined that you're going to spend $1500 on a guest speaker fee and $500 for travel and $500 for the miscellaneous cost, and you end up spending $400 for miscellaneous cost but you go over a speaker fee by $100, I don't care. As long as you meet your bottom line, I don't care how you spend the money in the budget. Now, if your miscellaneous charges were $900 and you were only going to spend $1200 on your speakers, I'd have a problem with that. You'd have to show me why you doubled your miscellaneous charges. But in order for the whole festival to work within budget, each person who spends any money has got to know how much they can spend.

But you're the one that looks at those budgets. The board of directors does not. Am I right?

I write the budgets up. I look at what we spent last year. Then, through what I saw, where I want us to go, with the feedback of that coordinator or that staff member of where they want it to go, and how they saw things happening, we'll add, delete, rearrange, that sort of thing, to their budget. I do that with all 50 areas and put them together to see what the festival's total expenses will be. Then I project income through growth and pricing. Sometimes after doing this income part, I have to go back and cut expenses somewhere. But finally it feels like it'll work and I take it to the board for their input, discussion, and approval. And we arrive at the next year's budget.

So the board understands that each area's budget is what it is, and so if people have objections to whatever budgets are they can raise them with the board.

Right. Well, if a coordinator wants her budget raised, she would come to me. It's not appropriate within our structure for her to go to the board and say, "I want more money." But if she came to me and she said, "I really want another thousand dollars this year in order to bring so-and-so in." And I say, "that is not feasible this year, because of this and this and this." She has the option at that point of going to the board to override me. And the board rarely overrides me. Or, what I would say to the board is, "OK, you raise a thousand more dollars then, and we'll put it in the budget."

Right. And that has happened, where board members took the initiative to raise the money for the women of color conference.

Yes. It's back and forth, back and forth. Rarely do I take my budget to the board and have them say they want me to change something. They may ask me why I did this, or why I moved that there, or why did this increase, or why did this decrease. That sort of thing. But normally, prior to me writing the budget, I get input from everybody on how last year ran.

What you've done is centralize the spending authority in order to have the control now to protect yourself from irresponsible women.

It's a little different. I've not centralized the spending. In fact, we've decentralized the spending and empowered the 50+ coordinators to do that. I've centralized the recordkeeping and the checkwriting with the budget, so I know what everybody ought to be spending and if someone is totally out of their budget. But I do rely on the managers. Like the day programming manager: she supervises and manages seven or eight different coordinators (and their areas). Her budget includes all of their budgets plus a budget for herself. Say that's $10,000. She has to be in contact with all of her coordinators to know where they are and what they're spending, because she wants to use all that. If the writers conference coordinator didn't pay any speakers, for example, but there was $1000 in her budget, the day programming manager could scoop that $1000 up and let the drama series and spirituality and women of color conference go over $1000. So the coordinators and managers are all aware of how much they can spend.

A nonprofit corporation with a board needs to set fiscal policies and procedures. The board members need to assure themselves that I'm not writing blank checks to people, to myself or to anyone else, because there's all kinds of ways that you can mess with books and hide stuff. So the board treasurer goes through at the end of the year and checks the receipts to the checks and does that kind of stuff. She can then be assured that if the federal government ever came in to audit us, that we would have our receipts, that I was doing the bookwork correctly, and that sort of thing. Ultimately the board is fiscally responsible, legally responsible, and of course they want to be sure we continue our tax-exempt status. That's their job. Their main job is to protect the organization.

I think that's important to everybody, in the sense that they want the festival to go on. We just don't realize how difficult it is financially.

There are four things that we tie together in the business/ structural/organizational end of the festival. First, people develop skills in an area, then they take on responsibilities in an area, then they have decision-making power over those responsibilities, and then they are held accountable for that power and those decisions. And if you have those four things, for every layer of the organization, what you end up doing is empowering people. I think that is the bottom-line basis for feminist business. Empowering people.

Empowering women.

They learn an incredible amount. You'd be just amazed at the number of women who join our staff who have never seen a budget. It takes a full year, for them to go from the very beginning through the process and then at the end for them to understand that budgeting process. I think that by going through that first year in our organization they learn a great deal about any kind of business. In fact, they all learn, to some degree, how to be producers, because you've got to budget, you've got to plan, you've got to make decisions. I think that by allowing people on every layer of the organization to have those four ingredients, the empowerment and learning comes from that.

I think that a lot of times in the mainstream what you find is that people are given responsibilities but no power to go along with them. Or maybe they're given the power and they don't have the skills yet. When you have an organization that doesn't have all four of those ingredients at the same time, it's very dysfunctional and you have a whole lot of palpable problems. Within our organization we can be flexible too. Like, if you don't want to be responsible, if you don't want to be accountable, then you won't make those decisions. People don't have to take any more responsibility than they're comfortable with, but what responsibility they do take over, they have the decision-making authority involved in that.

How do you get women to take only as much responsibility as they can handle? Do you give more authority to someone from a different area and have shared responsibility?

No, I don't do that. We very, very rarely let two women co-coordinate an area. We will have one coordinator and an assistant. There has to be one mind that all the information goes through. There has to be one person who is ultimately responsible. Now, that doesn't mean that one coordinator has to do all the work—quite the opposite, she needs to find help and delegate. The only time we've allowed two women to truly be co-coordinators is if they live together (and hopefully talk every day!). But you have a much greater probability of having problems when you share, because it's not as easy to be clear about the delineation of the responsibility. When you get a fuzzy area of responsibility is when you're going to have some problems.

It's difficult to determine beforehand whether a woman is going to be able to handle responsibility. Sometimes you get little feelings that something is not right or someone is not going to be able to do her job. And you really have to teach yourself to listen to those feelings. Sometimes it's a matter of needing to be more clear about what your expectations are. You may think they know what their job is and they don't know what you are wanting at all.

I think the business of not encouraging women to take on financial responsibility before they're comfortable with it is important.

You have to reassure them that they can do it, because they can. They may not feel comfortable with that. If somebody wanted to be the coordinator of an area, but they didn't want to have anything to do with the money, I don't know that we could have them be the coordinator of that area, because it goes hand-in-hand.

You started producing the festival in 1982. What was it like then, compared to now?

I don't remember what our budget was in 1982, but it was real small. No staff was paid. Graphic art, nothing. It was by the seat of our pants.

No one was paid but the printers of the program, right?

Yeah. We had nine Mainstage performers, one guest speaker, and we did have Showcase. We had seventy-five workshops and one series, and that was the Music Industry Conference. We had eighteen coordinators and probably between fifty and sixty volunteers. Now we've got somewhere around 3,000 participants, our budget is over a third of a million dollars, my position is almost full time, and I have eight staff members,

called managers, who work directly with me who get small
stipends.

That's 1994?

Yes. We have 44 coordinators, 9 board members, 550
volunteers. That's 550 people who got something from us in
exchange for doing something. That does not include all the
workshop volunteers. Quite a few workshop presenters just
write in and say, "I'd like to do a workshop on this." We have
16 different series of workshops, or conferences, with a total of
more than 200 workshops. We have 10 Mainstage performers
including the MC, so that's about the same, 22 speakers, and
then 15 other performers, which include Showcase and dances
and that kind of stuff. So, how does it differ from what I hoped
for? It's exactly what I hoped for. Except for the Music Industry
Conference. That developed into AWMAC, and then in
1988—in 1988 we had an internal staff problem.

What happened?

Two staff members got disillusioned with me as a producer
and rabble-roused to cause major problems at our annual
meeting, and that gave AWMAC the reason to leave the festival.

So AWMAC had been threatening to leave.

Yes. There had been talk about taking the AWMAC
conference into different regions of the country in order to pull
in that region's producers, performers and that sort of thing. At
that point, AWMAC had a half ,dozen "biggies" in women's
music who basically ran the show. It was a little clique, and it
wasn't very open. I think that they just used that internal strife
to do a very, very disastrous, for us, smear campaign as far as
racism.

Racism is a great tool for dissent and chaos, because there's
nothing that you can do to say you're not racist. If you really
want to smear somebody and not have a way for them to get
out from under it, you call them racist. Why they couldn't have
just left without doing the smear thing, I don't know, because
they really hurt us, and to tell you the truth, they really hurt
themselves. In women's businesses, and the women's
community, if there's any dissent or public problem, it hurts
everyone involved. If there's conflict, people avoid it. They

know enough not to particularly take sides. They know enough to know they don't know the story. But they avoid it. So the shit hit the fan in 1988.

And 1989 was the year that nobody came.

That's right. In 1988, all this shit hit the fan and people didn't understand, and the annual meeting—our normal annual meetings at the festival prior to 1988 included maybe a half a dozen people. We could not convince people to be on the board. We could not convince people to come to that annual meeting. In 1988, there were probably over a hundred, because these staff members solicited everybody and they wanted to know, why was this budget so little, or why weren't we doing this? It was a fiasco.

It was such a fiasco, and I was so disgusted that I left the meeting to lead a workshop that I had scheduled. It was one of the stupidest decisions in my life. The board of directors wasn't ready for it. No one had brought the by-laws. No one had brought the articles of incorporation. We didn't know the law; we didn't have an attorney on the board. And this group said, "The articles of incorporation say that you have to have thirteen members on this board of directors." And at the time we had seven. They got the board of directors to somehow think that they were in violation of the law to have cut down the members to seven, so instead of electing one board member, to go to seven, they elected seven to go to thirteen. Well, I cried all day Sunday. I literally cried the rest of the day. Because these were women who didn't know anything about the festival, they didn't know anything about business. I mean, you can train board members if you get a couple of them on at a time, as to how things function, how it works, how to read a budget. But seven out of thirteen—they would have a majority of people who didn't know anything. I felt like, okay, maybe we could last another year. Maybe two, and then it would just self-destruct.

After that year, if it had gone through, the festival would actually have died. In terms of finances.

That's right. Because 1989 was a complete financial disaster. But it didn't go through. Basically what happened was that I got home Monday morning after that annual meeting in 1988 and called a lawyer. I asked her to please research this, and give me some sort of legal advice as to what we could do. She came back and said, "Your bylaws state that you only have one vacancy. You call a board meeting, you dissolve the annual meeting, you hold new elections, or somehow you fill that vacant spot." And that's exactly what we did. We took the person who had the most votes at the annual meeting, which was Donna Jones, and she became the seventh board member.

But the dissent was still there.

That's right. We resolved it, but the shit had hit the fan. And the next year everybody just avoided the festival. They didn't want to take sides, so they just didn't show up.

But in a way, this is something that could happen in any organization. This wouldn't necessarily happen only in a women's organization, do you think?

Well, I think that the reason it happened to us was that we were not astute in business terms. The board of directors were these philosophically feminist and wonderful individuals who loved the festival but didn't have any idea that we needed a lawyer on the board, didn't have any idea why we would want to have an annual meeting. Our annual meetings previously had six people. Why would we know Robert's Rules of Order?

A lot of feminists believe that we shouldn't have to abide by those male kinds of things, like having an attorney, having to abide by Robert's Rules.

But it is a business. It is a business. We changed from 1989 to 1990. In 1989 we lost our shirts. But, because of the difficulty, the board realized that they're in a business, they are responsible, that there are specific legal ramifications, and I think that they started taking themselves more seriously. The whole organization went into being a business in 1990.

You started thinking of the festival being a business and not just a community function.

That's right. The festival's got a huge budget. You've got to take yourself—I mean, we're running a business. We can have all the feminist philosophical reasons to do it, but if we want it to continue, it's got to make money, it's got to be structurally secure for longevity. And if we're going to do things by the book, we've got to know what the book says. For example, do we indeed have the right to change the bylaws? That was what the whole crux came down to. It was a mob action in '88, personally attacking board members; they had all the board members on the defensive. And those board members would have done anything to quiet that mob. It was a horrible thing.

It was. I think it is amazing that you've gone on.

It was not easy for those six board members to get together after that annual meeting and say, as they basically did, "We are dissolving—the annual meeting is annulled." That took an incredible amount of guts for those six women to do. And they had to do that in order to maintain it. It would have been chaos to have allowed the seven new board members on. Oh, and they had board members from Washington, DC, and they were talking about flying these people in—where did they think we were going to get that kind of money?

Once people are aware that the budget is so large, they think they're entitled to a piece of it. My theory is that we have tended to view festivals just as part of the community, as opposed to as businesses. That's what we as a community expect of our own organizations, even though we don't expect it of male-run organizations.

We do need to keep costs down, which gets us to accessibility for women who don't have money. What do you think about that? Does work exchange work pretty well?

People call in or write in about work exchange—they say they can't afford to pay to come to the festival, can they have a job, and we give them to a coordinator. I think the rate is four hours a day plus $10 for a full day pass. So if you work four hours for four days and pay $40, you get a full festival pass. That's the way we work it out. We try to have fewer people do more, so that they're trained.

We've always done it that way. You know, Michigan gets most of their labor pool from everyone doing a workshift or two. I know this is going to sound weird, but we don't have the non-skilled jobs that Michigan does. A tremendous amount of their labor needs are parking, shuttle, and kitchen, which we don't have. All of our registration people, workshop care

people, security, all those people have a specific job. Still, when
I go to Michigan, I never resent my workshift. Because you
always meet people. It's the one scheduled way, one structured
way of meeting other people that you don't know. So I think
that we might move into that a bit more. We don't have the
areas that just take masses of people, but we have a lot of areas
that need people.

But you've had enough people.

Yes, but at a horrible cost. Even though those 550 volunteers
aren't costing us any money, say they translate into 300 full
festival passes. Times an average of $100 for a full festival pass.
That's $30,000 that we've not gotten in registration. We've
started having work exchange people pay $10 a day toward
their passes too, because we were having a problem with people
signing up for work exchange and then not showing up for
their shifts. The $10 seems to make people feel they've made an
investment so they need to do the whole thing, and it helps
take the bite out of all those passes we don't sell.

*Part of the idea is that you wouldn't have sold those passes
because these women can't afford it.*

That's the theory, but if I am in charge of headquarters and I
need two people there all the time, and I've been sent three
work-exchange people but I need six, I'm going to touch base
with three of my friends to see if they would work in exchange
for a festival pass. Now those people may be able to pay. But I
need them to work four hours a day.

*So at this point, probably half the people getting passes don't
need them.*

Yes, maybe half. It's not their economic level, it's our labor
needs. So it may well be that we will go—I don't really want us
to get into mandatory workshifts because the follow-up on it is
just—I cringe to imagine.

*It conflicts with our image of our community. Lesbians tend
not to have much money. But the pool of women who have too*

little money and want to go to the festival is not actually large enough to meet the labor needs of a festival of 3000 people.

That's correct. We don't get very many people who write in for work exchange.

Did you used to get more?

No. Any kind of production needs ticket-takers, or people to set up, or help with decorations, or clean up. But times when I know I'll need some people to help out on certain things, say Mainstage security, I'll call around and ask people, "Do you know anybody who's not coming because they don't have any money?" So you almost have to solicit poor women or people who are in between jobs or students, that sort of thing. I mean, we solicit many more than come to us and say, "I need this."

That's true. Even though there's a lot of talk about how poor we are, we're not really quite poor enough for all the work that needs to be done.

I think sometimes when you're poor, you don't think of your options. Women get so caught up in not having that they just kind of give up.

Are there other women you can reach to for work exchange?

I've been making it a priority to bring in as many young women as possible. These women that are under thirty right now need their eyes opened. They don't know what we've been through. They don't understand what the big deal is. A lot of them are not in our culture, and we have to capture them. And I'll tell you, when they get down there, and after they've worked the weekend at the festival, they are so excited they can't even stand it! They love it!

Are we, as feminists, more demanding than people in the mainstream?

I think that we're more demanding because of our political ideologies. You've got to provide community housing, access for people with disabilities, childcare—those are things that you have to do. The weird part, especially with accessibility, is that it costs you so much to have those people come in, and most of the time they cannot afford to pay anything. So you're really spending a great deal of money to involve people who can't support the festival financially.

I think that if you spread the costs out over many people, it's better. I think about, like, a utility company. They're always screaming their heads off about how much it's going to cost to clean up the goddamn air. Now look. So my electric bill goes up two bucks a month. I would pay two dollars extra a month to have them not throw all this shit out in the air. I assume everyone would. And if they just said, "We're going to do this," I don't think people would be upset about it.

People will respect you more for doing what's right than if you were to whine, "Oh, it's so expensive to make this accessible for women with disabilities." Do you think our community has done a lot to make events accessible?

Absolutely. We've had drastic ramifications on Indiana University. How a state university can be so inaccessible, I don't understand. But going back to your earlier question— yes, we're demanding. The demands are that you have to be politically correct.

Which means what?

There are more ways you can get shots taken at you. I think that with the audience, a charge from someone saying that you're an ableist or you're a racist or something like that is generally going to be believed. Or maybe people are just more likely to wonder if you are. A couple of years ago at Michigan, Diane Davidson got into a lot of trouble over a song about her nanny. I know she was coming from her own experience, yet it caused a furor.

When I think about that situation with Diane, I wonder whether all the issues haven't made the performers a bit more middle-of-the-road, a bit more vanilla, rather than speaking on issues.

Self-censorship, you mean?

Yes. I wonder if they won't try to just have happy songs. There's a lot of kind of back and forth about how non-lesbian women's music is getting to be, how there aren't very many people anymore just talking about women loving women. I don't know. Maybe our culture is getting mainstream. I think that there are financial implications to that. Or at least there should be. Teresa Trull's album, that one with "Rosalee" on it: when I heard that record, I thought "for God's sakes, if this doesn't get top-forty play, I don't know what will."

But it didn't. Why, do you think?

I don't know. Maybe they didn't market it right. Maybe she should have gone to another record company. I don't know. That one was very well produced, the arrangements were excellent, the music was great, but it was lesbian. I think that our audience is demanding something that they can put in the tape rack and have their friends listen to and not have to worry about what's on it.

So the closet market is still a concern to a lot of women. As a producer, how does that affect you? Do you try to get people who say things that are more lesbian, less lesbian?

I'll be frank with you. I group them on Mainstage. I put together nights that are more mainstream and less mainstream. To tell you the truth, I don't have to really worry about that too much anymore. I mean how many people are really out there, that are lesbian, lesbian, lesbian, lesbian?

Where do straight feminists fit in all of this?

Two of the women who started the NWMF were straight, so our inclusion of them is very intentional. That also is a juggling act. We want to include straight women, and in order to include straight women you can't lead them to believe that it's a lesbian festival, because they will assume that they will be uncomfortable. I think, politically, just as black women want to have some space separate from white women, and as women want to have space separate from men, I think that it's possible that aware, feminist, straight women may think that lesbians want to have their space and that they shouldn't come to the festival, in order to give that space to us.

Just out of being politically aware.

Yes. So we do not label it as a lesbian festival. The juggling act is how do you let people know what to expect. I know this is going to sound dumb, but I have a rule that we can have the word *lesbian* in the brochure three times. It's enough to let

people know that there are going to be lesbians there. Maybe if
we were to go through the 200 workshops we might find that
10 percent are of interest only to lesbians; that's 20. That leaves
180 workshops that I think straight women ought to be at, that
it would be very good to be at: how to write, how to manage
money, women's religion. I think that we need straight women
at the festival for a sense of camaraderie, that we're all women.
And I think that they need us a whole lot. They have to
continue dealing with men, so I would think that four days
away from men, with us, would be wonderful for them. I've
always felt very sorry for them. How in the world could you be
a feminist and have to go home to one—a man—and tolerate
it? Because even the most feminist man is still a man.

But the real problem is that nobody wants to put themselves
into an arena where they're going to feel uncomfortable. And if
you're comfortable being ninety percent of the population, then
you don't want to be put into a situation where you're only ten
percent of the population. As white women, we're comfortable
being in meetings or going to things that are eighty-five percent
white. If we knew, going to a certain concert or lecture or
something, that there were only going to be fifteen percent
white people there, we might have a bit of trepidation about
doing that and we might avoid it. So obviously the number of
straight women who are going to be comfortable at the festival
is not going to be very great.

Are there other political issues that affect the festival?

One of the things that we did deal with to some degree of
success is the inclusion of S/M. That was basically a decision
that kind of came from the volunteer ranks on up through the
coordinators and staff meetings to the board. The decision
basically was that although there are people who don't agree
with S/M, we're not the judges. We're there to facilitate all
aspects of women's culture, and we're not the people who are
to say this part of us is OK, and this part of us is not OK.
There are two very distinctly politically-correct ways of looking
at it. On the one hand, how can we be OK and say just some
of us are the abnormal ones? On the other hand, there's the
sexually abused people, the incest survivors, who see S/M as
very unhealthy and who believe that by giving them space we're

reinforcing that. If there is a political/ideological conflict that I
don't ever see resolved, this is it.

It's not a halfway issue.

It isn't. It isn't at all. You're talking about right to privacy
and what people do in their bedrooms and feeling good about
themselves.

*And you're talking about incest survivors and child-abused
people and their own personal need for safety.*

That's right. Just the existence of an S/M lounge can threaten
those people's emotional well-being. So it can be very definitely
a juggling act, trying to keep everyone safe and yet include
everyone. The nature of any music festival is that it is eclectic.
It represents the whole culture, so that there is something for
everyone, and some things that some women don't want or like
or need. You have 200 workshops, and if you don't want to go
to these 5, you've got 195 that you can go to. Ten years ago
the big deal was racism. But there's not another whole group
within the women's community that's saying racism is OK.
With this S/M thing, you've got people on both lines that have
political ideologies, and who's supposed to be the judge?

*Do you think that that discourages people from doing things in
our community?*

Yeah. You do something and you've got your neck out on
the line—and your pocketbook. There are more issues for
people to pick on us about. We have more political ideologies
that are coming from all these different directions. A lot of
times it's like walking on eggshells.

*Do you think this is a particular problem with the
lesbian-feminist community, or do you think this is the way
people in the whole world are?*

I think that it is something that has to do with our
community. I think that, in the mainstream, people like to give
their leaders the benefit of the doubt, sometimes way too much.

And in our community we do not.

I think we're very, very, very hard on our people that are out
there, doing stuff. For example, there was a producer who was

starting to do productions in Cincinnati. She was gonna have
Two Nice Girls, already had it confirmed, had a place to play.
At Michigan, they played some song that had to do with loving
boys, or something, I don't know. So the women's radio station
in Cincinnati was not going to promote it and there was talk
about a boycott. Now, maybe it hurt Two Nice Girls, but it
killed the producer.

Producers really set themselves up for potential smashing.
Even if it's innuendoes. Innuendoes and rumors hurt maybe
more than a direct conflict. 'Cause you can resolve a direct
conflict, and people hear the results of that. Whereas the
innuendoes float, the rumors float, and they don't get resolved,
and it just leaves this feeling of mistrust in people.

I know that being a producer, I'm a little skewed on this, but
I think producers make our culture happen. If you don't have a
producer willing to produce musicians, you're not going to
have any musicians come to your city.

What does AWMAC do for producers?

The music industry conference that we set up in 1982 is the
reason that I started working on the festival. In Champaign,
producers would get together, and we'd talk about budgets and
about marketing—of course, we didn't call it marketing—but
we'd talk about reaching new people and everyone would see
all these new performers on Mainstage. But, in 1981, when
Champaign didn't happen, I felt the music industry was going
to just wither away if we didn't have a place where these
producers could get together—where you can capture people
and let them know that they can also bring this stuff into their
towns. At the music industry conference, though, most of the
people we get are performers. We've got lots of these young
women out there who want to become women's music
performers. Lots of theater, lots of drumming, lots of dance,
lots of all kinds of stuff, but if there are no producers to bring
them in, there's no place for them to perform.

*Ann Reed pointed out in her workshop that they're turning to
men to do producing.*

That's absolutely right. And who are they going to produce?
They're producing Ferron, and Cris. It's the local coffeehouses

and small producers that we don't have anymore producing new women's talent.

There must be other reasons for producers leaving production.
Money.

They're not making enough money?
A producer is the person at risk. If they lose money, who pays the bills? If they don't have enough audience, they still have a light bill and a sound bill that they'd better pay.

So the audience is not large enough.
The audience is not large enough, or they're not getting enough on their ticket price, or whatever. They're losing money. It's hard work, it's a lot of time and effort. So they're stopping. They're not doing it anymore.

But the audience is also at fault. If we want the culture to continue and if we want to see new performers, the community is going to have to go out to concerts with performers they don't know.

Ann Reed was willing to use the word marketing in the workshop she gave. I thought to call it marketing was somehow taboo.
It might have been taboo at one time. When women's music got started, it was kind of a philosophical thing that we were doing altruistically. We don't think that we're worth much, so we don't charge much, so we don't make much, and then we don't do it anymore. I think that it may just be cycles. A lot of the performers who were performing fifteen years ago aren't performing anymore. Bookers, managers who kind of ran the music industry ten years ago are not in it anymore.

Do you think they got out because of the money?
I would assume so. I mean, it's okay to live in poverty for a while, and scratch by, but it's hard to do it, when you know that you can go out there and make decent money, or have a little free time.

All we have to do is look across the street, and we find somebody who is working half as hard as we are.

Yeah, working forty hours a week and pulling in thirty thousand dollars or more, and can go home and have a private life. You're not risking; you're not spending all this time and effort not making any money and then holding the risk. Sometimes the musicians will share that risk with you, and with the young ones, especially, they almost have to. You'll split the door, or something like that. Sometimes I think they almost have to do that.

But the bars are doing less music now than they were doing ten years ago. It's more consistent for them to have dance night every Saturday night. As long as people know that, they're going to show.

That's right. And as far as I can see, without a doubt, you're going to make more money dancing. So I hope that we can capture new people. I don't know how we're going to do that, but we've got to.

HAVE SHEARS, WILL TRAVEL

MARY WALLACE

"I can never find anyone who'll cut it short enough!" Kate Richards hears this refrain again and again from clients delighted to have found her at the womyn's festivals. "So," she replies, "find me 50 clients in your town and I'll fly to you."

This is a love story, a success story, a story of spreading fame and goodwill. What Kate is accomplishing through her work is to do something that she loves, to work with the community she loves, to live in a place she loves and to travel frequently, which she loves. And she supports herself, too.

Kate has been a haircutter for eleven years. Before that, she had started jobs only to lose interest in them within months. While working as a peer advisor at a local community college, Kate took the battery of computer tests and questionnaires she used to counsel the students on career choices. The computer spat out one job: "Insulation installer." Somehow that wasn't the answer she wanted. So she reworked the questions and "hairstylist" came up as one of the many possibilities.

She began to remember the summer she had spent hanging out at her hairstylist's shop, and realized that she'd spent time there not simply to be sociable but because she wanted to be cutting hair. Then there were the times she'd cut her brother's hair in high school. In those days, her image of women who cut hair was that they chewed gum, wore white uniforms, and did little old ladies' pink hair. There was a valid need for this service, but Kate did not want to be a beautician. It took her years to discover that she could actually be a barber. Once she started cutting hair and found out how much fun it was for her, she felt lucky. "Looking back, I feel blessed. How many people

Copyright © 1993 by Mary Wallace

work all of their lives at jobs they dislike? I'm doing something I love—and I get paid to do it!"

Kate worked in shops, either as an employee or renting space from a shop owner, for a few years. She began traveling with her services in 1985, when she moved back to the state where she had grown up. She asked all her clients in her mountain state if they'd like to try an experiment, and they all agreed to, so she started flying back to the mountains at intervals to cut hair. Some of her clients moved to different towns in the state, so her trips stretched a bit farther. When she decided to return to the mountains, she continued to travel to her client bases in three different towns, as well as to cut hair at the womyn's music festivals.

Kate's busiest times are at the festivals, and she goes to as many as four during the course of a year. "I would work only festivals, but it's impossible to do them all since on the major holiday weekends there are at least three going on at one time," Kate laments. Still, the festivals are where she can do her highest volume in the shortest period of time, so she goes prepared to work hard. "'Til dusk do us part," she tells clients asking what time she'll quit. She psyches herself up to cut as fast as she can, and as long as there's someone waiting in line, she will work.

How does she manage to work standing up for days in a row in the hot sun? "I try to eat right, and then have lots of good athletic fuel (PowerBar™-type products and drinks), drink lots of water, and try to get enough sleep—which is harder at a festival. I joke and tell people I'll cut hair until it's too dark, or no one's in line, or I fall over, whichever happens first. I've never fallen over. I find cutting hair invigorating, and that makes it easier to go for it, to see how many haircuts I can do in a day. One year I *did* have to finish a haircut by flashlight— when the sunlight ran out before the women in line!"

Kate was the one licensed professional haircutter at the festivals she attended for seven years. (Recently, more of the haircutters have become licensed.) Having a license meant that Kate had the technical training to do the range of hairstyling, from conservative to wild. But women who wanted haircuts they could wear to work on Monday morning tended to gravitate toward Kate's chair. As a result, she wound up doing most of the conservative cuts while her colleagues were happily creating wild hairstyles. "My clients would say, 'Make it look sharp, but nothing *too* radical—I don't think they'd appreciate it at the office.'" Finally, in her tenth year of festival haircutting, she was asked to cut a double women's symbol on the back of a woman's head—and she eagerly complied, scissors in hand!

Success at the festivals is part of what led Kate to her current traveling route, a swing every six weeks through the Midwest. She was feeling the need to build up her client base, which was difficult to do in her hometown. There are four lesbian haircutters that she knows of in her hometown of 500,000, three of whom are actively trying to tap into the lesbian community. But not all lesbians go to lesbian haircutters. It would be lovely if more lesbians could support their own community instead of straight women or gay men haircutters. "People get attached to their haircutters and a lot of people just won't leave. Whether they like them or not, they won't leave this person who's cut their hair for ten years because it's too traumatic to find somebody else." So the lesbian haircutters in her town are competing (though Kate says they don't really compete, because they all get along well) not only with each other but with every other haircutter in town for a comparatively small pool of lesbian clients.

Understandably, Kate felt that her hometown market wasn't big enough to support all of the haircutters, so she decided to go elsewhere. In thinking about where, she realized that she had been successful at the festivals, and decided to tap into that clientele. Kate's ten-year tradition of collecting names and addresses on her sign-in sheets made it easy to contact these womyn and establish centralized client bases. In the meantime she had offers of a place to stay and a space to work from womyn in each city, so things fell into place. Kate does between 75 and 80 haircuts per two-week trip. At home, she has five or six days of work spread out over the four weeks she stays there, traveling a day to each of the other two towns where her clients live. "Other people work where they live and go to the mountains for a vacation. I work where my clients live and go home to the mountains!"

It's an arrangement that suits Kate fine. She figures that, even with traveling costs and a high phone bill, her overhead is the same or less than it would be if she ran her own shop in town. She takes home more money than she would if she worked for someone else. It requires a minimum of 50 people to cover all the expenses and make a trip worthwhile, and she's been well above that minimum on her trips to the Midwest.

Scheduling is the most tedious part of her job. By booking appointments ahead, at the time she finishes a client's haircut, she minimizes the work she has to do from home. She lays out her schedule and then makes 70 or 80 phone calls which last from 30 seconds to 5 minutes to confirm the appointed times. She works with her travel agent to find the cheapest airfare, or, if money is tight, bus fare. (Kate works with a lesbian travel agent.) They can spend half an hour at a time on the phone working out the logistics—which plane will get in at what time to connect with which bus to get her to her destination how many hours (or minutes) before her first appointment—and who's going to pick her up? It takes about two hours to get the logistics settled.

Once she's on the road, Kate has to make the time to take care of her own needs. "When I first started traveling, I'd only be gone for five or six days, so I didn't necessarily have to work out or do the things I usually do. Now, on these trips, I'm gone for two weeks at a time—so I need to have time to exercise, time to rest, and time to play." It can be difficult to keep a balance, because she's getting new clients each trip. "I try never to turn down a haircut. Sometimes I am booked solid, but if I can get someone into my schedule, I will."

And if someone wants a haircut but doesn't have the money for her usual fee, Kate will cut her hair anyway. "If someone's going through a temporary hardship financially, I have her pay me whatever she'd pay for a cut at one of the discount chains. I find that helps me to maintain clientele. Womyn can still use my services and they will pay me more when they're doing better. But they've maintained the relationship with me, not with some discount service." Kate will also trade her services with clients. Her philosophy is that there is enough of everything for everyone, and she tries to put this idea into practice. "I really feel lucky that I love haircutting so much that the money people hand me is like a bonus. Yes, I have to make my living so I do need the money, but it's like a gift to me afterward."

Kate consciously avoids, especially at festivals where the fee is sliding scale, looking at the money someone hands her. She just puts it in her pocket and counts it all at the end of the day. That way she doesn't associate a particular amount of money with a particular person. She figures out on average how much money she makes per haircut and on average how much she makes per hour, which she needs to know to maintain her business. But by focusing on the people rather than on the amount of money each one brings her, she's able to keep a more wholistic perspective.

Kate tries to be conscious about where she spends her money. She tries to support small businesses rather than big corporations, and feels that she benefits from that choice. She banks at the neighborhood bank down the street from where she lives. She feels that the service they give her is more personal because they know her. Kate also tries to buy from lesbian-owned businesses whenever possible. By this, she means that if the lesbian product or service is as good as or better than the mainstream equivalent, she will try to buy it even if it's a little inconvenient or a little more expensive. "I'm trying to walk what I talk," Kate says. "If I expect dykes to come to me because I am a lesbian—if I can do as good or better a job as what they've been getting—then I have to do the same."

Kate sees her business as developing within a niche that's right for her. "My preferences in terms of haircutting styles is short hair—easy care, wash-and-wear styles. In the world at large that means working mostly on men, since the beauty industry caters to straight women's hairstyles, which generally require a lot of products and preparation. But as far as people, I prefer to work with lesbians. I'll cut anyone's hair if they want to come to me. But every hairstylist has a strong point or a different kind of thing that they do well. Most lesbians I know want a haircut that's easy to take care of, with not a lot of fuss and bother. They want to look really nice, and they want a good technical haircut that they don't have to mess with. And that's where my skills are."

Really listening to her clients is part of what helps Kate make them happy. She doesn't subscribe to the theory that the hairstylist knows best. "The client is the one who has to go home and look at her hair all month." So she tries to divine what they really want, even if what they say is a vague, "Do whatever you want, you're the expert."

"Most of my clients love what I do because I talk to them long enough to find out what they want. Some of them have very specific ideas, and I execute their concept. But others aren't as clear. I'll talk to them for a little while, then do the haircut. It tickles me when they say, 'It's exactly what I wanted!' I joke about being a psychic haircutter, but in reality most people know on some level what they are looking for. I don't really 'go for it' and do whatever I think best. I find out what they want and then give it to them."

As far as hairstyle trends, Kate thinks dykes are definitely among the risk-takers. Radical people who have employment that allows them to look wild set the pace for the mainstream, which can take years to catch up. "When I was in barber school, eleven years ago now, the only tails I did were on two lesbians who used to come into the school. Those hairstyles came out of the punk movement, when people wore safety pins as jewelry. It may already have been going on in New York before that, but those were the first women I'd ever seen with tails. And now, it's a big fashion in the whole country. You see straight, middle-aged males with tails on TV! Seven years ago, the mohawks I saw were at the festivals. These styles seem to have migrated from the big urban centers to the lesbian and gay community, to the men and womyn who didn't have to worry about what they looked like for their jobs. And then it becomes totally mainstream!"

Kate swears that she cut the *first* "shelf" haircut around 1982. One of her clients designed it, with two layers cut from the temple toward the back of the head. "It looked really good, but the client was so freaked out that her head was so bare on either side that she wore a headband for four months, wrapped around to cover the buzzed part." Now Kate cuts shelves all the time. If her client had waited eight years, she'd have been at the height of fashion.

As Kate's travels spread, so does her fame. A couple of friends told her a story about going to the hot springs in the mountains about 100 miles from where she lives. When they got there, three other women were lounging in the springs. The conversation turned to the topic of massages, and one woman said she would never feel comfortable going to get a massage. But then, stopping to think, she said, "Wait. The woman who cuts my hair does a little massage before she starts cutting. Her

is name Kate . . ." and the other two women finished, ". . .
Richards!" and her surprised friends said, "*We* know Kate
Richards!" It's the kind of name recognition that makes Kate
glow. What makes her business worthwhile to her is doing her
part for lesbian visibility, lesbian community—and lesbian good
looks.

THE ORIGINAL WOMYN'S WOODSTOCK

MICHIGAN WOMYN'S MUSIC FESTIVAL

DEBORAH R. LEWIS

When I began doing research about the Michigan Womyn's Music Festival, I had never been to the festival. I began my research with *Books-In-Print*. And found nothing. Then *The Reader's Guide to Periodical Literature*. Nothing. Had I not heard of the place, had I not spoken with women who'd actually been there, I'd have given it up as legend. How a festival sounding so important could survive eighteen years without showing up in *Time* was beyond me. I finally went to Gerber-Hart Library and Archives (a gay and lesbian library in Chicago). The back-issue periodicals there were impressive, and I finally settled down to the work of digging.

In the August 1976 issue of *Lesbian Connection*, there appeared an ad reading as follows:

> Women's Music Festival: In Mt. Pleasant, Michigan on August 20, 21, 22. Come and celebrate with the music of Meg Christian, Holly Near, Margie Adam, Ginni Clemens, Sally Piano, Andrea Weltman, Teresa Trull, CT and April, Maxine Feldman, New Harmony Sisterhood Band, Be Be K'Roche, and more. Camping and meals included in registration fee of $20 at gate. Write for tickets or more info (include SASE): We Want The Music Collective.

That August women arrived 2,000 strong. The seed money for the event had come from garage sales, car washes,

donations, parties, and small loans from many sources. The
means were modest, and receipts for the first festival covered
the musicians' wages and festival expenses (the producers went
without pay) with $400 to spare.

As time passed, the collective was renamed a cooperative,
and after several years of attempting to run as a coop, the name
was changed again, in 1979, to We Want The Music Company
(WWTMC). "In truth, we were never really a collective,"
explains producer Lisa Vogel, "because while many wanted to
take part in the decision-making process, not everyone wanted
to take responsibility. So not everyone was equally involved." In
1976, *collective* was the way to be, or at least the name to
have. "We didn't know," says Lisa. "We were young. We've
learned things over the years. It [the festival] can't be run any
other way, because we've tried it. . . . We've had to organize the
festival, not just politically and socially, but as a business, too."

WWTMC is an unusual business. It is a private corporation,
which, while it could claim not-for-profit status, has never
opted to file as such with the IRS—to avoid becoming
vulnerable to government interference. Its leadership structure
remains mutable, and festival producers remain responsive to
the women's and lesbian communities. Lisa likens the company
to a hybrid—the operating structure of a partnership with the
communication structure of a collective. The legal structure of
WWTMC is that of a corporation.

In the July 1982 issue of *Lesbian Connection* appears an
article written by Lisa and Kristie Vogel, who had been
producing the festival from its beginning:

> We are the producers of the Michigan Womyn's Music
> Festival and we want to let you know who we are now
> and a little about our progression over the past few
> years. This article is a statement about why we want to
> continue to produce "Michigan," as the festival has
> been affectionately named, and what kind of
> environment we are working towards.
>
> Festival "82" will be the seventh. . . . In the last seven
> years the festival and the womyn who have produced
> the festivals have gone through significant changes. We
> began in 1976 in what we defined as a collective to
> initiate the makings of the first festival. Over the next
> three to four years there were anywhere from three to

six womyn who produced the festivals, accepting
varying degrees of responsibility throughout the year.
We struggled with our definition of who we were and if
indeed we were really a collective. Eventually we came
to the conclusion that we were not a collective since
responsibility was not equally taken for the production
of the festival. This conclusion was long in coming, and,
as usual in these cases, seemed somewhat anticlimactic
and even inconsequential at the time. By the 1980
festival, production was being handled and organized
by us: Lisa and Kristie Vogel (yes, we are blood sisters!).
We have been with the festival since its conception in
1976, and have always taken major responsibility for it.
As in most cases, changes that happened
organizationally took place at a gradual pace. Any
womon who has ever worked collectively knows that
there are many personal and political ideals, conflicts,
and goals to work out among those involved. We were
of course no different. Many womyn participated in the
WWTMC "collective" during those initial years. Some
were more central than others but all were a very
important driving force that helped to bring the festival
to what it has become today.

Along with personnel changes, the festival as a
business was also growing and having to become more
refined to function as economically soundly as possible.
More and more we saw ourselves as a business even
though we really had not thought to actually "define"
ourselves as such. In reality we ARE a business, as
much a business as any other production company, and
it is BECAUSE of this that the festival is a reality. . . .

As the festival has grown, we have become more and
more financially solvent. This has allowed us to expand
and improve what the festival offers in many ways. One
major way is through the number of womyn that we are
able to pay for their services. The festival began and ran
on volunteer labor for more than three years. By the
fourth year we were able to pay a small salary to
womyn who coordinated areas of the festival. Each year
thereafter coordinator salary increased proportionate to
our financial status and the number of coordinators.

A coordinator is usually a womon who has worked at
the festival at least one year in some training capacity.

She will usually be at the festival grounds from two to
three weeks before the festival and stay one to three
weeks after the festival to complete her area and to
help "break down" and clean up. Some coordinators are
involved in "prep" work for their areas before they
arrive at the festival. They are the womyn that actually
organize and manage the festival at its site. The winter
work, administrative and yearly business planning, is
carried on by Lisa and Kristie Vogel, the two coordinating year-round staff persons. By early summer there are
additional staff person who work in the office and who
assist in the over-all summer management of the
festival. By July there is a growing number of womyn
involved. . . . Daily the staff grows, until in the weeks
prior to and following the festival, there is the paid
involvement and input of over one hundred womyn.

The making of policy decisions at the festival has
been an issue that we all have struggled with. Many of
the coordinators have worked with the festival for many
years. This is mentioned because it is this consistency
that has helped create a forum and a process for
debate, feedback, and decision making. . . . At present
there is an elected group that takes the responsibility to
solicit feedback, suggestions, and criticisms from all the
coordinators on important policy and organizational
issues, so they may be able to have a voice in the
decisions that affect the festival. Hopefully this process
will continue and be fine tuned as we progress. . . .

The festival began as a dream. . . . We thought, "how
exciting it would be to have a pleasant environment
that was attended and run only by womyn!" Well, it
happened, and it WAS exciting. . . . Many felt a kind of
support from this world that they had never felt before
in their lives. We were in control of our own
environment, and we were taking responsibility for all
aspects of our well-being. . . . We are trying to create an
environment where womyn feel safe, affirmed, can enjoy
themselves and each other, can share information, are
taken care of AND take care of each other, can be
themselves and in general have the opportunity for
many positive experiences.

We have worked hard to help create that kind of
environment. We of course cannot do that without every

single woman who comes making a commitment to create that environment also. The bottom line is that womyn must feel safe. We must be able to feel secure in this small community we create. . . . We are trying to create something different from our day to day living experience.

Michigan for many years has been an energizer and a high point in the year. It has helped give womyn strength and energy to go back into the world, a world that most of us need a lot of strength to live in. We are concerned with keeping Michigan a positive influence and effect on the lives of womyn who attend.

The idea is cooperative sisterhood. We ALL make the festival work. The only way an event like this can keep its ticket prices as low as they are is because womyn are asked to participate in work shifts at the festival. This was never intended to be a "catered" event. We are setting the stage for a cooperative event. Everyone who attends should know this and be willing to pitch in and do their share to make it work. The festival is a community of womyn working and playing together. We are ALL responsible for keeping the community in good shape. If only one woman shrugs her workload, it falls extra heavy on the shoulders of her sister who won't walk away from her responsibility. It is an environment where we all can help each other. . . . It is certainly a challenge—one that we hope every woman will accept when she decides to come to Michigan.

We are in the process of attempting to purchase land. . . . We plan to develop this site as a permanent home for the festival. There are of course other future visions for the use and development of this land: conference space for the many national political causes, gathering space for the womyn involved in womyn defined businesses, year round womyn's resort space, and well equipped resource and meeting facility. The possibilities are exciting and would greatly benefit the womyn's community at large. As the land becomes more developed we will be able to install more sophisticated systems such as permanent structures, water, septic, electrical, and communications improvements. Can you imagine taking a hot shower at Michigan? . . .

At the point where acquiring this piece of property becomes imminent, the actual ownership and administrative structure of this land and the various methods of incorporating national community access will be dealt with in a structure separate from the structure that now guides the festival. Since this is all in process, more information concerning this will be coming out when all of this becomes closer to being a reality. . . .

Over the years we have worked on improving and expanding staff, services, and other features of the festival. We have made mistakes. We will make mistakes in the future. We have learned a lot over the years about the needs of womyn, the need for good communication, process, and much more. We want to meet the needs of the womyn who attend Michigan. We feel that although we can't meet everyone's needs, . . . with your support and help we feel we CAN come close to creating an environment that is a good and safe alternative.

That the festival was still learning through experience was to become especially apparent during the 1982 festival itself. That year marked the beginning of a difficult period. WWTMC had found land to rent with an option to buy, still intending to have the 1982 festival at the "old" land. The owner of the old land, however, backed out at the last minute, so WWTMC had to scramble to create a festival in August.

1982 marked the end of WWTMC's attempt at a collective/cooperative organization. According to Lisa, "There was a large desire on many women's part to be a collective, but not to take the risks. Not many were willing to sign for the loans or to work off the debt if it didn't work out." Lisa and her sister signed for loans, and the land where the festival is currently held was bought.

Because of the last-minute change of place, there was barely time to prepare for the 1982 Festival. Then, 8,000 women showed up—significantly more than the organizers were ready for. In addition, the undeveloped terrain made wheelchair locomotion all but impossible, and the number of portable toilets set aside for disabled women was inadequate.

The portable toilets are still a source of controversy, because they can only be cleaned once a night. Lisa and Kristie's dream

of putting in permanent meeting places and septic systems has
not come to pass, but hot showers have been around since
1988.

▲ ▲ ▲

In the hard years, the women who ran WWTMC faced
accusations of being petty business women. In a utopian
environment, profits and business have evil connotations. "If
someone goes to a store and pays a hundred dollars for a pair
of Nikes," says Lisa, "They know they have to pay that much;
no one expects any different. But somehow there's something
about giving money to women. No one expects to pay a
woman a hundred dollars for a pair of handmade shoes."

Women who do business serving the women's community
seem to face more of this difficulty than women in the
mainstream: on one hand they often want to be socially
responsible; on the other hand, they must also make a living
(i.e., make some kind of profit). Yet some people see making a
profit as the ultimate in social irresponsibility, regardless of
what the service or product accomplishes for the buyer or how
much the business benefits the community.

The festival helps no small number of women musicians and
artisans make a living by gathering and developing an audience
for their work. Craftswomen have been at the festival since the
very beginning, and the crafts area has been a central part of
the festival for the past ten or twelve years. In 1993, there were
146 different bazaar booths listed in the program, and Lisa
reports that there are frequently 200 or more applicants vying
for space.

Some craftswomen use the festival to boost their income, or
as a way to "work away from work," while others make their
entire living from the various women's festivals, traveling
around the country from festival to festival. "These women
have also had to become more organized and professional over
the years. Many women have had to make the choice: 'Do I
want to do this for fun, or do I want to make a living from it?'
and act accordingly," Lisa says, "They tend to be alternative,
independent, artistic, a little vagabondish, and non-traditional
business women. They're a very important part of our culture."

In addition to the difficulties the festival faced in the early 1980s, it seemed that, as Lisa comments, "utopia lost its glow." The community had come to expect more—more polish, more access, more festival. Also, by 1983, other festivals had sprung up all over the country, so boycotters could boycott and still get their music, while others simply went to festivals closer to home. WWTMC took Michigan back to its essentials and over time, with dialog and trial-and-error, the Michigan Womyn's Music Festival has stabilized so that now an average of 7,500 to 8,000 women come annually. Of these, about 20% per year are "festi-virgins"—women attending the festival for the first time. For one week in August every year, women only populate the largest town in Oceana County.

▲ ▲ ▲

The community that arrives is diverse. WWTMC has had to face many issues as a result: making the festival accessible to disabled women, allowing/not allowing male children to attend with their mothers, helping heterosexual women cope with alienation (lesbians are a majority at the festival), barring or including the leather community without other women feeling intimidated or threatened, and, most recently, deciding whether to admit male-to-female transsexuals to the festival. Over the years, different people have threatened the festival with boycotts regarding these decisions and, while the producers take criticism seriously, Lisa says boycotts haven't much swayed attendance.

The festival has been a curiosity for the men who know about it, and, at times, an event to harrass. One year, after the permanent land was bought, during a time when no one was on the land, some men decided to blow up the electrical transformers—which are now stored below ground. Another year, the driveway outside the gate was strewn with nails. There have been petty acts of vandalism and harassment. "There's been definite loss," says Lisa, but she refers to the costs of repairs as part of the cost of doing business. "I don't think these things have affected the attendance, because even with these occasional incidents, festival week is one of the most secure weeks of the year in many women's lives—it's a boost. A large part of the festival is feeling safe."

In 1993, at the gate, $225 gained a woman entry to six days on 650 acres, complete with three vegetarian meals daily, more than 300 workshops, and 44 scheduled concert acts. There were also films, a shuttle service, assistance for disabled women, community tents for the tentless, a first-aid center ("The Womb"), an emotional support center ("The Oasis"), a sober support center, sign language and foreign language interpreters, and child care.

Tickets bought in advance are on a sliding scale; for instance, a six-day ticket in advance is $200–230. A one-day ticket was $50, and tickets could be had for any number of days, with the end of stay figured for Sunday. There are no tickets for, say, just Tuesday and Wednesday; a two-day stay is always Saturday–Sunday.

In addition to the ticket price, all women attending the festival are required to work one or two 4-hour workshifts, depending on how many days they are attending. This has been the source of some controversy and was explained as follows in the 1994 program:

> The Festival community expands from the five hundred womyn on staff to a greater village of six to eight thousand womyn from all fifty U.S. states, all ten Canadian provinces and two territories, and at least twenty other countries from around the world. The concept and structure of the Festival is built on the premise that we all provide the necessary village services for each other. There are a number of reasons for this but they all distill to the same value . . . building a community of womyn.

> We aren't a campground with entertainment, an amusement park or even a fair where womyn drop by to catch a concert, buy a sandwich and shop for a few hours. We are a gathering of womyn who represent many diverse cultures and experiences, but do share a common bond which is our desire to live a week of womyn-centered life. For this reason we are building our own community which means that everyone attending does some part of creating the whole, thereby making it her own, investing it with a part of who she is, and gifting other womyn with her contribution. It is

essentially how the Festival works and what infuses it
with its unique empowering quality. Each womon who
attends is proud to know that everything that exists
here is done by womyn for womyn and that she too is a
part of that.

The greatest need for workers is in the kitchen, which serves
three vegetarian meals a day. According to the festival program,
most of the women attending the festival do a workshift in the
kitchen, plus there is a staff of 31. A number of meat-eating
women bring coolers of steaks and hamburgers; others drive
out to restaurants, even though the closest town is 20 miles
away. There are also concession stands. One is run by the
Saints collective—a group of political working-class women
from Boston. Originally, the Saints, who ran the Saints women's
bar in Boston, wanted to set up a beer concession to raise some
extra funds. WWTMC didn't want to prohibit alcohol but
didn't want to have it sold at the festival either, so the SAINTS
run a general concession stand at the festival, selling coffee, tea,
soft drinks, juices, cookies, donuts, chips, and bagels with
cream cheese. Other foods, such as crackers, cookies, and ice
cream bars, are sold by the festival's general store.

▲ ▲ ▲

In some of the articles and letters from 1982–85, I found
complaints of festigoers regarding the working staff—which
includes the paid coordinators—and their privileges. Many
people believe that all festival staff are paid, but this is only
true of coordinators, not all workers. Riding back from my
workshift, I asked a bus driver what workers' benefits actually
were. She said they got free entry to the festival, and fish or
chicken once a week so that the meat-eaters of the group
wouldn't get sick. Other than that, they work basically because
the festival and the women connected to it are important to
them. They are on call twenty-four hours a day during the
festival week, and sometimes the work is exhausting. For that
reason, the festival workers' campground is roped off and has a
border watch—to keep it as a sanctuary.

The festival, from the arrangement of the camping areas to
the shuttle service, runs efficiently because of experience that

eighteen years has lent. Each year has had its issues, its weather, and potential for disaster, but Lisa and all the women working with her have steadily worked to improve the festival year by year. Improvements come through WWTMC's responsiveness to complaints, suggestions, brainstorms, and general feedback from the festigoers to the coordinators and producers. Lisa attributes the success of the festival to organization and communication. "The issues of communities everywhere are issues here as well." I heard a few sarcastic remarks here and there about political correctness ruling the festival, and clearly there have been misunderstandings over the years; it is now printed in the program that

> We want this gathering to be a safe place to broaden our experience, to make room for each other, to leave the learned prejudices out beyond the county roads. This is more than an opportunity, however—it is an expectation which underlies each person's welcome to participate. Acts or attitudes of racism, sexism, anti-semitism, classism, ageism, ableism, homophobia or violence against womyn in any form are not acceptable in this community, on this land.

I tried to talk a friend into coming to Michigan, and she thought I was crazy for asking. Who would go to a place, she wanted to know, that charged an entrance fee so you could rough it, eat like a rabbit, *and* have the guts to ask you to work? Not even the promise of good music and thousands of women could budge her.

Having gone, I can explain some of it. The days I spent there stretched out, and I sank into a complete ease with my own existence. I felt less self-conscious about my body. Bodies in general became more themselves, natural and erotic, losing their sexual-object charge. I felt less singular and more essential, connected. I gave a damn. I was curious. I felt secure. It was easy to find someone to hang out with, to make friends. Each could go as naked as she wished. No one was afraid to take a midnight stroll, or to walk alone at night. The music was great, the humor easy to laugh with, and the place had plenty of atmosphere—I slipped into it as easily as an old pair of shoes.

I asked Lisa if she thought the festival was workable on a larger scale, for longer periods of time. Her response was this: "Hopefully. We're brought together by common values. The

LESBIAN RICHES

KAREN WILLIAMS

I've just returned from a fabulous week at Club Med in Playa Blanca, Mexico. What made the trip so fab was the fact that there were more than 650 lesbians in attendance— of all races, creeds, and nationalities—relaxing on the beach, basking poolside, horseback riding, kayaking, dancing, playing ping pong, volleyball, and basketball, and yes, flying on trapezes and trampolines. What makes this all so amazing and alluring is that we as lesbians have evolved to a place where we can allow ourselves to have fun. And as we all know, fun does not come cheap. Which also means that some of us have, in fact, given up our vow of poverty and decided to go for it! Because, as you know, part of the unspoken vow that we took when we became lesbians was the vow of poverty.

The vow of poverty was necessary in the beginning days of lesbian feminism, when leaving home to become a lesbian often meant your only worldly possessions were your plaid shirt, jeans, and Birkenstocks (and your student loans). With two or three decades under our belts (and Capri slacks), we have, in fact, come a long way, baby, on the economic side. But it's been a struggle to let go of the good ole days when potlucks ruled and milk crates and futons were the decor of the day. The very notion of spending money to have fun for some of us is sheer heresy. However, I prefer to view having fun and spending money as a radical take-off on the *Do What You Love and the Money Will Follow* ideology.

For those of us who are used to going any and every where with a covered dish, the idea that one would actually spend hard-earned money to have a good time is indeed radical. But it

Copyright © 1994 by Karen Williams

is a necessary mindset if we want to launch ourselves into a new era of lesbian-being. The time has come where we must support ourselves as lesbians with our mouths and our money. It's one thing to talk lesbian and to spend mainstream. It's another to put our time, energy, and money into the support of our own lesbian culture, instead of worrying about the mainstream so much. Let's share information with one another about lesbian-owned businesses and products, publications and producers, and all people, places, and things lesbian, so that we can build a viable and prosperous community.

Feminists and lesbians must reevaluate our politics. Even more effective would be a rehash of Economics 101: Supply and Demand, where, say, the women's bookstores represent the supply and we, the lesbian consumers, represent the demand. Otherwise, our precious bookstores, which are more to us than mere places to make book purchases, will be forced to concede to the Barnes & Nobles of the world. Our commitment to feminism, to lesbianism, to womanist beliefs and goals, must reach beyond mere ideology. We must support women's businesses with women's dollars. There is no other solution for the safeguarding and institutionalizing of our women's culture. We must put our money where our mouths are (well, not literally, but it is a woman-to-woman thing)!

We must honestly evaluate our level of commitment not only to the women's bookstore owners and operators but also to the many lesbian, feminist, and womanist authors, poets, storytellers, playwrights, humorists, and theoreticians who rely on us to buy and read their work. Participation in the many festivals of women's culture produced around the country supports lesbian artists, performers, and producers, as well as participants. In years to come, we must make efforts to build a strong lesbian community with a viable economy filled with choices. Then we will be able to look back fondly on the days when a covered dish was not an option but a necessity. We may feel, because there are a few places where women's culture is being cultivated, that the women's movement is built. While our foundation has been laid, it will take more time before the edifice is secure. That security must be financed by us, its participants. Buy Lesbian, Feminist, Womanist, or be prepared to say Good-Bye to our Culture and our Heritage!

FEMINIST BOOKSTORES

PART OF AN ECOSYSTEM

Feminist bookstores have never been stronger. Numbering at
least 135 in the United States and Canada with combined gross
sales in 1992 of $35 million, feminist bookstores are a
formidable grass-roots industry. For over twenty years, feminist
booksellers have balanced sound business practices with
political commitment to their communities. The result has been,
in most cases, thriving bookstores that, in addition to providing
books, periodicals, music, and sidelines unavailable anywhere
else, offer a multitude of community services such as bulletin
boards, readings and community events, referrals to social
services, and meeting places for women. Who among us hasn't
gone to our local feminist bookstore to find a roommate,
support group, therapist, woman carpenter, or tickets for the
Sweet Honey in the Rock concert?

When Lioness Books in Sacramento, California, opened in
1981, our entire stock could fit on a few shelves; now we fill
2,500 square feet of store space with about 15,000 titles. Like
all feminist bookstores, we have grown with the proliferation of
feminist publishers, periodicals, authors, and most importantly,
audience. In the early 1970s a few publishers such as
Daughters, Diana, The Women's Press Collective, and Shameless
Hussy began publishing a few feminist and/or lesbian titles; we
now have at least 154 feminist or lesbian presses publishing
over 300 titles per year, along with 300 to 400 other
independent publishers producing feminist and lesbian books.

Copyright © 1993 by Theresa Corrigan   181

Having said all of that, I do not wish to paint an overly rosy picture of feminist bookstore land. Like all independent booksellers, we are facing tremendous predatory competition from the chains and superstores (huge chain stores carrying, on average, over 100,000 books in each location). Currently 40 percent of all books are sold by chains, primarily by Waldenbooks and Borders Bookstores (both owned by the K-Mart Corporation which had revenues of $39 billion last year), Barnes & Noble (which also owns B. Dalton), and the Crown Book Corporation. However, industry spokespeople predict that the voracious proliferation of superstores (Barnes & Noble plans to open 150 new superstores by the end of 1993) could mean the end of many independent and specialty bookstores. The *Sacramento Bee* (Nov. 16, 1992) quotes Lois Connelly, assistant director of investor relations at K-mart, "We think superstores will become the dominant channel of book distribution within five years."

The marketing strategy of superstores is to move into a location well established by one or more independent or specialty bookstores, target the independent's customer base, and use a combination of discounting, publisher-sponsored advertising, big-name author appearances, and, to many, questionable ethical practices to outsell their competitors.

A young man recently told me that you can never have too many bookstores in any community. Others add that the free enterprise system and competition are the backbone of excellence. That might be true if the playing field were level. The expertise and experience of feminist booksellers would provide the competitive edge. But the arena is not equitable. The superstores discount many titles at prices at or below what feminist bookstores pay wholesale. It doesn't take mathematical wizardry to figure out that a business cannot survive selling products at a loss. Nor are the chains taking a loss. They have special arrangements with publishers to purchase books wholesale at discounts independents can only dream of.

According to the Federal Trade Commission,

> Discrimination in prices and terms offered by major book publishers has created two categories of book retailers: favored book retailers (chains) and disfavored retailers (independents). Because disfavored retailers pay higher prices for their books and have limited access to

publishers' co-op advertising funds (where the publisher pays the store's advertising costs to promote their titles), it is very difficult—often impossible—for disfavored retailers to compete.

William Petrocelli, owner of Book Passage in Corte Madera, California, says that the price disparity between what chains and independents pay for books now appears to be 15 percent or higher.

Superstores also hope to entice customers away from feminist stores by offering readings by well-established authors, such as Adrienne Rich, Gloria Steinem, and Rita Mae Brown, whose original audiences were built in feminist stores. Mary Kay Blakely, contributing editor of *Ms.* magazine and author of *Wake Me When It's Over,* says that 70 percent of the sales of her books are in feminist bookstores, but her publisher ignored them when planning the tour for her first book. For her new book, she has chosen a publisher respectful of her wishes to include feminist stores in the promotion. "My career only stays alive because of feminist and women's bookstores," she says. "People like me stay in print because feminist bookstores are willing to carry backstock and to reorder." According to the *Chain Store Age Executive* journal, the chairman of Bookstop (a superstore in Texas and Florida), says that if a new release does not do well (in his stores) in its first few weeks, it is replaced. However, he adds, the classic works stay forever. We all know what he means by "classic." And he doesn't mean 99 percent of the books carried by feminist bookstores.

The chains are also capitalizing on the lesbian and gay markets since they discovered that we buy so many books. However, they primarily stock mainstream press titles, so don't expect to find most of your favorite authors at the superstores. Few lesbian authors are published by the big houses. Mainstream publishers want a track record before they're willing to risk money. Most lesbian authors now published by the big houses, such as Dorothy Allison, Sarah Schulman, and Jeanette Winterson, established their track records through the feminist presses and bookstores. Most new authors don't have a prayer of being published by the mainstream houses, or if published, won't be sold by the chain stores.

When the mainstream houses do publish lesbian titles (which isn't often—of the 1993 Lammy nominations, mainstream presses published 65 percent of gay men's titles compared with 19 percent of the lesbian titles), they publish stories they think will play in Peoria. Victoria A. Brownworth, in "Desexing the Story," a recent article in the *Lambda Book Report*, describes what happens when lesbian authors go mainstream—the lesbian sexual content is absent, and lesbian characters are presented stereotypically as non-sexual friends or obsessed and dangerous. She quotes a gay male editor at a mainstream house, "Who wants to read about two girls getting it on?" If mainstream publishers and chain stores do indeed damage the feminist bookselling and publishing industries, they will destroy the source of literature that reflects the richness and diversity of lesbian lives.

Carol Seajay, publisher of *Feminist Bookstore News* (the trade journal for feminist booksellers), describes the interrelationships among feminist bookstores, women's music labels, feminist and lesbian publishers, feminist periodicals, and authors as an ecosystem. When each part thrives, the entire system is healthy. When one part suffers, the rest feel the effect. Feminist publishers are dependent upon feminist bookstores to carry their books; the chains will only order those books they can get at discounts most feminist publishers cannot offer. Without feminist bookstores, one would probably never have encountered the works of Cherríe Moraga, Kitty Tsui, Chrystos, Katherine Forrest, Barbara Wilson, Jewelle Gomez, Dale Spender; or even the works of authors who are household names like Alice Walker, Gloria Naylor or Robin Morgan, whose writing was first promoted through feminist networks. Many first books are hand-sold by feminist booksellers. We know what is important to our political and literary movements, and we promote books as cultural and intellectual expressions, not merely as commodities.

Corporate America views books as just another commodity to be sold in mass quantities. Mary Morrell, co-owner of Full Circle in Albuquerque, New Mexico, says, "When price becomes more important than substance, we get cardboard tomatoes, cheap but tasteless. Then when we want real tomatoes, we have to pay through the nose." Mary adds that the issue is difficult because women don't make the "big bucks" in society and cost is an important factor, but she compares women's communities to ethnic communities: "Ethnic communities that have supported their own businesses have created healthy endeavors that have reinvested in their own communities." Feminist bookstores reinvest in their communities every day through all the services they provide.

Feminist bookstores are a resource the chains can never be, according to Gilda Bruckman of New Words in Cambridge, Massachusetts. "We have twenty years of history about our communities and our movement; people come to us to make use of the knowledge we have acquired. We are consistent. For example, we don't suddenly alter our face for gay/lesbian book month; we are there for lesbian and bisexual women all the time."

When asked how feminist bookstores are dealing with the competition from the chains, store owners all emphasize customer service, knowledge of the literature and their community resources, and dedication. Lammas in Washington, D.C., is not waiting for customers to come to them. "We are going to lesbian bars, women's studies instructors, and any place else to reach women," says Jane Troxell, the new co-owner. "We also organize special events for the community, such as self-defense classes, financial planning workshops, camping and rafting trips, and will soon exhibit the only existing lesbian dollhouse (based on *Heather Has Two Mommies* by Lesléa Newman)." She adds laughing, "We may carry fewer of the mainstream bestsellers, but Crown doesn't have menstrual goddesses or Margie Adam tapes."

Pokey Anderson of Inklings in Houston, Texas, points out that "the demands on a feminist bookstore are high; as well as running a business, we do referrals, sell tickets, provide emotional support, listen and lots of other things that can only exist if customers matronize the business. It's hard, sometimes, when you know someone buys lots of feminist books, but the only time they come in to the store is to post a flyer."

Tollie Miller from A Reader's Feast in Hartford, Connecticut, is going one step further in defending her store from the onslaught of the chains. Connecticut has the largest concentration of chain stores of any state, and most of the independents are sorely feeling the results. A Reader's Feast, along with fifteen other independent bookstores from around the state, have organized the Connecticut Independent Bookseller's Day, during which local authors will read at each

of the participating stores. The stores will pool money from the
events to place ads in national media to celebrate the diversity
that independent bookstores bring to the intellectual
environment of the country. They have even gotten financial
support from some publishers. Tollie echoes the sentiments of
other feminist booksellers when she says, "we have a
commitment to carry and disseminate progressive ideas, not
merely to sell commodities." She adds, "We do so much more
than sell books; over the last ten years we have helped
innumerable women through life crisis, not by counseling them,
but by empowering them about the choices they have."

Many people assume that one sale here or there won't make
a difference. So what if someone buys *Backlash* or *Revolution
From Within* at a chain? The independent book business, unlike
many others, operates on tiny profit margins. Most feminist
bookstores are lucky to have a 1 to 3 percent yearly net profit.
Some feminist bookstores have experienced a 10 percent or
more decline in sales after a chain store moves into the
neighborhood. When a business operates on such small
margins, it can ill afford even small fluctuations in sales.

To have intellectual, political and literary diversity, we must
have diversity in the marketplace. Without feminist bookstores,
the kinds of books you see at your local store will cease to exist
for the most part. Every time each of us invests in a feminist
bookstore, we are helping to protect the range of literature
available: from lesbian and gay novels, to nonsexist, nonracist
children's books, to goddess-centered books, to feminist theory.
The future of progressive and quality publishing is in our
hands—simply by making conscious decisions about where we
spend our money.

Sally Owen, co-owner of Judith's Room in New York City,
describes the potential effect of the superstores quite simply: "If
people buy books at Barnes & Noble, small stores (including
feminist stores) will go out of business, presses will suffer and
books will disappear." This process she calls "economic
censorship." "We are contributing to our own censorship by
supporting the chains," she adds: "If we allow this to happen,
Barnes & Noble (and the other chains) will decide what gets
sold, what is in print, the size of the print runs, and ultimately
what people have access to. The question is not who gets a
piece of the pie, the pie itself will be drastically changed."

Now time for a parable. Twenty-five years ago I first went into the Off Key, Sacramento's only women's bar, which was huge, grungy and owned by a man, but ours to do with what we wanted. It had been there for as long as anyone could remember and hadn't changed much. The neutral cultural borderlands between the traditional gay women's world and the emerging lesbian/feminist one, populated with diesel dykes, hippie lesbians, politicos, butches, femmes, and an occasional queen, the Off Key was home to all of us. We had performances, marriages performed by the old preacher woman Mama Lou, pool tournaments, birthday parties, and protest meetings.

Then four years later, some men from San Francisco opened a glitzy new bar about a mile away. The new bar had everything we thought we could want: a rotating glitter ball over the dance floor, a hard liquor license, a restaurant, a live DJ, and fancy everything. Most of us shifted loyalties and became regulars at the Hut. The Off Key did not survive, but we hardly noticed. Only a few weeks after the Off Key closed, the owners of the Hut put a sign on the front door, "Men are welcome. Women will be tolerated with three forms of ID." The harassment escalated with aggressive male bouncers, mandatory drink policies, and verbal abuse. We clearly were not wanted but had no place to go. Sacramento, by the way, hasn't had a successful women's bar since.

This experience taught me a valuable lesson about loyalty, not necessarily to a particular person or place, but to an alternative that I, as part of a community, had created. The Hut courted women only as long as they needed us to establish the business. I know that the book industry (publishers and mainstream bookstores) will only court lesbian and feminist communities as long as it is in vogue and profitable.

An editor from Penguin, USA spoke at the Publisher's Triangle meeting at the American Bookseller's Association convention this year. At one point, he said, "Let's face it folks, we're in this business to make money." That was his bottom line. This statement is the fundamental philosophical difference between the Off Key and the Hut, between feminist bookstores and chain stores. Feminist stores are not in the business to make money, but we need to make money to stay in business. Those of us who operate feminist bookstores are very smart women; if making money was our priority, we would all have chosen more lucrative means. We are in the business to educate, to end sexism, racism, homophobia, classism, ageism and all the other inequities that threaten our society and survival, and to create a safe place for our sisters and brothers. We are in the business to change the world. That will never be profitable or in vogue. Feminist bookstores are in it for the long haul and proud to be part of a larger movement for social change.

For a complete list of names and addresses of feminist bookstores throughout the U.S. and Canada, send $1.00 and a SASE to Feminist Bookstore News, PO Box 882554, San Francisco, CA. 94188

A TALE OF TWO FEMINIST BUSINESSES

WOMEN & CHILDREN FIRST
WEST END WAX

ALICE LOWENSTEIN

What may we ask of a business owned by women? Furthermore, what do we expect of a feminist business, or one that caters to women? These questions arose in my interviews with the female owners of two successful stores. As I asked about community interaction and creative economics, I realized the questions themselves imply certain expectations of women or, more specifically, feminists, in business. Indeed, we must question the meaning of the term *feminist* when applied to business. For example, must a feminist business see positive community interaction, or some form of reciprocity, as fundamental as profit to a successful venture? Or can female ownership of a business exist as a strong feminist act, in and of itself, regardless of the operating principles of the establishment? I found some illumination exploring these issues with two women-owned businesses that operate in very different environments.

Women & Children First, a bookstore in Chicago, Illinois, is a bustling, brightly lit, well-stocked testament to the literary woman. Its owners, Ann Christophersen and Linda Bubon, decided early on that the store was to be a place for all women. To that end, they carry a wide array of work by women and of interest to women, including fiction, feminist theory, romances, mystery novels, lesbian erotica, recovery literature, self-help

Copyright © 1995 by Alice Lowenstein   189

books, and more. As a result, the store is a popular spot for the local women's community as well as a highly respected independent bookseller.

Women & Children First embodies a feminist principle of inclusiveness. Co-owner Linda Bubon says, "We wanted the mix to be so broad that no one would be put off, so that any woman, of any age, could come in here and find something that related to her life and that honored the choices she had made in her life. Our bottom line is that all women live in a patriarchy and need to feel a link with all other women. That's one of the reasons why we've always had [only] one store. It feels so good to bring all kinds of women together in one kind of space." The store's chosen area of specialization, its varied stock, and target market represent a dedication to empowerment and community building.

When they went into business in 1979, the idea of opening a women's bookstore rang true for two main reasons, says Ann Christophersen. It would provide for "the community where our hearts and interests were beginning to lie primarily. And also it seemed to make good business sense."

From the store's beginning, Bubon and Christophersen were aware that in order to succeed, they would have to ensure the store's economic health. To that end, the owners chose a focus that was not "anti-business," as some early women's bookstores had been, says Christophersen. She adds that the store's location, in the large and diverse city of Chicago, contributed to an expanded notion of what a woman's bookstore could be. "That's all to say that when we opened, we were clear from the beginning that we were a business and we organized as a corporation. We didn't intend to compromise, and don't feel like we have compromised, feminist principles in the process. Our understanding of it from the beginning was that the only way we could serve the community was if we could exist."

So the two decided to run a *business*. But, as Christophersen goes on to say, they were not business people and so the resulting business was very personally defined. For them, the idea of running a business meant that they could provide an important resource to their community which also allowed them to survive financially. "It was never as reductive as 'the bottom line is profit.' The bottom line was shifting all the time, but it always had to do with how we could fulfill our mission," says Christophersen. That mission includes providing a viable livelihood for the store's owners and the others involved in the project.

Before starting the business, Bubon and Christophersen considered the possible financial difficulties that could arise for the business as a result of the economic injustice in women's lives. The fact that, at the time they began, women were paid 59 cents to every dollar men were paid was something they had to weigh in opening a store that appealed primarily to women. Women still have less discretionary income than men. Christophersen says that issue was not viewed as a problem, however, but as an important awareness that they shared. They also knew that women read. "Women don't have as much disposable income as their male counterparts because of economic disparity. But we were also fairly confident that what disposable income women had, this was one way they wanted to spend it." This belief has proven true.

Women & Children First has grown in size from its original location with 800 square feet, to a 1600-square-foot space, into its current size of 2300 square feet. It celebrated its 15th birthday in 1994, having been incorporated November 10, 1979. The two owners originally staffed the store and held down other jobs. Now they each maintain a forty-plus-hour work week at the bookstore, and they employ five full-time and four part-time workers.

While clearly a very successful business in terms of finances and longevity, Women & Children First is also committed to its community. Due to its nature and focus, the business and its owners are called upon and want to be more. Women & Children First gives directly back to its customers and its community, demonstrating that a feminist notion of reciprocity can apply to economics. The combination of feminist consciousness and business acumen, in this case, reflects a far-reaching commitment to women.

From their initial years in business, Women & Children First found that a consistent way to give to the community as well as to the business was through public programs at the bookstore. Christophersen says the idea of opening the store to the community, in ways beyond a simple retail relationship, was crucial. The store hosts famous women authors such as Alice Walker, Gloria Steinem, Susan Faludi, and many others, as well as providing space for local women writers to share their work. In addition, the space is made available for community forums. "We've had discussions here on probably every issue of concern to the feminist community and/or lesbian community over the years. We've [hosted] every speaker we could possibly get our hands on. . . . That's the way in which, on an ongoing basis, we and the community have interacted, on a formal level," says Christophersen. She adds that the community knows the bookstore has this space available. Whether it's a Feminist Writers Guild reading or the airing of a topic of importance to lesbians, it can and does happen at Women & Children First.

The programs are a way the bookstore reaches out to underemployed and poor women. All the events are free. Says Christophersen, "We cover all the costs of producing. We pay for the staff, we pay for the advertisement, we pay for the electricity, we cover the overhead of having programs here, and anybody can come to those."

This is one method of navigating the sometimes tricky issues of economics in a feminist establishment. Feminist businesses often work to address the question of access to their products. But they must balance the desire to eliminate economic barriers for women with the need to maintain a focus on the business's own financial health. When a business fails because it gives too much away, it loses its ability to serve anyone.

The bookstore makes frequent donations to organizations that assist women. Christophersen notes that they have just begun keeping track of these gifts, and the amount exceeds what she and Bubon realized. "It's literally three or four a week of a gift certificate for a raffle, or an autographed copy of something. . . ." As the owners work to share resources with women, they illustrate an aspect of feminist economics. We can assist others, only as we provide for ourselves.

Women & Children First now adjoins Womanwild, a women's gallery and store, and is building ever stronger ties with the women's community. Its owners are able to have lives outside of work—a real mark of achievement, as any small business owner knows. Their success has come through a willing mingling of feminist principles and sound business decisions. Women & Children First is a feminist business which, in this case, means a woman-focused store that actively works for the empowerment of the populations it serves.

▲ ▲ ▲

West End Wax, a thriving St. Louis record store, is also a feminist business. It, however, doesn't cater primarily to women, nor does it share the same operating principles as Women and Children First. It is an example of a woman's success in a historically non-female industry. West End Wax owner, Pat Tentschert, is a strong, feminist, woman.

Tentschert began in the record business on her nineteenth birthday. Always an avid collector of music, she recalls the first song she ever heard as Elvis' "Hound Dog" in 1956, when she was two years old. "Music," she says, "was my escape and also my salvation."

Tentschert decided to open West End Wax after a plan to co-own a store with a group of people fell through. Some early employment experiences, many of which are familiar to women, also helped spur Tentschert to start a business. She recalls feeling underappreciated, doubted, and overlooked in her first jobs.

West End Wax opened 1982. Like Women & Children First, West End Wax has grown, from its original 900 square feet to a current size of 2700 square feet. The business began as a sole proprietorship and was incorporated in 1991. Each year to date has brought an increase in sales. Customers often tell Tentschert that they've never seen a store quite like West End Wax.

Tentschert recalls her lean early days with a chuckle. She says that the store had only about 200 records in stock when it opened. The business was makeshift and extremely undercapitalized, as are many women's businesses. Tentschert and the store's general manager Debby Mikles (who is still with the business) were not able to hire employees in the beginning, so they staffed the store themselves. Says Tentschert today with a smile, "By sheer will, brilliance, tenacity, sweating blood, putting every cent right back into the business, and some good decisions," the store has grown into its current success. From this vantage point, she takes an organic view of her achievement. "I have to remember that success is a gift. Not that I didn't work for it, but I do thank the Goddess for it."

From the store's beginning, it has occupied a central position in its owner's life. "Once it opened, it really became an extension of me. It was like giving birth. It is still my child. I

gained a lot of strength from it, and gave my strength to it,"
says Tentschert. West End Wax is packed with stock—CDs,
tapes, posters, t-shirts, and more. It exhibits a quirky sense of
humor and reflects Tentschert's philosophy of creating the most
enjoyable surroundings possible for shopping. "The atmosphere
is about freedom, outrageousness, and sensory overload," she
says. "I want you to be bombarded by sensation in a creative
presentation that reflects the store's sense of humor."

The store's early motto, "All styles served here," still
holds true. While initially well known for dance music and
imports, West End Wax has expanded its merchandise
assortment to cover a broad spectrum of music. The store also
tries to carry stock that is often overlooked by other record
retailers. Tentschert and the store's employees regularly get
compliments from customers, both St. Louis locals, and those
visiting from elsewhere. It is not uncommon for tourists
shopping at West End Wax (even from such big cities as New
York or Chicago) to state that they can't find the breadth of
selection at their local record stores that they find at West End
Wax. All this, with a strong, dynamic, outspoken woman at the
helm.

While she does not have the exact figures on the number of
successful women record store owners, Tentschert believes the
number is fairly low. More women are in management with the
various record labels today, she says, but store owners are "on
the frontlines." She recalls encountering gender-based
discrimination in her first years of business. The landlord of the
building her store has occupied since it opened, originally asked
Tentschert, who was 27 years old, to have her father co-sign on
the lease. She told the landlord flat-out, "no way." The request
was a real slap in the face, she recalls, and became an
important point in the development of her feminist
consciousness. She also remembers getting mail and telephone
calls from companies for *Mr.* Pat Tentschert, to which she
would always respond, "How dare you assume I'm a male
because my name is Pat!" Those companies never got her
store's business, she says adamantly.

Tentschert's strength of spirit has come out in other ways as
well. She has been known to "wrestle to the ground" male
shoplifters. A serious body builder, she says with a chuckle,
"I'm a big boned gal." In her retail neighborhood, the story still

goes around of a multi-mile chase on foot and in car with Tentschert after a shoplifter. The city area West End Wax occupies can be dangerous, and Tentschert is aware of the need to temper her instincts toward defense at all costs with the need to proceed with caution. "I try to channel my strength in a positive way and not let it be too negative," she says. She nonetheless appreciates her power and finds it a valuable asset in many areas of business.

The issue of neighborhood safety has led Tentschert to community involvement. She holds a government-appointed volunteer position as chair of an otherwise all-male safety commission. Her activism came out of the anger and frustration she felt at seeing her store and others victimized by violent crime. In her current role, Tentschert feels her assertiveness is especially tested. She leads large meetings and is often responsible for mediating heated debates among the men on the commission.

Tentschert calls herself a radical feminist and fervently believes in the possibility of combining feminism and business. The visible manifestation of feminist principles at West End Wax differs in some ways from the practices of Women & Children First. One reason for this is that West End Wax is patronized by a general sample of the population, and often largely by men. The store cannot, therefore, focus primarily on meeting the needs of women. However, West End Wax is resolute in its dedication to women's empowerment.

Tentschert's feminism and that of her employees is given high priority in the business. The store is run by a female management team, and Tentschert sees the need for fostering women's leadership and educating the community to supersede business when necessary. She has no qualms about calling her customers on their sexist behavior, and she backs up her employees who do the same. She says, "I have to do that, I'm committed to it. That's beyond business. That's political and that's important to me. Some things are more important than making money." At West End Wax, "we don't bite the bullet. We have to educate people [customers] about women, and that we are feminists [the store employees] and we will be treated with respect."

Tentschert's commitment to upholding basic feminist principles may not be unusual. Many women do this in our daily lives. But her behavior is of importance for two reasons: First, it illuminates another definition of feminist business—incorporating and supporting the daily practice of feminism into a business situation. Second, this feminism exists within the context of a mainstream business that is very successful by even the most traditional definition. Tentschert is quick to note that West End Wax has an excellent reputation in the record industry. She and the other representatives of the store are known as being knowledgeable, straightforward, honest, and strong. West End Wax is also a reporter to *Billboard* magazine on trends in music, a rare position for an independent record store.

Like Bubon and Christophersen, Tentschert combines good business skills with appreciation for and increasing her business interaction with the feminist and lesbian communities. One of Tentschert's pleasures in owning a successful business is that it allows her to support women in many ways. She donates to feminist causes personally and through the store. She also observes a growing awareness in St. Louis that it is empowering and self-affirming for women to support women-owned businesses. She has been pleased to see her lesbian clientele increasing over the past few years. Tentschert is, herself, a presence in the women's community, and perhaps a role model for some.

Another strong characteristic of West End Wax is its out "queer" image. Recent ad slogans, such as "Queer spoken here," and "West End Wax, where the men are pretty and the women are strong," are only the latest in a long history of the store's presence in the St. Louis lesbian and gay community. Says Tentschert, the store has always had a "huge gay clientele." The store's sense of humor as well as its "outness" is empowering to lesbians and gay men. Describing West End Wax, Tentschert says with a smile, "it's a place for lesbians to go and be gay, to kiss women, and to see queers." In this way, West End Wax provides the invaluable resource of safe, non-judgmental space to an often disenfranchised population.

By providing that space, West End Wax moves beyond the role of retailer to serve its community more fully. The store is an exciting and open place. Because, in the minds of many, St. Louis lacks a large variety of lesbian and gay or women-centered activities, West End Wax is a vital gathering place. It is a place to cruise, listen to music, shop, and hang out in an atmosphere of warmth and humor. Tentschert talks excitedly of the armchair she recently added to the store which she imagines will highlight even further the welcome West End Wax offers.

Women & Children First and West End Wax are but two examples of women-owned business. The two stores are similar in their degree of success in their fundamental commitment to women and in traditional businesses terms. Their self-definition and practice of feminist business differs, and each store brings its own answer to the question of community and personal expectations. But from these two stories of hard work and triumph, we may formulate a definition of *feminist business* based on the realization that the term may apply less to specific practices and more to the idea that women empowering themselves and their communities through women-owned businesses is, in itself, *always* a feminist act.

FEMINISTS AND HEALTH CARE

A MIDWIFE'S PERSPECTIVE

KARIN KEARNS

The cultural taboo that prevents women from discussing their money can make it difficult to run a business based on feminist principles, serving women's needs. This article describes two womens' attempt to consciously transcend the obstacles that keep many women from obtaining health care, specifically quality midwifery care.

STARTING OUT

In April 1990, I left a salaried position as a liscensed midwife in a birthing center owned by a male physician because of internal politics that I believed were affecting patient care. The two women I worked with also left, in solidarity and protest for being emotionally manipulated. It was, of course, a major stress for us all.

One of the women, Anna, consiously chose to continue to work with me, and we now co-own a midwifery practice. Most decisions regarding the maintenance and development of the practice are made mutually. We pay ourselves for all of our out-of-pocket expenses, Anna draws her childcare expenses, and we share the insurance payments, as they tend to come in large lump sums. I am a single head of household with a dependent son, so my need for steady cash flow has been greater than Anna's, and I draw a larger salary. As we finished

Copyright © 1994 by Karin Kearns   199

our second year, both of our finances had become more stable as our client base developed.

Setting up the business bank account was a struggle. My personal bank required us to spend a considerable sum to run an announcement in the local paper to accommodate our DBA (doing business as) status. Also, as a war tax resister, I was unable to show income documentation to the bank's male-based standards for loans, so we were unable to get a loan. We borrowed a typewriter for the first ten months. We have had to obtain all of our office and lab equipment slowly over the years on a cash basis. Setting up and operating our business has been a very instructive journey, showing us just how oppressed women are, both externally and internally, concerning their finances.

GOVERNMENTAL OBSTACLES

I am a midwife licensed by the state of Florida. The governing organizational structure that oversees licensing has a long history of not supporting direct entry (non-nurse) midwifery. It harrasses most of the more successful midwives through legal reprimands. There are currently 29 licensed and actively practicing direct entry midwives in the entire state of Florida. With the number of us, it is hard to form teams or group practices. This effectively deters any attempt to seek and gain solidarity, or to get any relief for time away from one's practice.

At the time of this writing, Florida does not allow any new licenses to be issued to direct entry midwives, nor does it grant any licenses through reciprocity—that is, the recognition of licenses held by women already licensed in other states or countries.

The other obstacle created by the government is related to funding. Although more and more women qualify for government-subsidized medical care, in this state, licensed midwives are not Medicaid-reimbursable. This is due to the lack of a national standard for midwifery training, the lack of a legislative understanding of the benefits of midwifery, and the strong lobby for the status quo. Restricting funding is an important tool that enables the system to manipulate women, by disallowing them another birthing choice. Also, when state-run health departments offer their services on a sliding scale, women must burden themselves with the task of coordinating all the documentation required to prove their financial status. This keeps women running from office to office, as opposed to providing them with necessary care, and discourages them from considering a sliding scale system.

For these and other reasons, most trained midwives do not try to make a living through midwifery. I have had to be very conscious of my work load in order to avoid burnout.

WOMEN'S ATTITUDES ABOUT FINANCING HEALTH CARE

Most of the women we work with have their own jobs outside the home, and also work within the home: cooking, cleaning, home schooling their kids, and of course providing child care. I can think of only one of our clients who personally considers her work within the home her career option and respects herself for that choice. She is fortunate enough to have the financial freedom to make this choice. The rest of our clients tend to minimize their financial contributions to their homes and almost always defer to their spouses to make financial decisions. Sometimes the spouse is a husband, sometimes a boyfriend, sometimes a boyfriend who becomes a husband during the pregnancy. Sometimes there is no spouse of any kind. Rarely, there are girlfriends or women partners.

I have seen women with limited financial resources, who are often the sole moneymakers of their households, sit passively during a visit with us and watch their partners agree to and sign impossible-to-adhere-to financial agreements. Frequently these women cancel their next appointment or just won't show up. It seems their partners provide an emotional distance from us that allows them to cancel their agreements and feel safe doing so.

When we started, a small number of women from the male-run birth center decided to remain in our care. We had set our fee at $2200 for our package of care and services. This made us competitive with the birth center and very competitive with the doctor/hospital route, which usually costs $5000–7000. When these women came to us, we decided that we should charge them either their unpaid balance or their refund amount if they had already paid in full. This way, the clients weren't paying more for their births than they had originally planned. Although I believe this was the fairest thing to do, and we were building a client base, we weren't making any money.

Eventually we decided to go with a sliding-fee scale: the package of services that we offer is not negotiable, but the fee is. We started out asking women (and their spouses, if any) what they could afford on a weekly or monthly basis. We continue to be puzzled by most people's inability to answer this question. Unfortunately, self-selecting a reasonable payment and negotiating to a mutually agreeable end seems to catch most people totally off guard. Health departments, banks, and other credit lenders determine payments even for sliding scales that are based on an inflexible fee-to-income ratio. We refuse to set up this kind of policy because we feel that developing self-determination is vital to the kind of quality midwifery care that we want to offer.

Our current approach is to secure a realistic monthly payment plan with optional extension of payments in special circumstances. We are paid through direct client payments, barter, insurance reimbursement, or a combination of these. Although state law requires insurance companies to reimburse licensed midwives, I have had to endure a myriad of discriminating, paternalistic, and sexist comments, critiques, and requests. Sometimes the bureaucratic red tape can hold up payment for several months, even though insurance companies are required to pay within a mandated period of time.

When contracting for barter, the first step we go through is deciding whether the people involved offer a service or skill that we need. We learned that we cannot simply trust that the service will be rendered to our satisfaction. So we first get a clear picture of what is being offered and whether the client or someone else will be rendering the service. Then we determine whether that person is actually capable of doing the work and how much experience they have. We feel that it is important to honor a bartered service at its regular rate on the cash-paying market. We also find that it is important to state in the contract which party will pay for any supplies that are needed, where the work will take place, and most importantly, when we can expect the job to be finished. Once we had to finish a job because the person bartering the service was not skilled enough to continue.

Occasionally, someone will make an outrageous financial proposal. Most often, in a case like this, a couple will tell us that although they have a regular income, they have become overextended and therefore want us to accept a ridiculously low amount for services. Despite this, we come to a mutually acceptable agreement with almost every interested client.

PRACTICAL PROBLEMS

One of the ways we make our practice more financially accessible is by allowing women to continue making payments for up to three months after their babies' births. At first, we just trusted clients to keep up with scheduled payments. Unfortunately, people have a tendency to get lax about the amount owed, and some stop paying altogether. As a result, we have done a lot of problem-solving regarding the collection of payments due. After consultation with other midwives, an attorney, and a few doctors, we finally realized that we could not offer extended payments to all women. We also contract with a collection agency to obtain payments and occasionally to collect on bad checks. We utilize the State's Attorney's office for "fraudulent check" enforcement.

As the practice grew and we set out to lease office space, we had to be savvy about placing responsibility for building code maintenance, pest control, theft prevention, and other space issues in the landowner's hands. We had the support of a self-employed lawyer, who coached us through a lot of the difficult business decisions so we could spend our energy on client care. She also scaled down her fee at the outset of our practice in order for us to have affordable access to legal advice.

CONCLUSION

Although there have been difficulties, we acknowledge that we are very fortunate women to be able to make a living doing what we do best and what we want to do most. We are dedicated to facilitating the empowerment of individual women.

We work to support and develop the concept that women have
an obligation to become informed consumers of health care and
that they can and should be in control of their options. Of
course, we hope to empower all of our clients through the
experience of birth—as each woman discovers that birth,
without doctors, works.

GOOD BUSINESS VIBRATIONS

JOANI BLANK

Joani Blank is founder of Good Vibrations, a retail and mail order concern that sells products to enhance people's sex lives. She also publishes books that teach sex education in a sex-positive way, as owner of Down There Press. Here she responds to a few questions from the editors of *The Woman-Centered Economy*.

What is your typical day like?

I don't know that I have a typical day. I spend lots of time on the phone. I go to my office only 2–3 days a week and then often at odd hours. But I spend several hours at my desk doing work-related stuff at home. My personal life and work life are very mixed up together. I would be hard-pressed to do a time motion study that separates the two.

What is your least favorite part of running your business?

I don't do any unfavorite tasks except occasionally writing things that only I can write. One of my privileges as founder of a 17-year-old business with more than 30 staff members now is that I don't have to do any work I don't enjoy.

How do you feel about working in the women's community?

I don't work exclusively in the women's community. A few women of the lesbian community in San Francisco occasionally act as if they own us—that is, they feel that the store should never sell anything that would offend some lesbians, or that we should have women-only shopping days, or we should not allow men in the store at all. Some heterosexuals, especially men, think we are a lesbian store, but we make efforts to

Copyright © 1994 by Joani Blank

promote our store as a place that is especially, but certainly not exclusively, for women.

What kind of legal entity is your business set up as?

My business was a sole proprietorship for the first 10 years of its life. We were incorporated with me as the sole stockholder in 1987. In 1992, we became a wholly worker-owned business—a worker cooperative, not a collective—with an elected board of directors and with each owner (16 to start, including me) owning one share of stock. I am also carrying a note for the "buyout" with a 20-year term, representing my 15 years of investment (sweat equity, not cash) in the business. The current profits of the company will be partly kept in the business and partly distributed to the owners on an equal basis varying only by the number of hours worked in the year, not related to seniority or salary level.

Is your business lesbian-identified? What difficulties have you encountered being woman-identified?

Many people believe our business is lesbian-identified, but we certainly don't self-identify that way. However we have had marketing problems through the years because we are in the sex business. These hassles from the straight world may have occasionally been exacerbated because we are woman-owned and -operated, but more often being woman-owned has been an ameliorating factor. We have experienced some discrimination by women's businesses and events, especially women's music festivals and crafts shows, and to a lesser extent women's publications where we might wish to exhibit or advertise. The "problem" for some straight folks is that we deal unabashedly with sex, and that changes all the rules of a business relationship. The "problem" for some lesbians is that we sell products that support a broad diversity of consensual sex styles, not just monogamous, vanilla, egalitarian, intimate, and politically-correct sex (whatever that may be).

How do you feel about other women-run businesses?

We feel very sisterly toward other women-owned businesses in the same field as ours, but there aren't many of them that are really very similar. And frankly we do not always find that the feeling of sisterliness is reciprocated. It has been my observation that women's businesses often move in one of two directions, neither of which I personally am comfortable with. Many become just like a typical mixed or men's business in the way the boss relates to her employees, the way coworkers relate to one another, and the way they all relate to vendors, customers, and "competitors" (real or imagined), i.e., with hierarchy, suspicion, secrecy, and competitiveness. It seems "natural" and "normal" for women business owners to behave like this. After all, this is what they teach in business school. This is the way they saw their fathers and grandfathers go about doing business.

The opposite direction with which I am (almost) equally uncomfortable has a group of women in a collective or two women partners (often lovers at first) trying to run a business like an all-adult family—with so much attention and energy devoted to relationships and purposes (not to mention political correctitude) that none is left to actually run the business. If the business consists of a couple of lovers (or the lovers are business partners with one or more employees), they usually do not have a written partnership agreement or a well thought-out plan for possible future dissolution. Therefore, the business may not survive these women breaking up, should that occur. In the case of the collective, I can tell you that even though the fantasy of totally egalitarian management is most appealing, I believe that it rarely works—certainly not for more than a year or two and not with more than six or seven people.

Are there ways that you work with women who might not ordinarily be able to afford your products?

Not really, but our products come in a wide price range, including some as inexpensive as $5. However, our more expensive products are often costly because they are made by women artisans—not mass-produced. The workshops we hold at the store are inexpensive, however, and we often do free presentations in the community.

What kinds of things do you value that makes your business different from a mainstream business?

I believe we are moving toward a near-perfect balance between hierarchy and democracy, between productiveness and doing "good works," and most important, between taking care

WIMMIN BUSINESS OWNERS!

TIRED OF NOT BEING TAKEN SERIOUSLY BY PROSPECTIVE MALE CLIENTS?

CALL NAN'S RENT-A-BOB!

Nan's Rent-a-Bob provides clean, tie-wearing white men with briefcases for those icky meetings that involve white male clients or suppliers. Our Bobs are screened and bonded, discovered through the finest outplacement services. Bobs talk about all the male topics, such as:

- ▲ golf!
- ▲ personal sports injuries!
- ▲ the "bottom line"!
- ▲ huge companies with impressive acronyms!
- ▲ Republicans!
- ▲ suburban office plexes!

All Bobs can be trained to spout any well-known business cliche, including 4 cliches from your own line of business!

Best of all, our Bobs know they're only there for the meeting—then they're happy to take their *Wall Street Journals* and go home. Nan herself screens every Bob for just those sorts of attitudes that she knows might cause you to do him bodily harm.

Nan knows you're trying to change the world, and you don't want to hire fatuous men just to be taken seriously. But you can't change the world if your business isn't making enough to feed you! Keep our card on file!

NAN'S RENT-A-BOB   1-800-RENTBOB

Copyright © 1995 by Loraine E. Edwalds

CREATING AND SHARING WOMAN-CENTERED SPACE

WOMEN'S BED AND BREAKFASTS

ELEANOR MORTON

According to *The Wall Street Journal* (July 1, 1992), "many openly lesbian women . . . are rushing to start their own businesses. With a broad array of products and services, they are targeting an increasingly visible market of women like themselves." Although I personally don't know any lesbian business owners who are rolling in money as the article suggests, dyke-owned businesses are on the increase. We see a need in our community, an economic need, a cultural need. And so we start businesses that fill it. We sell to lesbians; we buy from lesbians; and we create our own economy. Sisterhood meets supply and demand.

Women's bed and breakfasts (B&Bs) are part of this movement. They are woman-operated, woman-owned women's spaces. Some of these B&Bs offer resort-like accommodations, others offer secluded rural settings, and others sit in the middle of big cities. A recent issue of *Lesbian Connection* included 65 advertisements for women's bed and breakfasts. Ferrari's 1993 guide to *International Places of Interest to Women* listed 111 bed and breakfasts especially for women and only for women in the United States. That's double the number listed in the 1991 guide.

Women's B&Bs first sprang up in New England. There were a few in the Northwest in Oregon and Washington, and a few in scattered tourist areas like Florida and Hawaii. Except for

Copyright © 1995 by Eleanor Morton   211 small areas of the Southwest, women's B& Bs were mostly on the coasts. Slowly, however, they have started moving toward the Midwest.

A typical example is the Inn at Pine Ridge, owned and operated by Joanne McGibbon and Charlotte Gervais. Located in Wisconsin half-way between Madison and the Twin Cities, the Inn sits on a square mile of Christmas tree farms. The Inn itself is an old renovated farm house purchased by the two women in 1988. Using money from McGibbon's divorce settlement and Gervais' savings, the two women bought the place after looking at close to eighty different properties. The property had been on the market for four years. The owners wanted a very large down-payment. While McGibbon and Gervais did not have enough for the total asked price, they did have enough for the down-payment. In this way they brought the price down tens of thousands of dollars. The Inn opened for business in April 1989 and business really started to roll in around September.

After spending years raising children, having a husband, and doing family day care, McGibbon, the oldest of ten children, had plenty of experience taking care of people. She says that she remembers thinking about women's space years before the Inn ever became a concrete idea. "After spending endless hours listening to women, I felt that women needed a place where they wouldn't have to change the diapers, where they wouldn't have to answer the phone, and where they wouldn't have to take care of their husbands," she says. She envisioned a sort of retreat center.

When her divorce went through and she met her partner, McGibbon began to reconsider her retreat center idea. McGibbon had been an intern at the Women and Minorities Business Enterprise in Minneapolis so she knew about small business. "At WMBE I learned not to be afraid of the paperwork," she says. So after they bought the land and the house, McGibbon saw to it that they got licensed, registered with the state and got a sales tax number. She also wrote a business plan for the Inn. McGibbon and Gervais realized that the small house could never support two people with benefits. So McGibbon lives and works full-time plus at the Inn, and Gervais lives and works in Minneapolis. All the profits from the Inn go back into the business. A portion of Gervais's income goes straight to the Inn too. McGibbon says that she doesn't find the work difficult. Her only problem was asking people to pay for it. Fortunately, she says, that's not a problem anymore.

McGibbon and Gervais are experimenting with ideas for new ways to bring in income connected with the Inn so that they can both live at Pine Ridge. They have an antique loom they have been fixing up. They also have a building that they have discussed renting out to groups to be used for a menstrual lodge or for an artists studio or for a paper-making lab. They would like to do more organic gardening of vegetables to sell and to supplement the guests' meals. It's difficult, McGibbon explains, when "one person has to deal with the emergencies and with the daily work, and be charming too. There's not enough time."

Most of the Inn's business comes from the Twin Cities and Madison. One woman comes and stays at the Inn and tells her friends about it, so they come and stay, and so on. As a result, the Inn has become a sort of local lesbian resource center. Word-of-mouth is their best form of advertisement. They also advertise in gay and lesbian papers and in local and area women's centers. Business is generally slow in the summer and then picks up in the fall when the leaves start changing colors. They're always busy around Thanksgiving and Christmas. The Inn becomes a home for some and get-away place for others. Many women spend anniversaries or birthdays there. A few guests have made a tradition of spending special days at the Inn.

McGibbon and Gervais wanted to create a space for women. One of the ways they've done that is by gearing their prices toward a female clientele. Most bed and breakfasts and most hotels charge per couple; a room will cost $75 per night for one person or two. McGibbon and Gervais felt it was important that they make themselves easily accessible to single women, who make up a large portion of their business. As a result, the Inn charges per person to keep prices down.

While the clientele is almost all women, the Inn is not exclusively for women. Two or three men may stay there during the year. McGibbon explains that they will register a male if no women are registered for that day. Then any women who call for reservations on that day will be notified that a man will be staying there as well. It works the same way with children. This

CONSUMER ETHICS IN THE WOMAN-CENTERED ECONOMY

MARGARET VAN ARSDALE

In the U.S. economy, I have several functions—taxpayer, consumer, producer (small business owner). When I function in the economy in any of these roles, I try to be as ethical as possible about my choices. As a consumer, that means I am constantly struggling to maintain a balance between (a) the Puritan/Dutch part of my heritage that urges me to make sure I don't pay a cent more than I absolutely have to for anything and (b) the feminist/humanist/egalitarian side of me that insists that I must buy recycled, woman-made, minority-made, or locally-made goods. And then there's the whole issue of the concept of *consuming*: when you consume something, it is gone; yet what we prefer to do in the woman-centered economy is pass things along.

I try to practice mindfulness in all things, including awareness of the ripple effects of my purchasing. When I buy some kinds of products, I know exactly where the money goes. When I buy a pair of shoes from Sara's Shoes, for example, I know that Sara uses some of that money to buy the materials to make the shoes, some to maintain her business (tools, advertising, electricity, and so on), and some for herself to live on. (I like that.) With others purchases, the destination/ultimate function of the payment is less clear; those are the ones I worry about. When I pay the electric bill, the power company takes that money and uses some of it to pay its employees (who are my neighbors), some to maintain service to my house, and some

Copyright © 1995 by Margaret VanArsdale   215 to build electric-generating facilities (and in my neck of the woods, that means nuclear). When I pay my long distance telephone bill (or my tax bill, for that matter), I'm not sure quite what happens to the money (although I have a better idea about part of it now that I've switched to Working Assets Long Distance). Some of it goes to provide the service I receive (Working Assets renting phone lines from Sprint), but a lot of it goes to support amorphous company activities (of Sprint's) that I don't know about and that I might or might not really want to be supporting.

I prefer to buy woman-made goods or at least to buy from a woman-owned and -run store or company. But sometimes that's not possible. I don't know of any woman-owned grocery stores near where I live, for example. Nor are there any woman-owned automobile manufacturing companies (or utility companies!) that I know of, though I can make sure that I at least buy from a woman sales rep (easy enough) or maybe a woman-owned dealership (which might mean doing some homework and travelling some distance).

▲ ▲ ▲

I have a loose hierarchy of principles, things I revere, in making purchasing decisions. It goes like this: first choice, woman-made, -produced, -sold stuff; second choice, environmentally-conscious stuff; third choice, locally (or minority) -made, -produced, -sold stuff.* And in all cases, I try to be aware of how the company I am buying from treats its workers. Of course, I can't always know this about a company, but often I can get a pretty good idea just by watching how employees interact with each other—is there blaming and anger

---

* I'm not suggesting that this is THE hierarchy of principles that everyone should use, only that it's generally mine. I am suggesting that in fact everyone does set priorities (even if the only priority they set is "I have to be able to afford it") and that to function responsibly we must all be conscious of what those priorities are. It's kind of like the old "think before you speak" adage; instead it's "think before you buy."

and fear going on, or is do I get a sense of general respect and good will among peers.

A couple of mail order catalogs I've looked at recently (Footprints, a retailer of Birkenstock and other footwear, from Kansas; and Far & Wide, a worker cooperative and resource catalog for large women, from Canada) have mentioned in their copy about their companies that they know their prices aren't low, as much as they'd like to make their wares accessible to people with low incomes, but that they buy products of good quality and they try to buy them from places that they know do not exploit their workers. I like the fact that these folks are thinking about these concepts, that they consider them important enough to mention in their catalogs, and that they are trying to do something about it. For example, Far & Wide makes the following statement (in their fall 1994, very first catalog), which I consider exemplary:

> A study reported in the *New England Journal of Medicine* (1993) has shown that fat women are more likely to be living below the poverty line with lower incomes than average-sized women. Far & Wide would like to be able to price our goods lower than average, but can't at this time. Our prices are partly determined by the quality of construction and the amount of material used: they will last longer and fit better than cheaper products. We also try not to buy products of underpaid labour and this increases the cost. When we receive price breaks, however, we will pass them on to you. We hope that those of you with low or limited incomces will be able to purchase our goods. We are creating opportunities for women to act as Far & Wide representatives and earn clothing credits and cash in return for assisting us with sales. Please get in touch to talk about this option.

On a practical level, all of what I've been talking about means that if I am out running errands and I want to stop at a fast food place for lunch, I choose the hot dog stand run by the guy who went to high school with a friend of mine rather than going to a chain hamburger stand; it costs me a little more, but I'll get a slightly better product and I'll be directly supporting someone I know rather than some anonymous corporation. It means that I buy recycled toilet paper (I did it even when recycled toilet paper was more expensive and when you couldn't buy it at the grocery store, on the theory that if people bought it enough the producers would get the idea of producing more and thereby making it cheaper—which actually happened). It means that I used to buy my Jockey-for-Her underwear from Travis Place (a woman- owned mail-order company in North Carolina) rather than from a department store (and now I'm looking for a new source because Travis Place has disappeared). It means that before I buy something, I think about the consequences.

It doesn't mean that I never shop at Target. Maybe it should, but I haven't evolved that far yet. As frustrating as all of this might sound, and as impossible as it is to make the "right" choice every time (because sometimes there's just not a clear "right" choice), I do think that the effort of awareness is worthwhile. I have a limited number of dollars to spend and I want to spend them where they will do the most good. When I can spend my money in my community (whatever community that may be), I have at least a chance of knowing what I'm supporting.

Often I have to strike a balance between what I'd like to do ethically and what makes practical sense for me financially. If I really need a case of typing paper and I have only twenty dollars to spend, I can't buy the recycled paper that costs twenty-four dollars; instead I buy the paper that costs sixteen—and maybe save the extra money toward being able to buy recycled next time. It's a matter of setting priorities (as so many things are) and of being flexible enough to know when the priorities have to be bent.

PLAYING TO THE HIGHEST COMMON DENOMINATOR

TONI ARMSTRONG JR.

This is an edited transcript of an interview by Loraine Edwalds with Toni Armstrong Jr. of Chicago, Illinois. Toni Armstrong Jr. is a long-time activist dedicated to the promotion and documentation of what she calls "woman-identified music and culture." She published *HOT WIRE: The Journal of Women's Music and Culture* from 1984 through 1994, and was on the staff of *Paid My Dues: A Journal of Women and Music* during the late 1970s. Toni's *Women's Music Plus* directory first appeared in 1977 and is the only ongoing, comprehensive listing of resources in feminist women's music and culture available today. In addition to Toni's editing and writing, hundreds of her live-action photos of women entertainers have been published. She also coordinated the Music Industry Conferences at the National Women's Music Festival in the mid 1980s, a series of gatherings that led to the formation of the Association of Women's Music and Culture (AWMAC). As a musician, Toni has appeared on three albums and played bass in the women's bands Surrender Dorothy and Starkissed Tunaband. She performs with Alix Dobkin and Kay Gardner whenever they do Lavender Jane reunion shows; most recently, the trio played Carnegie Hall in June 1994 as part of the Stonewall 25 celebrations. At press time, Toni was beginning to produce albums of uptempo women's music (the "Slammin' Amazon Saturday Night" series) with June Millington, and was setting up the Amazon Arts Foundation, a group dedicated to funding women's projects and events that prioritize lesbian and/or feminist content and ideals.

What were your initial fantasies about finances when you started HOT WIRE?

When I first started *HOT WIRE* in 1984 with my three partners—Michele (Etas) Gautreaux, Ann Morris, and Yvonne Zipter—we all thought the magazine could make a go of it

Copyright © 1995 by Toni Armstrong Jr.

219

financially without compromising any of our feminist ethics. We were all very hot on the idea of providing the lesbian feminist cultural community with a publication we could be proud of, one that would bring "woman-identified women" of all persuasions together in positive ways.

By late 1985, when I became the sole publisher, money was already becoming a problem. I was never unrealistic enough to imagine I'd be able to quit my day job and live off the magazine's proceeds; by 1984, musicians, producers, festivals, and record labels had already started desperately treading water in their own seas of red women's-music ink. As is usually the case in the arts, enthusiasm was high, but money was in very short supply. It was clear that almost nobody would be able to make a living solely from working in women's culture.

Nonetheless, I *had* hoped that the magazine would be able to pay its own bills and have dollars left over to compensate the creative contributors for their writing, photos, and cartoons. I'm sorry to say that never happened. Postage and supplies kept costing more, even though we were relentless about buying in bulk, reusing every envelope and box, and not wasting so much as a 2¢ stamp. We should have been awarded PhDs in "making do." But it got to the point where we simply had to buy technology, like a computer and a laser printer, and the printing bills kept creeping up despite the best cost-containment efforts of our socially conscious and extremely generous printer—Janeen Porter of C&D Print Shop in Chicago. In years that were "less lean" than others, I was able to send token cash payments—tiny, "gesture-size" amounts—to some of the cartoonists and writers, but generally the creative contributors had to settle for copies of the issue in which their work appeared, plus either a subscription or free advertising. Like our Chicago-based office volunteers, the creative gals basically donated their time and talent because they shared the woman-identified vision.

HOT WIRE worked in a classically feminist way in that it provided community for women in exchange for labor. What are your thoughts on that?

Lucky for us, there were always local women who were willing to donate labor. We maintained a volunteer base of approximately sixty women who lived in and near Chicago.

The entire operation was basically run by volunteers working in my basement, at night, when we were already tired from working at our full-time nine-to-five careers. During any given month, about a third of us would be doing some sort of labor—opening and answering mail, packing and shipping orders to bookstores and subscribers all over the world, editing, reading through magazines and newspapers for "Hotline" news items, doing paste-up, unsnarling computer snafus, typing articles, printing photos, shopping for office supplies, producing the soundsheet recordings, proofreading, updating ledgers, gathering inventory to haul to festivals, selling magazines at the local women's coffeehouse . . . the work was endless.

One of the main payoffs was knowing we were making a significant contribution to the health and well-being of the national lesbian-feminist cultural community. And you can't minimize the appeal of being able to meet women in an environment other than in a bar, on a softball field, or at a political-action demonstration.

The organizing principle—supporting, promoting, *reveling in* the creativity of feminist and lesbian women—was tremendously gratifying, but not particularly lucrative for any of us. As publisher, managing editor, writer, and staff photographer, I was never paid for any of my work—in fact, I heavily subsidized the project from the beginning. For the first few years, I paid more for *HOT WIRE* each month than I was paying in rent. But I always had the feeling that it was somehow my *destiny* to do this work, to make it happen regardless of cost, so I was willing to be the "number one volunteer."

On the down side, though, volunteer-run organizations often experience a high degree of turnover, which creates a logistical nightmare when you're trying to run a business in a responsible way. Procedures get established, and people get trained but it all falls apart when someone quits suddenly, or gets careless, or is having trouble with a lover who also volunteers for the organization. Despite the large amounts of time and money I put into the business, it seemed like I was constantly making apologies for things that were late, or wrong, or missing. I found this aspect of doing *HOT WIRE* to be excruciating, and it was one of the primary reasons I decided to stop publication. When considering the "cost of doing business" where money isn't the only bottom line—as is so often the case in feminist and lesbian enterprises—the emotional toll paid by the women in charge really needs to be factored in.

One of the biggest and least pleasant surprises about running the business was that volunteers actually were, generally speaking, better workers than paid help. I had fantasized that if we could only pay people to *coordinate* the work and keep volunteers scheduled to come in and do the tasks, the business would run well. As it turned out, more than half of the paid workers didn't work out very well—they didn't take responsibility for carrying out their duties. Most of the paid coordinators ended up doing the work that volunteers should have been doing, because it was easier to just do it themselves than do the often frustrating organizing, planning, and supervising they were hired to do. We were never able to successfully keep all of the business details straight or stay on top of billing people who owed us money, let alone launch an effective promotional campaign—although I still believe these things *should have* happened once we started paying people to come in for set numbers of hours each week.

A few of the paid workers were nothing short of goddess-sent, like my partners Lynn Siniscalchi and Susan Waller, who worked with the project until 1993 when they moved away to Seattle. But these were women who already believed in their hearts that the culture *HOT WIRE* represented was a valuable, fun thing that should be in the world. Their commitment was more to the project than the paycheck. The money they earned made it *possible* for them to do so many hours of work, but it wasn't the prime motivator. After ten years of experience, I now believe the only way a magazine of *HOT WIRE*'s size and caliber can succeed is to have at least one full-time worker with full benefits; the magazine has to be someone's primary commitment.

How did being a lesbian-feminist affect the economics of running the business?

Good business practice dictates that you set a budget, don't spend more than you earn, and get the most money possible for your product and your advertising space, right? Well, *realistic* business practice from a lesbian-feminist point of view dictated that those bottom-line-oriented business practices not prevail, or the magazine would have been small and cheaply produced or else affordable only for the most affluent readers.

There were several options we considered, things that would have helped make the magazine financially self-sufficient, but we ultimately rejected them all. We could have cut back size, frequency, and paper quality; increased the cover price; charged much more for advertising and for time on the stereo soundsheets; sold the mailing list; gone after corporate advertisers; or become a "tax write-off" publication of some organization. These options, while viable and certainly advisable from a capitalistic point of view, would have priced women out of the market, or violated confidentiality. We also didn't want to compromise the editorial content by making it accountable to some outside entity. And the big advertisers who want the "women's" market usually advertise cosmetics and diet products; corporations going after the "entertainment" market are usually pushing alcohol and cigarettes. No thanks.

The basis of *HOT WIRE* was the creation of a national forum for like-minded women. Entertainers, writers, photographers, theater people, and filmmakers (and their products) made up the bulk of the articles in the magazine; the lioness's share of advertising was purchased by them and by the businesses that sprung up to support and showcase their work—bookstores, festivals, production companies, distributors, and so forth. We were determined to avoid pricing out of the market the perpetually underpaid creative women the magazine was for and about, so we kept subscription prices and ad rates ridiculously low.

I had many discussions over the years with staff members who wanted to raise prices—and I always held the line on the above thinking. I was also advised more than once to lie about our circulation, since it's standard practice ("everybody does it") to inflate the numbers to entice potential advertisers. I could never swallow the idea of lying, though I agree that we would have gotten more advertising dollars if we claimed a circulation of, say, 50,000 readers. The reality I dealt with was that for many individuals and businesses, even our "low-low bargain prices" were a stretch; long-term payment plans were common.

Fortunately for all of us who valued *HOT WIRE*, I was childless and able to siphon off money from my professional day job to plug up the holes whenever the magazine began to financially hemorrhage. Still, I never had the resources to just carry the publication; we had to "depend on the kindness of strangers" to give us money.

What role did finances have in closing down HOT WIRE?

I think if we could have found the money to hire even one full-time worker and pay for her health insurance, we could have kept the magazine going indefinitely. But like most alternative periodicals, we were chronically underfunded from the beginning. "Women's culture" has never been perceived to be political enough, important enough, or valuable enough to be given grant money, even by gay or feminist funders. Over the course of our ten years, we applied for a gazillion grants but got only one (from the blessed Harmony Women's Fund). Let me read you something from an all-too-typical letter we received toward the end of our ten-year run: "On April 22–24, the [lesbian-gay grant foundation] met . . . to allocate grants for our 1994 funding cycle . . . [the foundation] awarded a total of $100,000 to eleven projects . . . sorry to inform you that the board did not award a grant to your organization. Though the board acknowledged that your project was important, they felt that it did not represent the kind of organizing project that is defined by [our] mission. [We] focus on grassroots organizing efforts that attempt to identify the root causes of social injustice and that are actively organizing for social change by connecting their work with other social justice groups dealing with issues of racism, sexism, homophobia, ableism, etc. . . ."

HOT WIRE and the grassroots, highly inclusive, fervently political women's culture we supported and represented fit their profile exactly. But there was always *some* reason what we were doing wasn't important enough to warrant financial support from grant-givers who were supposedly funding projects like ours. There were trendier causes during our ten years—for a while it was Nicaragua, then homelessness, then AIDS, now women's cancer projects. Grant-givers were quick to give lots of seed money to impressive-sounding projects that didn't even last two years, but they didn't value lesbian-feminist culture enough to support one of its most important institutions. Oh, well. Thank heavens for the fairy godmothers who sent their hard-earned money month after month to keep us afloat. "Sisters are doin' it for themselves," and all that.

The generosity of individual women was amazing, demonstrating the kind of altruism that's in operation when people support religious institutions, children's sports teams, and educational scholarships. One of our more saintly volunteers, Kris Johnsen, took over our "Fairy Godmother Program" a few years before the magazine folded and coordinated it until the end. Her efforts raised approximately $10,000 in income each year from our extraordinary women donors. I'll always be impressed with the generosity they displayed. Most groups lure potential donors with bonus gifts and other perks. In keeping with our austerity program—i.e., "every penny goes into *HOT WIRE*"—we listed the names of our Fairy Godmoms in the magazine, but they got nothing extra for their money, not even a "free" subscription. And at least a dozen of them chose to remain anonymous, not even getting glory for their donation.

To what extent did closetedness among lesbians affect a periodical like HOT WIRE? Did that make it harder to market?

Ah, marketing. One of the most difficult aspects of women's music and culture for the past twenty years has been marketing it. Success in entertainment depends on many factors, not the least of which is reaching the masses with the product—radio airplay, TV exposure, interviews and reviews in widely read newspapers and magazines, and so on. Keep in mind that society has been most interested in promoting only certain limited images: feminists as ball-busting shrews, homosexuals as child-molesting AIDS carriers, and lesbians as women with men's names and men's haircuts who only think about sex, or more chicly as homicidal bisexuals. It *hasn't* been a good environment in which to try to market nice, normal, garden-variety lesbian-feminism—what comic Sara Cytron calls "the culture of gentleness."

Lesbian events and products ran into incredible resistance—publications refusing to run gay-related ads, concert venues unwilling to rent to women-only events, papers unwilling to print reviews, radio shows refusing to play lesbian-specific lyrics, TV shows not allowing accurate portrayals with happy endings, things like that. The supposedly more open-minded segments of the media were usually disinterested in us unless our culture could be presented as a sensationalistic freak show.

To do business in a feminist way, the concept of marketing had to be examined closely. Traditional marketing basically means a company has a product that it convinces the public they need. Traditional "salesmanship" means you do whatever you have to "close the deal," even if you have to manipulate, intimidate, or deceive customers to get them to sign on the bottom line. Obviously I didn't want to run *HOT WIRE* in those ways.

Our marketing depended on getting the word out to women who were already interested in the existing feminist cultural world—those who went to festivals or local women's concerts, who shopped in feminist bookstores, who belonged to their local women's choir or women's film/video collective, who made crafts and visual arts with "womyn's" imagery, and so on.

We found print advertising to be ineffective in marketing our magazine, with the exception of ongoing classified ads in other feminist and lesbian publications.[*] Occasionally women would also contact us after they'd heard a particularly glowing description of the magazine on a feminist or gay radio show, so word-of-mouth was effective.

Ultimately, though, the only marketing that really worked for us was to get a copy of the magazine into a potential customer's hands. When we had a booth in the crafts area at a festival—especially the National Women's Music Festival[**] and the Michigan Womyn's Music Festival[***]—we found that it worked best to get over our discomfort at being pushy. Once a copy of the magazine was in the hands of a woman standing in front of our table, we felt our "hard sell" job was finished. I can't tell you how often women who had no apparent interest in the magazine—who were looking at it only out of female-conditioned politeness, really—would end up saying, "Wow! I never knew this existed! This is great!" Our job, see, wasn't so much to manipulate someone into buying a product she may not need, but to be sure she *knew what it was* before she decided if she wanted it or not.

---

[*] *HOT WIRE* exchanged classified ads with other periodicals, so it didn't cost us or them anything for this publicity.

[**] NWMF is held in early June in Bloomington, Indiana.

[***] "Michigan" is held in mid-August near Hart, Michigan.

Keep in mind that during our ten-year run, especially in the Reagan-era '80s, there were almost no famous lesbian celebrities out in the mainstream, except Martina, Rita Mae Brown, and, to a limited degree, Lily Tomlin. And the few well-known women who weren't afraid to embrace the word *feminist*—Whoopi Goldberg, Susan Sarandon, Kathy Najimy and Mo Gaffney, Alice Walker (who coined the term *womanist*), and Roseanne [Barr/Arnold]—were pretty much out there alone on a limb, not getting support from the mainstream. This was simply not a welcoming climate in which to market lesbian-feminist culture.

In terms of marketing the culture itself, it didn't help that women's events and recordings were routinely ignored by the mainstream media, and then panned by feminist and gay publications. It became an easy sport to write snide reviews and to stereotype "the Birkenstockers" as a bunch of granola-crunching, crystal-wearing, politically absurd folksingers. It was very, very difficult to promote all the exciting multicultural things that were happening at festivals, for example, when the average reader either heard nothing or read long diatribes focusing on some minor negative point. I'm sure most women were truly surprised to hear that there was a mosh pit at Michigan in 1994, for example—but those of us who go each year know that the festival has *always* pioneered unusual, thrilling entertainment. Over the years, the end result of the bad press was that many women never even tried lesbian-feminist music and culture because they'd been poisoned against it *by our own* publications. Sad, really.

Did political pressures affect you in terms of the content? Did this affect sales?

Political pressure had very little effect, because we were an independent publication that didn't owe anything to anyone. I always felt that as an editor I had everyone's best interest at heart—so I trusted my own editorial judgment. But I'll admit there was a certain ethical, visionary pressure . . . to not turn *HOT WIRE* into a tabloid sleaze fest and to not just cover the "hot" celebrities.

Again, "good business sense" dictates that you pick the most exciting, sensationalistic thing possible for your magazine cover—to grab the attention of people in bookstores and make

them pull out their wallets. Thus, the mind-numbing frenzy of
O.J. Simpson covers we were all subjected to during 1994. But
I didn't want to gratuitously put famous women on our
covers—which I probably could have done, and made more
money. And sometimes when the money situation was
especially bad, I seriously considered it.

Part of the difficulty for *HOT WIRE* was being a specialty
magazine that covered performers, events, filmmakers, writers,
etc. who were having a difficult time making names for
themselves for all the reasons I've already mentioned. It was
challenging sometimes to find someone to put on the cover
who'd have enough face recognition to be able to sell the
magazines in bookstores. I feel good about all of our cover-girl
choices, though; some of the less-easily-recognized celebrities
who graced our covers weren't that great for sales, but from a
historical perspective they absolutely deserved the
recognition—cartoonist Alison Bechdel and sign language
interpreter/actor Sherry Hicks would be in this category.

We probably could have sold truckloads more issues if we'd
followed the rest of the national media down the trail toward
lurid tabloid journalism—you know, "An INSIDER'S look at
the SECRET LOVE TRIANGLE of k.d. lang, Cris Williamson,
and the women in Tribe 8!!!" Or perhaps "Sneak photos of
KATHERINE V. FORREST researching how to write lesbian
sex scenes at the Naiad Press Tallahassee LOVE NEST!!!" Or
how about "Exclusive coverage of the BIZARRE costuming
rituals DOS FALLOPIA learned from Maile and Marina, who
are really LESBIAN ALIENS!!!"

But we tried to adhere to higher journalistic standards. Too
bad ethics aren't always best for the bottom line. We really
tried to produce a publication that would play to the highest
common denominator, not the lowest.

I'm happy that so many issues of *HOT WIRE* are in libraries
and archives the world over. Long after concerns about paying
those old debts are forgotten, long after we've all faded into the
mists of history, people of the future will be able to read about,
see photos of, and listen to the wonderful women's music on
the soundsheets. *HOT WIRE* made sure that for at least one
ten-year slice, some of the best of who "we" were was
documented without resorting to tabloid gossip. This is so

much more important to me than whether or not we turned a profit in any given fiscal year.

So in the final analysis, it was successful? It was worth the effort and expense?

Oh, yeah—if you're not counting financial profit as a measure of success. I believe there are specific eras in time that arise, thrive, and then fade, and these eras are radiant spots on the timelines of cultural history—Paris in the '20s is a great example. All eras are by definition specific historical periods when like-minded people work in unison to create something vibrant and new. Their efforts become so well known in society that their peak years are labeled a specific era: the "Harlem Renaissance era" or the "big band era." It's an incredible privilege to be involved in something that ends up being exciting and influential enough to be called an era, which has *undoubtedly* been the case with lesbian-feminist cultural activism during the past twenty-five years; the face of American society has been forever changed because of our efforts. We have already left in our wake literally hundreds of thousands of books, films, recordings, pieces of artwork, plays, photographs, festivals, and publications.

As I've said many times, I like to think that in the 1970s the feminist and lesbian movements married each other, and their most beautiful and powerful daughter was named "women's music and culture." From coast to coast in the U.S., across Canada, and in little enlightened pockets around the globe, woman-identified performers, concert producers, technicians, recordings, record labels and distributors, festivals, radio shows, theater troupes, choirs, and sound and light technicians sprang up. Paralleling this was the growth of the women-in-print movement, characterized by an explosion of writers, periodicals, feminist bookstores, writers' groups, conferences, and publishing ventures. Documenting and interpreting all of this were the photographers, cartoonists, filmmakers, visual artists, archivists, and craftswomen. During the years when the mainstream was nowhere "near" recognizing lesbians as chic, thousands of creative, feminist, woman-loving women "just said yes" and provided for ourselves.

HOT WIRE not only documented women's music and culture, we promoted it and provided links for like-minded

women to be inspired by each other's work. It also provided a
high-quality project that brought together some of the most
exciting feminists and lesbian-feminists of our generation, as a
perusal of our mastheads over the years proves. Our staff
included writers who are respected by their peers today and
destined to be famous in the future, including Bonnie Morris,
Claudia Allen, Jewelle Gomez, Jorjet Harper, Pat Parker,
Rosetta Reitz, Suzette Haden Elgin, and Terri Jewell.
Performers like Jamie Anderson, Janna MacAuslan and Kristan
Aspen [who perform together as the out-lesbian classical music
duo Musica Femina], Judith Sloan, and Kay Gardner were on
staff, too, as were lesbian-household-name photographers Irene
Young, JEB, Marcy J. Hochberg, Sharon Farmer, Susan Wilson,
and Vada Vern'e. Even the cartoonists—Alison Bechdel, Andrea
Natalie, Diane Germain, Kris Kovick, Laura Irene Wayne—are
making names for themselves. There were so many talented
women involved, actually, that I can't even list them all here.

It's important to remember that the women of our generation
were willing to put themselves forward as proud feminists and
proud lesbians during the years before society accepted these
things or thought them chic—certainly before it was possible to
make money from it. It's far from perfect today, but at least
there are decent portrayals of lesbians on TV, and legit stations
like Comedy Central air all-gay shows such as the annual *Out
There* specials. Society is definitely changing; the more tolerant
world is now allowing some safety for people to come out as
lesbian or gay. And as celebrities like Melissa Etheridge,
Martina, k.d. lang, and Amanda (*Married With Children*)
Bearse continue to come out, the public gets a more realistic
look at what lesbians are actually like, and young lesbian girls
and women have some healthy role models.

The women of *HOT WIRE* did their share to bring us all
this far into the mainstream—and they did it without pay.
We're hoping the next generation, which is starting on a more
level playing field because of us, won't have to make the same
kind of financial and emotional sacrifices we did. Remember
that song in Mary Poppins, which goes, "Our daughters'
daughters will adore us, and they'll sing in grateful chorus, well
done, Sister Suffragettes"? My hope is that *our* daughters'
daughters will adore us, and *they'll* sing in grateful chorus,
"Well done, lesbian-feminists!"

PART 3

REAPING OUR HARVEST

If this book were a piece of music, this third part would be big and booming and glorious, dealing as it does with the future. The future would be before us, blue and sunny and wide and clear. Unfortunately, this is a book—and a book about women and money, at that—so it doesn't quite work that way.

Part 3 includes two types of articles: those that push us to look at different directions we might go in the future, and those that consider the directions toward which we seem currently to be going. It's important to note that those aren't necessarily the same. Reaping what you sow means that sometimes what you reap isn't what you might really have wanted—sometimes you've sown the wrong seeds, and sometimes you realize after they've come up that you really don't need that many cucumbers after all.

The articles in this section of the book are not upbeat, for the most part, much as we might like them to be. They are pointers to the future in their analysis of things we need to do differently. Many wonderful things can be said about where we've gotten ourselves so far, but there are some significant problem areas—for example, race and class. And in fact Julia Penelope edited an anthology that focuses on these issues, called *Coming Out of the Class Closet* (Crossing Press, 1994). Although the focus of *The Woman-Centered Economy* is different, some of the articles included in this book add to that discussion.

The woman-centered economy, which is a reflection of and a part of women's culture and the women's movement, has been predominantly white and middle class. Gloria Joseph's "White Promotion, Black Survival" in Part 1 of this book describes some of the ways black women feel alienated from feminist culture; bell hooks' "Third World diva girls," in this part, talks about how our culture pedestalizes some black women, which alienates them from one another. Jamie Lee Evans, in "Aunt Lute Books: Theory and Practice in Action," writes about one company where women of all colors are trying to make multiculturalism real, an effort that offers us hope for the future.

Another thread in Part 3 is the concept of the gift economy, which is "The Philosophy Behind Stonehaven" as described by Genevieve Vaughan, founder of Foundation for a Compassionate Society, and alluded to by Sonia Johnson and Laura Burrows in their respective articles. The gift economy they propose is an alternative to capitalism, but it is one that can be practiced to a certain extent even within our existing economy. Toni Armstrong Jr. offers the gift of a list of business and financial resources for some of the many projects and companies women are developing, particularly though not exclusively those projects that might be eligible for various kinds of grant funding (and don't be too sure that your project or company isn't).

Finally, in "An Alternative to the Economics of Threat," Mary Kay Blakely reports briefly on some of the heart-warming developments among the economics of women around the world as she learned about them at a conference on Women and Economic Development organized by the Ms. Foundation for Education. She concludes this way: "You want to believe that by taking up our pitchforks, one by one, women could turn the face of the earth." We are.

I'LL SHOW YOU MINE IF
YOU'LL SHOW ME YOURS

TONI ARMSTRONG JR.

I know what I *should* do . . . but I really don't *want* to, for
selfish reasons . . . and I can probably get away with not doing
what I should . . . how will I decide?

This universal human conflict has been the grist for countless
creative mills, providing a central theme for literature, music,
theater, and the big and little silver screens. It also plays out in
women's culture when it comes to sharing resources—
something every feminist knows she *should* do.

Feminist and lesbian enterprises are almost always hampered
by lack of money—no surprise there. Historically, women have
always been paid less than men. Sustained feminist activism
over the past three decades has made significant inroads to
equalize this inequitable condition—and has raised the "glass
ceiling" to a higher altitude in professions such as law,
medicine, and business—but complete pay parity remains a
future dream. It follows that women trying to do things for
women simply have fewer dollars available to seed, promote,
and maintain their endeavors.

Meanwhile, specifically feminist and lesbian-feminist cultural
projects and events have been historically undervalued and
underfunded. If we've wanted to produce a record, publish a
book or magazine, put on a festival, make a video, keep a radio
show on the air, buy women's land, or anything along those
lines, we've had to scrape to find ways to pay for it ourselves.
The feminist cultural industries have generally been lucky if

Copyright © 1995 by Toni Armstrong Jr.

233

they could afford the proverbial shoestring to hang the budget on!

A key characteristic of feminist economic philosophy is that cooperation rather than competition is valued. It would be naive to assert that because a woman is a feminist or a lesbian she automatically shares scarce resources, but at least there's more of a willingness to *consider* working together for the good of all (instead of as rogue individuals with conquest in our hearts). Feminists try to replace the traditional "I've got what it takes to win, and screw you" with "If we put our resources together, we will all be better off."

Information is a commodity that is jealously hoarded in the entertainment industries. And that's completely understandable; if a producer can only do three women's concerts a year, Ms. Musician is loathe to give that producer's name to other musicians. What if the producer likes someone else better, and then Ms. M doesn't get booked? What a bitter pill to swallow when that producer was Ms. M's exclusive contact in the first place!

The bottom-line economic realities of trying to make a living in the arts are such that sharing what you have may in fact help other women, and will probably strengthen the overall culture—but may very well cut *you* out of the game.

Nonetheless, the level of cooperativeness and trust has been amazingly high in the women's music and culture world over the past twenty-five years. People don't share everything, and some won't share anything, but there's been substantially more passing around of info than one might expect, given the harsh economic realities. Hundreds of women have been willing to trust their feminist sisters and have given away precious contacts in the belief that they're *trading,* not getting ripped off.

It's a case of "I'll show you mine if you'll show me yours" at its finest.

Early in the game, it became apparent to me that having one central source of information was essential to the continued growth of the feminist cultural network. As someone whose priority has always been the care and feeding of the whole network, and as someone who's always had a knack for being organized, I assigned myself the job of creating that source— publishing a directory.

The first edition (entitled *We Shall Go Forth*—inspired by Margie Adam's anthem) came out in 1977. I've kept expanding it and putting out new versions every couple of years. Now called *Women's Music Plus,* the directory includes contact information for more than 5,500 individual women and groups who are involved in most aspects of what we've come to call "women's culture." New categories for 1995 include Cyberspace, Riot Grrrls, and Zines.

For the most part, it's been logistically difficult to *collect* the information, but emotionally easy to *publish* it. My feminist ethics could operate almost in a vacuum, because sharing the resources didn't impact *my* career. (I'm not a performer trying to keep my producer-contact list private so I'll get all the gigs, you know?) There was a major exception to this, though, which propelled me into the arena of conflicted emotions along with everyone else.

The one list I have always felt fiercely protective of was the foundations that give grants. That list took a great deal of research to compile, for one thing. For another, we had a business to run too, and we had perpetual problems with money. We sure didn't want any competition for those scarce grant dollars.

In the end, I always decide I just have to put my money (literally) where my mouth is, and I print the list. I'm glad to know my work helps other feminist and lesbian women.

With that spirit, here's a list of financial and business resources. Go forth and prosper!

GRANTWRITING

GUIDE TO PROPOSAL WRITING, The Foundation Center, 79 Fifth Ave., New York, NY 10003-3076. (800) 424-9836. *By Jane C. Geever and Patricia McNeill. Advice on grant proposal packages, advice from grant-givers, documents, excerpts from successful grants, pre-proposal planning, etc.*

KC BUSINESS DIRECTIONS, 500 N. Michigan Ave. #430, Chicago, IL 60611-3701. (312) 280-8887, Cathie. *Financial and grantwriting advice.*

KORKY VANN, The Ghostwriter, 20 S. Quaker Lane, West Hartford, CT 06119. (203) 233-7394. *Grantwriter.*

RAISE MORE MONEY FOR YOUR NONPROFIT ORGANIZATION, The Foundation Center, 79 Fifth Ave., New York, NY 10003-3076. (800) 424-9836. *Guide to evaluating and improving your*

*fundraising by Anne L. New. Launching a development campaign,
effective fundraising involving multiple sources, bibliography, resource list.*
  SUSAN WALLER, 821 Third Ave. No. #201, Seattle, WA 98109.
(206) 217-9738. *Grantwriter.*
  WHERE THE MONEY IS, The Foundation Center, 79 Fifth Ave.,
New York, NY 10003-3076. (800) 424-9836. *By Helen Bergan,
published by BioGuide Press. How to find info on wealthy donors. Basics
and finer points of prospect and donor research, how to use your local
library.*

INFO ON GRANT-GIVERS

  AIDS FUNDING, The Foundation Center, 79 Fifth Ave., New York,
NY 10003-3076. (800) 424-9836. *450+ foundations and charitable
organizations.*
  ARTS, CULTURE & HUMANITIES GRANTS GUIDE, The
Foundation Center, 79 Fifth Ave., New York, NY 10003-3076.
(800) 424-9836. *Info about grants to arts/cultural organizations,
historical societies, media, visual arts, performing arts, and music.*
  DIRECTORY OF FINANCIAL AIDS FOR WOMEN, Reference
Service Press, 1100 Industrial Rd. #9, San Carlos, CA 94070. (415)
594-0743. *By Gail Ann Schlacter. Biennial; more than 2,000 funding
opportunities for women.*
  FILM, MEDIA & COMMUNICATIONS GRANTS GUIDE, The
Foundation Center, 79 Fifth Ave., New York, NY 10003-3076. (800)
424-9836. *Info about grants for film, video, documentaries, radio,
television, printing, and publishing. Includes censorship issues.*
  FOUNDATION CENTER (THE), 79 Fifth Ave., New York, NY
10003-3076. (800) 424-9836. *Extensive resources on grant-giving
foundations. Several (but not all) of their publications are listed here.*
  FOUNDATION CENTER'S USER-FRIENDLY GUIDE, 79 Fifth Ave.,
New York, NY 10003-3076. (800) 424-9836. *Booklet for the novice
edited by Judith B. Margolin. Answers commonly asked questions about
grantseeking. Jargon explained.*
  FOUNDATION 1000 (THE), The Foundation Center, 79 Fifth Ave.,
New York, NY 10003-3076. (800) 424-9836. *Info on 1000+ grant-giving
foundations. Includes info for initial contact, application procedures,
funders' true interests and priorities, more.*
  FOUNDATION DIRECTORY & SUPPLEMENT (THE), The
Foundation Center, 79 Fifth Ave., New York, NY 10003-3076.
(800) 424-9836. *Designed for nonprofit groups; info on grants from
mid-sized foundations (those with annual grant programs from $50,000
to $200,000). 4300+ foundations.*
  FOUNDATION GRANTS TO INDIVIDUALS, The Foundation
Center, 79 Fifth Ave., New York, NY 10003-3076. (800) 424-9836.
*Info about grants to individuals for arts/culture programs, education,
awards/prizes/grants by nomination, medical assistance, etc.*

JUDITH LeBOLD, 214 Levick St. #2, Philadelphia, PA 19111. (215) 342-8104. *Fundraising consultant, grantwriter; has given workshops at festivals on raising money for women's projects.*

MONEY FOR VISUAL ARTISTS RESOURCE GUIDE, American Council for the Arts Books, 1 E. 53rd St., New York, NY 10022. (212) 223-2787, fax (212) 223-4415.

NAT'L DIRECTORY OF CORPORATE GIVING, The Foundation Center, 79 Fifth Ave., New York, NY 10003-3076. (800) 424-9836. *Info on 2300+ corporate philanthropic programs.*

NAT'L GUIDE TO FUNDING FOR WOMEN & GIRLS, The Foundation Center, 79 Fifth Ave., New York, NY 10003-3076. (800) 424-9836. *Info about grants for feminist issues, including arts, rape/domestic violence, health, reproductive rights, equal rights, and athletics.*

NAT'L GUIDE TO FUNDING IN ARTS & CULTURE, The Foundation Center, 79 Fifth Ave., New York, NY 10003-3076. (800) 424-9836. *Info on 4200+ foundations and corporate direct giving programs with histories of awarding grant dollars to arts and culture-related projects. Includes sample grants, grantmaker portraits.*

WOMEN'S PHILANTHROPY, Nat'l Network on Women as Philanthropists, 1300 Linden Dr., Madison, WI 53706-1575. *Info on philanthropic groups and individuals.*

GRANT-GIVERS

ACT UP NETWORK, P.O. Box 16899, St. Louis, MO 63105. *AIDS-related grants.*

AMAZON ARTS FOUNDATION, 5210 N. Wayne Ave., Chicago, IL 60640. Fax (312) 728-7002. *Starting in 1995. Grants to ongoing feminist/woman-identified creative projects and events (music, film/video, theater, comedy, publishing, festivals, radio, media activism, etc.).*

AMAZON AUTUMN EDUCATIONAL FOUNDATION, P.O. Box 2104, Union, NJ 07083. (201) 354-9054, (201) 568-8518. *Grants to projects that benefit the lesbian community.*

ASTRAEA FOUNDATION, 666 Broadway #520, New York, NY 10012. *Gives a variety of grants to creative women.*

BOSTON WOMEN'S FUND (THE), Adult Education, Florida Education Dept., 31 St. James Ave. #902, Boston, MA 02116.

CHICAGO FOUNDATION FOR WOMEN, 230 W. Superior St. #400, Chicago, IL 60610-3536. (312) 922-8762. Marianne Philbin. *Focus on feminist projects.*

CHICAGO RESOURCE CENTER, 104 S. Michigan Ave. #1220, Chicago, IL 60603-5907. (312) 461-9333. *Focus on lesbian/gay projects.*

COMMUNITY ARTS COUNCIL, 837 Davie St., Vancouver, BC V6Z 1B7, Canada. (604) 683-4358. *Grants for specific projects to arts, heritage, or multicultural organizations.*

COMMUNITY INVOLVEMENT PROGRAM, Womontyme Distribution, P.O. Box 50145, Long Beach, CA 90815. *Grants to social service projects and self-help groups committed to helping women and children.*

CROSSROADS FUND (THE), c/o Culkin Fund, 3411 W. Diversey #20, Chicago, IL 60647-1245. (312) 227-7676. *Focus on social change projects.*

DESIGN INDUSTRIES FOUNDATION FIGHTING AIDS, P.O. Box 180, Orangeburg, NY 10962-0108. (212) 727-3100. Rosemary Kuropat, executive director. *Funds AIDS-related organizations nationwide.*

FELLOWSHIPS FOR VISUAL ARTISTS, Southern Arts Federation, 181 14th St. NE #400, Atlanta, GA 30309. (404) 874-7244, fax (404) 873-2148, TTY (404) 876-6240. Lisa Richmond, visual and media arts coordinator. *30 $5000 fellowships given annually to Southerners; since 1984.*

FRANCESCA FORT*f*, Earth Light Visual Productions, P.O. Box 2, Hayward, CA 94543. (510) 733-5629.

GLOBAL FUND FOR WOMEN (THE), 2480 Sand Hill Rd. #100, Menlo Park, CA 94025. *Gives funds to seed, strengthen, and link women's groups working for the empowerment of women. Has given $3,302,832 (612 grants to 484 groups in 97 countries).*

HARMONY WOMEN'S FUND, P.O. Box 300105, Minneapolis, MN 55403. (612) 377-8431. *Major focus: women's arts organizations and women's safety.*

LEGACY, 147 W. 79th St #4A, New York, NY 10024. *Financial support for projects that promote the civil rights and well-being of lesbians.*

LESBIAN NATURAL RESOURCES, P.O. Box 8742, Minneapolis, MN 55408-0742. *Dedicated to the development of rural lesbian communities. Grants for land purchase/development, community development programs, individual self-sufficiency.*

MIRABELLA GRANTS FOR WOMEN PROGRAM, Mirabella, 200 Madison Ave., New York, NY 10016. (212) 447-4600. *Annual, in June; funds to groups "that pursue particular endeavors with the utmost conviction."*

MONEY FOR WOMEN FUND, Barbara Deming Memorial Fund, Inc., P.O. Box 40-1043, Brooklyn, NY 11240-1043. *Grants to individual feminist women active in the arts whose work speaks for peace and social justice; since 1976.*

MORGAN PINNEY TRUST (THE), 434 Liberty St., San Francisco, CA 94114. Jim Hicks. *Gay political projects; occasional funding for cultural projects if deemed political enough.*

MS. FOUNDATION FOR WOMEN (THE), 141 Fifth Ave., New York, NY 10010. (212) 353-8580.

NAT'L ENDOWMENT FOR THE ARTS, 2401 E St. NE, Washington, DC 20506. (202) 634-6369. *Major U.S. government arts-funding program.*

NAT'L NETWORK OF WOMEN'S FUNDS, 1821 University Ave. W. #221-S St. Paul, MN 55104. (612) 641-0742.

NAT'L WOMEN'S STUDIES ASSOCIATION (NWSA), University Of Maryland, College Park, MD 20742-1325. (301) 454-3757. *Grants include Pat Parker Poetry Award (co-funded by Woman in the Moon Press); Lesbian Studies (co-funded by Naiad Press); Jewish Women's Studies.*

PAT BOND FUND (THE), 545 Douglas, San Francisco, CA 94114.

PAT PARKER POETRY AWARD, NWSA, University of Maryland, College Park, MD 20742-1325. (301) 454-3757. *$250 grant.*

PRIDE FOUNDATION (THE), 2820 E. Madison, Seattle, WA 98122. (206) 323-3318 or (800) 735-7287; fax (206) 323-3318. *Focus on lesbian/gay projects in the Pacific Northwest. Has granted nearly $600,000 to more than 100 organizations since 1987.*

STADTLANDERS FOUNDATION, 600 Penn Center Blvd., Pittsburgh, PA 15235. (412) 825-8118 Karen Jacobi, or (412) 825-8105. *Focus: gay and/or AIDS-related.*

RESIST, 1 Summer St., Somerville, MA 02143. (617) 623-5110. *Focus on grassroots organizations working for social change.*

SHARING OUR ASSORTED RESOURCES (SOAR), P.O. Box 22112, Lansing, MI 48909. *Small grants to lesbians for emergencies.*

STONEWALL AWARDS (THE), Anderson Prize Foundation, Barrett Comm., 1555 N. Astor #23, Chicago, IL 60610. (312) 751-0148, Paulette Barrett. *"Honoring achievement for gay and lesbian America" since 1990.*

SUE SANIEL ELKIND POETRY CONTEST, Kalliope Journal, Florida Junior College, 3939 Roosevelt Blvd., Jacksonville, FL 32205. (904) 387-8211. *$1000 first prize and publication in* Kalliope—*poetry in any style/on any subject. SASE for guidelines/deadlines.*

UNCOMMON LEGACY FOUNDATION, 150 W. 26th St. #602, New York, NY 10011. (212) 989-5029. *Provides financial support to the lesbian community. In 1994, provided 30 student scholarships and honored eight women for their contributions to the social, cultural, health, and educational needs of women (Alison Bechdel, Rita Mae Brown, Kate Millett, the Hensons, Barbara Giddings, Joyce Hunter, Hilary Rosen).*

WOMEN FOR FELINES FUND, Women's Energy Bank, Inc., P.O. Box 15524, St. Petersburg, FL 33733-5524. (813) 823-5353. *Limited financial help for emergency vet services for pets.*

WOMEN FOR WOMEN FUND, Women's Energy Bank, Inc., P.O. Box 15524, St. Petersburg, FL 33733-5524. (813) 823-5353. *Limited emergency funds for women in crisis.*

WOMEN FOR WOMEN IN BOSNIA, 1212 New York Ave. NW #300, Washington, DC 20005. *Helps support women who have survived the genocide and war in former Yugoslavia. Financial/emotional support regardless of religion or professed ethnicity. Looking for financial donors from all over the world.*

WOMEN'S MONEY NETWORK, P.O. Box 90683, San Diego, CA 92169-2683. (619) 275-1378. *Network for the lesbian community that matches women who have funds with those who need money for business, community projects, etc.*

WOMEN'S RESEARCH AWARDS PROGRAM, c/o M. Abrams, Jefferson Community College SW, 1000 Community College Dr., Louisville, KY 40272. (502) 935-9840. *$750 grants to encourage/support excellence in research by, for, and about women/girls.*

FILM-VIDEO

EVE FUND (THE), Frameline, 346 9th St., San Francisco, CA 94103. (415) 703-8650, fax (415) 861-1404. *The Eve (Erotic Video Education) Fund supports lesbian-oriented erotic film/video projects that promote safer sex. Up to $500 and/or other resources to women who are first- or second-time filmmakers; up to $1000 to women with demonstrated professional experience.*

FRAMELINE FILM/VIDEO COMPLETION FUNDS, Frameline, 346 9th St., San Francisco, CA 94103. (415) 703-8650, fax (415) 861-1404. *Up to $2000 to artists in last stages of production; any format or genre.*

PERFORMING ARTS

COMMUNITY ARTS COUNCIL, 837 Davie St., Vancouver, BC V6Z 1B7, Canada. (604) 683-4358. *Grants for specific projects to arts, heritage, or multicultural organizations.*

AMAZON ARTS FOUNDATION, 5210 N. Wayne Ave., Chicago, IL 60640. Fax (312) 728-7002. *Grants to ongoing feminist/woman-identified creative projects and events (music, film/video, theater, comedy, publishing, festivals, radio, media activism, etc.).*

DANCE ON TOUR, Southern Arts Federation, 181 14th St. NE #400, Atlanta, GA 30309. (404) 874-7244, fax (404) 873-2148, TTY (404) 876-6240. *Provides fee support to nonprofit Southern producers engaging out-of-region/out-of-state professional dance companies/artists. Grants range between 15% and 35% of the company/artist fee; in 1993, 51 grant awards were recommended, distributing $222,457 in fee support.*

HARMONY WOMEN'S FUND, P.O. Box 300105, Minneapolis, MN 55403. (612) 377-8431. *Major focus: women's arts organizations and women's safety.*

INSTRUMENTAL MUSIC GRANTS, Alpha Delta Kappa, 1615 W. 92nd St., Kansas City, MO 64114. (816) 363-5525. *$5000 grant; $3000 alternative grant. Submit a recording of 30-60 minutes in length. Grants every two years; 1995 grant will be for strings.*

MEET THE COMPOSER, Southern Arts Federation, 181 14th St. NE #400, Atlanta, GA 30309. (404) 874-7244, fax (404) 873-2148, TTY (404) 876-6240. *Fee support to Southern nonprofit producers to help bring composers for master classes, lectures, conducting performances,*

interviews, and other activities that bring the composer in contact with
the general public. Funds up to 50% of the composer's fee; in 1993,
46 grants were recommended, distributing $21,600 in fee support.

MONEY FOR WOMEN FUND, Barbara Deming Memorial Fund,
Inc., P.O. Box 40-1043, Brooklyn, NY 11240-1043. *Grants to individual
feminist women active in the arts whose work speaks for peace and social
justice; since 1976.*

NAT'L ENDOWMENT FOR THE ARTS, Music Division, 2401 E St.
NE, Washington, DC 20506. (202) 634-6369. *Major U.S. government
arts-funding program.*

PAN AMERICAN MUSICAL ART RESEARCH, P.O. Box 863 Village
Station New York, NY 10014-0863. (212) 644-5131. Jan Hanvik.

**PEGGY GLANVILLE-HICKS COMPOSER-IN-RESIDENCE
PROGRAM,** 56 Kellett St., Potts Point, NSW 2011 Australia. (02)
358-2464, fax (02) 357-3112. *The late Peggy Glanville-Hicks willed her
house (45 Ormond St., Paddington) as a haven for full-time professional
composers. Residencies from one to three years.*

PERFORMING ARTS TOURING PROGRAM, Southern Arts
Federation, 181 14th St. NE #400, Atlanta, GA 30309. (404) 874-7244,
fax (404) 873-2148, TTY (404) 876-6240. *Promotes touring in Southern
states. Fee support grants; grants range between 15% and 35% of the
company/artist fee. In 1993, 89 grant awards were recommended,
distributing $106,000 in fee support to producers.*

FINANCIAL & BUSINESS RESOURCES

AMERICAN WOMEN'S ECONOMIC DEVELOPMENT CORP., 60
E. 40th St. #405, New York, NY 10165. (212) 692-9100. *Holds seminars
for putting together loan packages.*

A.Y. UYEDA, Hagakure Images, P.O. Box 2866, San Francisco, CA
94126-2866. *Consultant on fundraising, development, and planning for
arts agencies and performing groups.*

ARTISTS' BOOKKEEPING BOOK, Chicago Artists' Coalition, 5 W.
Grand Ave., Chicago, IL 60610. *Tax booklet for the self-employed.*

BRENDA GOLDSTEIN, Vega Travel, Chicago. (800) FLY-THER. *See
what a dedicated travel agent can do to help you plan business and
pleasure trips. You pay no fees. Experienced with complicated tour-type
scheduling. Keeps track of vacation packages aimed at the women's
market.*

BRYNNA FISH, Bluefish Productions, 2256 Rexwood Rd., Cleveland
Hts., OH 44118-2880. (216) 371-9714. *Consultant to nonprofits and
other organizations for fundraising and events.*

CHERIE DONLIN, Global Affair, 285 E. 5th Ave., Eugene, OR
97401. (800) 755-2753. *Lesbian feminist travel agent; works with
producers and performers to control costs and minimize hassles.*

DEB MURPHY, 3442 N. Southport, Chicago, IL 60657. (312)
404-8401. *Lesbian CPA serving wimmin nationwide.*

EQUAL MEANS: Women Organizing Economic Solutions, 2512 Ninth St. #3, Berkeley, CA 94710. (510) 549-9931. *"Strategies women are developing around economic justice/development and empowerment, while stressing multiracial, multicultural international linkages." 3x/yr., 32 pgs., published by Ms. Foundation.*

NAT'L ASSOCIATION OF WOMEN BUSINESS OWNERS, 600 S. Federal, Chicago, IL 60605. (312) 922-0465. *Information and counseling.*

NETWORK OF WOMEN ENTREPRENEURS, P.O. Box 298, Winnetka, IL 60093. (708) 835-8911, fax (708) 835-8913.

POINTONE LINK VISA CARD (THE), 635-B Pennsylvania Ave. SE, Washington, DC 20003. (800) 764-6866. *Each time you make a purchase with the PointOne Link VISA card, a contribution is made to The PointOne Foundation, a nonprofit organization supporting lesbian and gay causes and organizations.*

QUEER MONEY, P.O. Box 59856, Dayton, OH 45459. *Financial planning.*

RUSTY GORDON, Rustron Productions, 1156 Park Lane, West Palm Beach, FL 33417-5957. (407) 686-1354. *Expert on many aspects of the music/entertainment industry. Fundraising consultant.*

SANDY RAMSEY, 881 Contra Costa, Berkeley, CA 94707. (510) 527-8036. *Experienced music festival accountant.*

SUSAN K. FRANZ, Franz Financial Planning, 5801 N. Sheridan #19A, Chicago, IL 60660. (312) 769-9244, fax (312) 769-9253. *Registered investment advisor, broker/dealer; tax preparation. Special interest in helping women become financially secure.*

TRIANGLE INTERESTS CREDIT UNION, P.O. Box 35145, Philadelphia, PA 19128. (215) 844-6348, fax (215) 844-1506. Michelle MacKinnon. *National nonprofit lesbian membership organization has filed for a charter from the National Credit Union Association (October 1994). If approved, TICU will create the first national credit union run by and for lesbians.*

UJAMAA, 6116 Merced Ave. #373, Oakland, CA 94611. (510) 255-2155, Annette Martin; (510) 832-0531. Suzanne Lovest. *Women of color; focus on cooperative economics/survival.*

LILIES OF THE FIELD

SONIA JOHNSON

I chanced one day upon what may have been the world women knew before patriarchy, that world of wholeness and unity so lost to us. One glorious spring day while I was still a Mormon wife and mother and a baby feminist, I was driving down a road in rural Virginia on my way to the supermarket. The closed car began to grow uncomfortably warm with the bright sun beating upon it, so I turned my attention to rolling down the window.

As I did, I suddenly realized that through that opening window I was not merely looking at but was caught up in and participating with a breathtaking world. Now, a dozen years later, I remember best the woods that were ablaze with a green so intense that like a leafy wildfire it sprang through my eyes into my body and burned along every nerve and bone and muscle until I felt as if I *were* its green-hot glow.

Totally part of that dazzling world for a few seconds, I felt released from time. Whether the whole experience lasted a century or a split second was irrelevant; the conventional designations were meaningless. The timelessness affected me strongly, though, and unexpectedly. In it I felt whole and large and real, very deep and rich. I awed myself and was awed by everything around me. I wanted to laugh and clap my hands for joy. I wanted to weep. I wanted to remain the rest of my life in that state of complete knowledge of myself and of intimate, loving participation with the earth. I knew for those few moments that if I could figure out how to do it, this was fully possible.

Copyright © 1989 by Sonia Johnson

If the scrim between me and the world as it truly is and can be is able to part for one magical moment to let me experience again a little of what is possible for human consciousness, my assumption is that it parts for others, too. So perhaps many of us know absolutely to what dim and muffled numbness patriarchy has reduced our senses and our minds, and something of what the "real" world is like.

That blazing green, timeless forest is one of my touchstones. Recollecting it, I am reminded of the possibilities for my life. It buttresses the other reference points that over the years have verified for me that joy, actual and readily available, is my human legacy. It fills me with incentive and hope, infuses me with energy and purpose. Who would choose to suffer in patriarchy if they understood that right at hand, all around us where we stand, a wondrous world *already exists* for us to step into and make our own?

Sometimes I think that we need not worry about creating a world at all but only about recreating ourselves so that the world that is there, that is in us, that *is* us, can become our external, concrete reality. I also know that as a universal gender class we have already moved into a different spiritual dimension, onto our own unique moral plane. Despite how crucial our inner transformation is, however, I know that it must manifest itself in some integral, external activity.

What that activity might be is becoming clearer. Thousands of us now believe that we have no choice but to build together an actual, physical society to our own specifications. Prime among these specifications is that each one of us has enough of what we need to live; specifically, as in the archaic world, plenty of *time*.

To establish hierarchy, the antithesis of women's world order, patriarchy had to create scarcity—of respect, of honor, of food and other essentials, but primarily of time.

All around me every day I hear people complain, "I don't have time." "There's not enough time." "I need 36 hours in every day." I say it myself, although I know that there is plenty of time, all the time we could possibly ever need; time is what there is an infinite supply of in the universe, and time is life. Perhaps we should ask ourselves the obvious question, "If there is plenty of time and *I* don't have it, where is it, who has it, and how can I get my share of if back?"

That this scarcity of time has seemed inevitable until now is instructive. If you can persuade people that there isn't enough time, if you can persuade them that this time deprivation is unchangeable "reality," and if you can simultaneously organize society in a way that bears out your contention that there seems in fact to be very little time, you can steal people's lives from them.

The initial time/life you would steal would be from their *minds*. Your success in getting people to *think* there is no time would cause them to limit themselves. By causing them to behave *as if it were true*, you could effectively establish time-poverty as their reality.

What would happen to tyrants if slaves refused the concept of limited time? What if they believed that there was all the time they needed, and freely partook of it to think, to talk and listen to one another, to dream, to love fully, to create music, art, and literature, to play games and climb mountains? Tyranny, nonfreedom, means primarily having no time for oneself. Ownership of others' bodies means dictating how those bodies spend their *time*.

When I hear everyone moaning that they have no time, I am made freshly aware of how patriarchy tyrannizes us all by taking from us our time. Free people need not only space— rooms of their own—but time of their own as well. Any beneficent society, therefore, that is not simply the old one under a different rubric must first free our time, give us "free time." That such an expression as "free time" exists is evidence that the rest of our time is "slave time."

Thinking about the necessity of time deprivation to patriarchy led me to examine the underlying assumptions that we must accept in order to participate in the delusions, the absurd beliefs, that only brainwashing could have made appear reasonable.

One of these is that we must spend most of our precious time/life working. Not only that we must do this in order to live, but that as men have narrowly defined it—whether enjoyable or not, whether mind- or spirit-expanding or not—work has been made to seem desirable in itself. We have been programmed to consider ourselves "good" if we work and "bad" if we don't. Our strong work enculturation teaches us that if we are not working—which usually means producing something saleable or in some way facilitating the movement of money through society—we are idle, not doing anything of value, and are worthless, good-for-nothing parasites. We have also been strongly indoctrinated to consider work done for payment superior to that done freely.

But what if we stopped believing the calculated nonsense that each of us has to work eight or more hours a day simply to survive? Think what we could be and do! What would we do if we didn't feel hurried, if we didn't suffer from chronic time-panic? What would we do if we had endless hours of freedom stretching out before us as far as we could see?

It seems to me that we might come to know ourselves and one another. We might relax into a deep connection with our own planet and the multitudes of other stars in our galaxy. We might begin to move to rhythms long since muted by hurry-scurry.

I believe that reframing our concept of time, diminishing it to a straight line between two points, and then goading us mercilessly along it has been one of patriarchy's most substantial successes. This revolution in the concept of time was absolutely necessary for patriarchy to gain a hold on the human mind and thence on the world. I am certain that it remains essential to retaining control of the planet and its inhabitants. As long as we live our daily lives according to unexamined patriarchal assumptions about time, we are at the mercy of the cruelest taskmaster of all the fathers, "Father time."

"Father time" forces us to live each day within such strict brackets that most of what is desirable and possible in life is outside them. Lashing our psyches with his whip, he maintains the necessary lie that we have no time for and therefore can't do most of the things we genuinely *want* to do. At the same time, his terrorist keeps our creativity so suppressed that we can barely imagine what we *would* do if we had time. It keeps us so automatized that we seldom even think to question his twin assertions that time is scarce and that we have no choice but to use up the little we have of it slaving to maintain the patriarchal state.

"I don't have time" is the single most frequently given reason for living fractional, perpetually indentured lives, for not living fully or freely. Because time is life, when we say we don't have enough time, we are admitting that we don't have enough life.

Even the little time we *do* have is Father time, froze time, dead time, rigidly, obdurately linear time, adamantly cause-and-effectful, swift, superficial, and anxiety-producing, like walking an unraveling tightrope high above the ground.

The assumption enforced by Father time's whip is that time is an external given to which we must adjust our collective and individual pace. But I am beginning to believe rather that time is within us and therefore controllable by each one of us.

I have spoken of time as surrounding us, as the element in which we live, as the ocean surrounds fish and is their element. Now I think that perhaps instead each of us swims in our own personal, internal ocean of time rather than in a communal bath. If this is true, then time literally *is* life and life is time, and both are ours to do with as we wish. On the other hand, if we conceive of time as the ocean in which we all swim together, then it is not under each individual's control and goes on whether any one of us lives in it or not. This latter way of thinking about time not only contributes to our general feeling of powerlessness in the universe, but by making life dependent upon time but not time upon life, blurs the fact that for each living person time and life are indissolubly merged.

Understanding that time and life are one is particularly essential as a starting point in uprooting the wrong-headed and calamitous exchange economy patriarchy has so carefully taught us to believe is inescapable. In the Western world we often hear the phrase "Time is money," and every successful socialized adult knows that this is not meant metaphorically but literally. We blur any distinction between time and money thoroughly and unconsciously every time we talk about "spending time," or deplore what certain activities "cost" us in time, or always try to "save" time, or "give" time in the place of money to charities or volunteer organizations, or when we pay a fine with money rather than with time in jail.

If time and life are in many critical ways synonymous, and if in patriarchy time really *is* money, then it follows that on planet Earth money is life.

This, of course, is not news. On many levels we've known it for a very long time. We would have had to be insentient to have missed the connection, living as we do in a world where people literally cannot live now without money, in a world where millions of moneyless people are doomed to certain

death and the rest of us to lives restricted in direct proportion
to our access to money.

In fact, because we believe that money is necessary for life
and have been so terrorized for so long by the chronic lack of
it, it is the one assumption of the considerable battery of
assumptions the fathers' term "reality" that is most frightening
for us to face and difficult to challenge dispassionately. More
than any other, it has the power to defeat women's
deprogramming methods. Though many of us have known with
certainty for some time that everything men have taught us
about the world is either wrong or a deliberate lie, in the past
not only I but obviously other feminists have not dared to
extrapolate from this that money must be tossed out with men's
other dangerous nonsense.

But that doesn't mean I have felt comfortable about my
cowardice. Women have been saying to me for a long time, "I
can't stand to work in patriarchy every day; it's killing me."
They have been terrorized by money scarcity for so long that
when I suggest that since patriarchy is killing us we should flee
from it and try our hand at society-making, almost always their
first questions come out of the mind that equates life and
money: "But how will we make money? How will we *live*?
How will we earn a living?"

Though I have always understood and even shared their fear,
I have known that that question sidestepped the
difficult-to-believe possibility that no woman needs to work in
the patriarchal system if she does not wish to. I have become
progressively more convinced that believing in the actuality of
our desires is necessary for them to appear. So I choose to
believe that neither I nor any woman has to work in patriarchy
in order to live, and that our conviction that we do is part of
the brainwashing that keeps us imprisoned here.

That question also prompts me to make clear that I am
determined to live in a reality in which the concept of "earning"
a living seems as bizarre and sad to everyone as it has come to
seem to me. The language of that phrase reveals our
programming to perceive ourselves as inherently worthless and
consequently to accept work as a rational and even welcome
atonement for some imagined inadequacy. From that language
the irony is evident: by making us perceive success at work as

proof of our value, patriarchy tricks us into working long, hard hours to maintain it as a system.

But more than that, that phrase exposes the fathers' cruel lie that we must earn the right to live. Though the fathers have got away with their deception for centuries, the mothers know that at birth life is a free gift of the universe. We know that life doesn't need to be—in fact, *can't* be—earned, and we are destined to recreate that reality.

Like the birds of the air and the lilies of the field, we do not need to toil to be allowed to live. In living out their lives as they wish, they faithfully abet the cycles and flow of all life, scattering seeds, controlling pests, providing beauty, enriching the soil and holding it together, perfuming the air, providing materials—such as pollen—that enable other creatures to live in their appointed ways, in their turn becoming food for others and ultimately for the soil.

Though the birds and flowers, the fauna and flora, contribute a great deal and are indispensable members of the world community, they do not "toil." With them as our model—though ultimately we may be less essential—perhaps we can begin to trust that if each of us does what gives us pleasure and what we do well, if each of us follows our natural bent and honors it, we too will enhance the flow of life, facilitate its cycles, meet all human needs, and have all that we ourselves require.

Though I struggled with it womanfully, I wasn't able in the past to answer the question, "How shall we earn a living?" no matter how often or how urgently it was put to me. After listing my objections to it, however, I finally realized why neither I nor any other feminist could answer it. Not because we weren't smart enough—we were twice as smart as we had ever been, thinking at last both with our heads and our intuitions—but because it was once again the wrong question.

The right questions do not ask how we can be more comfortable in patriarchy. They do not seek to discover how we can "pass." Knowing this, I realized that someday I would have to ask what were for me certainly some of the right questions: what *is* money? Is it necessary? If not, what else is possible? How might I begin to live in a moneyless world?

But I wasn't ready to ask them then because I wasn't ready for the answers. Once answers come, if I wish to be a woman of integrity, I have no choice but to act on them, and I was afraid. The shift from money-thinking and money-fear had to take place first in my mind. Further than that, I had also to stop believing that exchange itself was the only or even the best path to survival.

A handful of feminists has understood from the beginning that money and the philosophy underlying and sustaining it are profoundly patriarchal and therefore inimical to all they valued. I'm certain they have attempted to rid their lives of these most blatant evidences of the workings of the male value system. But I have not asked them about their experiment because until recently my fear caused me to regard these women as rash and uncredible and to dismiss them summarily.

But in the few months that I was finishing this book and sifting down through layer after layer of my brainwashing residue, my flinty refusal to examine my assumptions about money continually impeded my progress. I sabotaged my work not only by ignoring these looming assumptions but also by not recognizing money, price, and related concepts as patriarchal artifacts that prevented my personal liberation.

Though I believe that change must always take place first on the metaphysical level, I also think we are required to study whatever physical alternatives we can find. When I ran for President in 1984, I did a crash course in economics during which, to my delight, I discovered Hazel Henderson, a self-taught economist and advisor to heads of state the world over. Her book, *The Politics of the Solar Age: Alternatives to Economics*, is the best readily-available initial deprogramming about patriarchal economics that I know.

In this book she asserts that there is no such thing as economics; *there are only values.* As I read that, I knew she was right. But how did this simple fact become so obfuscated? How did "economics" grow so arcane that it slipped out of our individual control, leaving us at the mercy of others?

Henderson offers one clue. She maintains that economists, eager to be viewed as belonging to the scientific community— so important for men—first invented and then ghettoized economics. By mystifying it they made themselves indispensable as experts to explain it to the rest of us, and also put themselves in a position to control and manipulate us.

This behavior is so typical of patriarchy that it should elicit no more than a "ho hum" from feminists, a bored "What else is new?" It is so like the fathers to send up continually larger and denser smokescreens to shield their most vulnerable flanks. And "economics" is one of their weakest. Imagine if dreaded "economics," instead of appearing frighteningly complicated and beyond the grasp of most of us, were understood to be merely values. Recognized as eminently mutable—*and by us*—it could no longer reduce us all to powerless pulp.

For this to happen, we would first have to lose our respect and fear of it and our belief that "economics" really *means* something, that it really *describes* something necessary and useful, that it has the capacity to teach us something true about the world. Second, having become totally unimpressed and even a little embarrassed that we had ever perceived it as anything other than patriarchy's ugly values in drag, we would be ready to get rid of men's "economics" by substituting women's "economics"—women's values.

Henderson foresees this, positing "the coming era of post-economic policy making." "From now on," she writes, "as the economic and price-system levers become ever more divorced from reality, industrial societies will need to refocus their attention on policy levers that are nonmonetary, nonfiscal, and nonprice-oriented."

This is where women come in, this is where we are the gifted, the geniuses—in *value*-based decisions; that is, in decisions that are nonmonetary, nonfiscal, and nonprice-oriented.

Although men have increasingly used economics to terrorize women (and one another), it is equally true that their "economy" is doomed. Soon everyone who is not already doing so will have to rethink radically the ways we live and work together.

Henderson's demystification helped me begin this rethinking by releasing me from much of my anxiety about "economics." But it took another woman's courageous departure from herd-mentality to enable me to understand *how* women can create our own "economy," *how* we can substitute our values for patriarchal values in actual, physical ways in our lives and the world. Because of her thinking, I was finally able to leap over the barrier and erase money and all exchange dogma from my vision of women's world.

Genevieve Vaughan has a brave and original mind. Her papers, "The Philosophy Behind Stonehaven (An Attempt to Preach What We Practice)," and "Gift Giving: The Feminine Principle of Communication," advocate a nonmonetary, nonexchange economic model so simple, so evocative of our own personal power, and so in harmony with every idea I had laboriously come to in the past few years, that as I read it, I thought with profound relief, "Of course."

Briefly, Vaughan suggests that the surest escape from the economic scarcity and terror necessary to patriarchy lies in the overt establishment of a gift-giving society. She maintains that such a society already flourishes worldwide in the form of women's free nurturance—flourishes that is, as a *covert* system.

To make certain that this female economic order *remains* covert and invisible, patriarchy overvalues paid labor and assigns status to people and things on the basis of monetary worth. Men's economic philosophy and behavior is in this way the antithesis of and thoroughly reactive to women's values—a fact that helps to explain its devastating effect on the planet and its inhabitants. Reaction is based in fear, and fear, unable to produce anything but more of itself, has spawned a fearful, terrifying reality.

Convinced that men's exchange economy is an aberration in human interaction (and a recent one at that), Vaughan holds that the very idea of exchange, including barter, is based on invented rather than on real need—"a manipulated use of need satisfaction," as she puts it. It is also completely conditional: I will only give to you if you give back to me in exact measure. Extending this idea, she maintains that because the values underlying exchange—competition, manipulation, exploitation, justice, and self-aggrandizement—are inherently patriarchal (i.e., hierarchical and oppressive), exchange inevitably produces scarcity, violence, and death.

Mary Ann Beall, another creative thinker, interprets and expands upon Vaughan's work. In her opinion, women's model of society is a replication of the global ecosystems of Earth. Specifically, this means that, understanding the interconnectedness of all things, women cherish, preserve, and facilitate the flow of energy from one life form to another. We instinctively know—in our viscera, that is—that in damming up that flow and creating surpluses for the benefit of the few, the possibilities for interacting with its life-giving elements are destroyed for the many.

Beall gives the example of the Aswan dam which was designed to block the River Nile's flow so that cotton and other cash crops could be grown in hitherto unarable soil. In addition to decreasing the size and fertility of the delta, and spreading disease, this blockage stopped the flow of nutriments from the upper Nile that fed the aquatic and other life of the Mediterranean Sea, catastrophically disrupting the food chain for all living things in that area. In their blindness to the intertwining networks that support and sustain all life, men continually and with devastating effect block the ecosystems' energy flow.

Men's economy is designed on this same model—the blockage system of surpluses and dearths in which surpluses are not recycled into the flow. As the adage puts it, "stealing from Peter to pay Paul." But systems, including economic systems, are living things, and all living things need flow for survival; they all require the continual movement and recycling of energy. Instead, what we see on the planet today is that all men's systems—capitalism, communism, socialism—are energy dams in multiple ways, drastically interrupting the natural order of things and causing calamities. They can no more succeed for humankind that can the Aswan Dam.

Neither the natural nor the "economic" ecosystem can long sustain the effects of the dams men have built across every living river, physical and metaphysical. Because strife is a major characteristic of blocked flow and violence the inevitable result of a dysfunctional system, we could say that war is a state of advanced global arteriosclerosis.

Money is the congealed energy that clogs society's arteries. In creating it as a symbol of the transformative powers of both physical and spiritual ecosystems, men lost track of what it stood for, where the source of its value originally lay. When they no longer paid attention to the real things that money symbolized, money itself became "real." It took on a life of its own and began to have value in and of itself. In this way men disconnected money from the ecosystem that once generated its value, a disastrous move.

The trouble is, of course, that money is *not* the energy it once symbolized. It is not a member of a community that provides natural checks and balances, give and take. Unlike living things in a healthy life web, it has no internally disciplined flow. It accumulates in pile here and there at the same time that it is almost totally absent from vast areas. Having no inherent life force, like a vampire it can live only on stolen energy.

By cutting down the Amazon forests, for example, men are destroying something inherently valuable to the maintenance of the planet's energy network and turning it into a pot of money. What they are left with is a pot of money and a barren, wasted land. This is the kind of exchange that is necessary in order to energize money.

Money, or any other medium of exchange, is simply another artifact of the patriarchal mind and more evidence of the deadliness of its values. It is, among other things, the concrete manifestation of the ubiquitous, thoroughly iniquitous, and deeply entrenched belief that inequitable distribution— hierarchy—is unavoidable and even desirable. By forcing everyone constantly to compare the noncomparable—values, objects, ideas, people—on the basis of criteria established by external judges, it encourages the hierarchical, dichotomous mind. In this way, exchange crawls off the same dungheap of values as "an eye for an eye and a tooth for a tooth," the dungheap where reciprocation, comparison, retaliation, greed, and control sit enthroned side by side.

From this and from all else that we know and intuit about men's dammed economy, most of us would conclude, as Vaughan does, that any biophilic way of filling the needs of humans and other living things (i.e., any genuinely workable economy) must be based on such radically different values from those of exchange that exchange drops out of the human economic repertoire altogether.

We would also agree that such an economy or value system has already originated with women. Women's economic answer to exchange—nonreciprocal, nonadversarial gift giving—is based on our foremost value, a value that does not even exist in patriarchy: that the needs of living beings and our life systems be met.

Vaughan contends that if women were to behave in the way most comfortable for us and most supportive of our integrity, we would give freely without requiring repayment, establishing gift giving as the exclusive mode of satisfying human needs. In addition, if we had our preference we would assume and expect that because others shared our values and would respond in the same reasonable way, our own needs would also always be met. We would trust in the deep instinct of living things to maintain their delicate, powerful, generative networks.

Strong evidence for this as a probable scenario is that it is the way women have traditionally interacted—though admittedly often one-sidedly—with others and with the earth.

It could be argued, of course, that gift-giving behavior is not necessarily "natural" for women but instead that men, who benefit most from our habit of lavish sharing of our resources, have craftily programmed it into us. Insofar as women have capitulated to men's brainwashing to be selfless and subservient, this is no doubt true. But the likelihood is that men, as is their historically uncreative wont, have in their subjugation of women again merely seized the main chance. This was—and is—to capitalize upon and exploit for their own nefarious purposes women's already existing, ancient, aboriginal altruism, communitarianism, and predilection for anarchy, as well as our sense of deep and immediate spiritual interconnectedness with and attitude of responsibility for all other life.

There are those who insist that women are no more generous or life-loving than men. But such persons cannot have looked around them with open eyes. In most households of the world women work daily from dawn to late night attending to the physical, emotional, and spiritual well-being of immediate as well as extended family members, often in addition to neighbors, friends, church associates, employees and employers, animals, and plants. We do this not merely because we are coerced—though we often are—but because our connections with and the facilitating of life itself is what gives us deepest joy.

Perhaps whatever widespread limiting, debasing, and warping of our generous natures *is* now evident, however, can be traced directly to men's exploitation of this characteristic of female being.

According to Vaughan, gift giving—concentrating on satisfying needs rather than on receiving payment—is for all

people "a normal, healthy way to behave," and that, freed from
the taint of bribery or blackmail, both giving and receiving can
be highly pleasurable. But she is aware that pleasure, though
necessary, is not the most important result. Gift giving, she
maintains, is a real solution to the moral chaos inevitable in
patriarchy's exchange mentality. Giving and receiving gifts, we
can eliminate the greed, egomania, and fear that are part of the
competitive exchange system.

Gifts open the sluice gates of the universe and allow its
abundance to stream out. Giving gifts, we can unlock the Nile
and let its nutriment-rich flow nourish every part of Earth's
ecosystem, physical and spiritual.

Other radical differences between the value systems
represented by gift giving and exchange become apparent in the
behavior they evoke and the short- and long-term effects of the
transactions on individuals and communities. Gift giving creates
abundance; exchange produces scarcity. Gift giving protects and
nurtures the environment and other species; exchange
necessitates their exploitation and destruction. Gift giving
encourages ethical, compassionate, and humane individual and
group behavior; exchange disconnects and isolates, and
encourages expediency. By not assigning value to the gift itself,
gift giving discourages greed; by valuing products for their
exchange value, exchange promotes avarice and covetousness.
Gift giving, by assigning value to the satisfaction of the need
and to the connections that are established as the need is met,
expands human connections and unity; exchange isolates
individuals and encourages an adversarial stance.

A look at bartering as an example of exchange reveals how it
discourages community, how its exclusivity creates a closed
circuit of interaction and blocks the natural flow of human
energy.

Two women exchange objects or services that they agree are
of approximately equal value in time or money. Even though it
is gentle and barely noticeable, an adversarial attitude is
inescapably built into this transaction, coloring the tone of the
entire proceeding. When the transaction ends, the experience is
over; neither woman ends up with more than she came with,
physically or metaphysically. Few spiritual, emotional,
intellectual, or ethical ripples go out from it into either their

lives or the life of the community. Exchange is like dropping a stone into wet concrete.

On the other hand, since in gift giving no expectation of equivalent returns exists to limit or break connections, the gift flows on and out, the circle of givers and receivers expanding exponentially and overlapping in all directions. Every receiver is also multiple giver, every giver receives many gifts. Giving a gift is like tossing a handful of stones into a calm lake.

In addition to the material plenty that results from gift giving, riches of spirit attend and follow upon it, riches that are permanent and available to everyone. In order to give good gifts, for example, people must first notice what others need and care how they feel. Studying what gifts will in fact fill needs or truly give pleasure, they arrive at a common understanding of human needs and how to satisfy them in all their variety, an understanding that links them to all other human beings. This in turn makes their interdependence visible and reveals to them its enormous value.

Equal benefits follow upon the act of receiving. In a gift-giving society, everyone is a receiver from birth as well as a giver. Because both giving and receiving are prized for their indispensable roles in maintaining the free flow of life-sustaining energy, receivers are as conscious as givers of their worthiness. They receive in the sure knowledge that they deserve to have everything they need simply beaus, like the birds of the air and the lilies of the fields, they are living beings.

In addition to ensuring material abundance, therefore, gift giving/receiving yields metaphysical gifts that also flow into the gift stream, blessing everyone in perpetuity: gifts of understanding, compassion, wisdom, and connection. In this way, the female mode—giving as the means of satisfying needs—creates bonds of trust and security on a practical level.

Gift giving's terrific subversive potential, therefore, lies not only in its ability to satisfy all needs—a condition of abundance that is anathema to patriarchy and would be enough in itself to spell its doom—but also to automatically establish connections among people, unite them, and encourage and strengthen community. Because patriarchy depends upon keeping people isolated from and suspicious of one another, it cannot withstand genuine community.

The antithesis of patriarchy is a world of community, and a global community or ecosystem is what women have come to organize.

Vaughan's view that women's nurturing is the basic underlying value system, and one that, though rendered invisible by patriarchy, is alive, venerable, and global reinforces my belief that the model for the world we want is already well-developed among women. What we need to do now is to replace men's constipated "economy" and all its attendant pain and deprivation with our abundance model. Continuing to use Earth's ecosystem as our blueprint, we need to make gift giving the standard method on this globe of converting energy into life.

First, facing the painful reality that for hundreds of years women have not respected femaleness or taken seriously anything associated with women, we must acknowledge the beauty, simplicity, and integrity of our basic way of being. Only then can we acknowledge its value and its incredibly transformative potential. Then we must believe in ourselves and our wisdom so fiercely that we begin *now* to practice gift giving on a larger scale than we ever dreamed would be required. Only immersion in it, only daily passionate and courageous experimentation with it by enough of us, can expand women's "economy" into a global reality.

But how do we break out of our transfixed minds, out of what Mary Ann Beall terms "the conservatism of inertia"? We are so embedded in the end game of this particular failure of the fathers called patriarchy that it seems impossible even to frame how we might begin to move out, how we might shift the blockage and start the flow of life again. Nevertheless I believe we must.

I say this in full awareness of the difficulty; I myself cannot see an inch around the corner of this world into the new. But I know that before any blockage disappears from the world, it must first disappear from our minds. Therefore, our initial challenge is to free the possibility of a women's world by making it real to ourselves. In the very act of *perceiving* and *feeling* ourselves as not trapped in men's exchange system, our energy will be unblocked and we can begin to break out. In fact, in some way not amenable to logic this change in our perceptions of what is possible is *in itself* our exodus.

To begin this exodus, we must imagine in broad terms how a nonexchange, gift-giving society might function. Trying to conjure such a society in detail will defeat us; we take tainted specifics into any imagined scenario. It is the *spirit* of a women's anarchic world we must imagine, the feeling of it. As visionaries dream, we must dream it sweepingly and unreservedly, anticipating it from our cherished principles and out of the desires of our hearts. Such a combined undertaking of intuition, passion, intelligence, and spirit, by changing our beliefs about what is possible, can free us to turn principle and desire into physical reality.

As a rough start, let us imagine a small town where the foremost desire of the citizenry is that everyone have everything necessary for health and joy. In order to achieve this, everyone in town *does what they want to do all the time,* loyal first to their own welfare while remaining fully aware of their critical interconnection with everyone else's. Under these circumstances chances are very good that, like a gigantic feminist potluck dinner, there will be enough of everything and all needs will be met with minimum time or effort spent by any one individual. It is only a matter of maintaining the flow. Functioning within the design of the natural world is always the simplest and most effective plan.

Nature's gift-giving design requires neither printing of money nor elaborate schemes for figuring out equivalent values. It necessitates no bureaucracy at all. What it does require is a deep love for life and all living things, for their individual and interconnected, interdependent rhythms, cycles, and energies. It requires a profound respect for oneself and faith that the springs of one's inner power loop through and among those of every other part of the universe, from the Milky Way's innumerable systems to the newborn kittens under the porch. It requires the fearless delight in ambiguity that comes from immersion in the present and that renders regulation and its requisite hierarchy not only irrelevant but odious.

Let us look at a young woman in this town who has recently arrived from a house of contemplation in the countryside without a definite idea of what she might enjoy doing now. She looks the community's situation over, perhaps consulting with others, to see what talents are in short supply and what the community needs. Finding a need that pleases her to turn her abilities to, she prepares to fill the gap.

Let us say that in this case the town needs another shoe-maker and that she becomes one, but only for as long as it gives her satisfaction. In this town, no one is expected to repeat the same creative act their entire adult lives unless they wish to.

Now that she is a shoemaker, she offers to make shoes. When anyone in the town needs shoes, they can now go to her workshop. She measures their feet, listens to their description of the style, color, material they prefer, and then makes shoes for them. They do not give her anything in return when they take those shoes home with them. But each of them also has some function (or functions) in the community from which she will benefit in turn, though perhaps not directly. Like them, whenever she needs something, all she needs to do is get it from the appropriate person or place.

In this town, I'm a dentist. Because my daughter makes wonderful shoes for me, I have no need to request shoes from any of the shoemakers in town. But when the new shoemaker needs her teeth repositioned, she nevertheless comes to me and I make braces for her. The wire for the braces is drawn by a local metal worker with perfect teeth (who will therefore probably never need my services) who, among other things, supplies toolheads to the woman in the community who crafts their wooden handles and makes them available to the rest of us.

Because everyone in town does what they enjoy all the time, when you, who are a poet, are having a professional haircut, you have the satisfaction of knowing that the woman cutting your hair isn't forced into doing it by the necessity of feeding her kids. You can be sure that she chooses to cut every hair she cuts because she likes and wants to. You can assume that she is there also because she enjoys sharing her gifts with others, because she understands her connection with them, aware that by contributing to their well-being she contributes to her own, and because she gets satisfaction from being an integral part of the life of the community.

Knowing the philosophy of the town you therefore know that if she didn't want to be cutting your hair, she wouldn't be. She would be doing something else. Or perhaps she would be doing nothing at all while she thought over what she would like to do, or while she merely contemplated the miracle of her existence.

No one in town keeps track of anyone else's activities—what they contribute to and take from community resources. It is assumed that everyone is a responsible person and perfectly able to regulate themselves. No one questions whether others are "working" enough or doing "their share" because no one presumes to understand better than the person in question what is meant by "working" and what "their share" might be. In fact, the word "work" cannot be found in the town's vocabulary. People simply do what they enjoy doing, and in the natural flow of things their every need is met.

In a society where everyone monitors themselves, no one presumes to know what anyone needs more than that person herself. Everyone's decisions are respected and honored. No one needs to give or to get permission. This society works because everyone respects everyone else, everyone cares about everyone else, everyone desires everyone else's happiness and health as much as they desire their own, and everyone understands the interconnectedness of their well-being with that of others and of all living things.

Artists make art, music, literature, drama for their own and the community's pleasure, and even many of those whose major focus is something else take their artistic talents seriously and use them for their own and others' delight. Philosophers think; they may also write and talk to one another and to anyone who comes by for that purpose. And many *do* come by because people here know that each of them is not only capable of important thinking but also of finding excitement and satisfaction in rigorous thought. Contemplatives meditate, and everybody else knows that they too can take however much time they want simply to drift and dream. No one automatically assumes that if someone sits quietly under a tree day after day for months or even years merely gazing out upon the scene that she is not "doing" anything useful or enriching for the community. Everyone knows that such times—and sometimes many such times of gathering one's life around oneself in silence—are crucial for every living thing and therefore for the ecology of all systems, including their own community. They know that whole lifetimes of such quiet inwardness are needed by some people.

People in this town, in fact, have found that they enjoy life more and are more likely to flourish when they model their cycles of energy upon the cycles of the natural world. During the winter, therefore, everyone slows down, sleeps more and eats less, spends more time in quiet reflection—retreats into a sort of physical and spiritual hibernation. When this gestation time gives way to germination in the spring, creative projects of all sorts burst forth. These blossom throughout the summer. Then in the fall, a great winding up of affairs takes place, a cleaning off of the slate so that winter's rest may be uncluttered, peaceful, and replenishing.

Because the value that above all others informs behavior in this town is that everyone have what they need for health and joy, and because there is no hierarchy to block the flow that provides this, there is no incentive to consume more than one needs. Neither is there any motivation to create artificial needs in others by inflating their desires; no propaganda, that is, dedicated to confusing and separating wants and needs— tricking people into believing that they *need* things when they really only *want* them to satisfy some externally engineered craving for superiority and control.

When needs are real, not manufactured and manipulated to provide a surplus for someone else, wants and needs are identical. In this town, therefore, people know what they truly need. Nobody hoards 40 pairs of shoes in their closet, for instance. They want shoes for the purpose shoes are needed— to beautify and protect their feet. The paradox is that when ownership is inconsequential, everyone feels as if they own enough.

In addition, since "things" are no longer believed to have the ability to fill up emotional emptiness—no ads persuade subliminally that certain perfumes or clothes or copiers guarantee intimacy or success—acquisitiveness is not mistaken for a shortcut to healing sickness of the soul.

For this and other reasons, the things the townspeople *do* own give them a great deal of satisfaction. They probably know personally most of the artisans and crafters, the artists and musicians who make what they use. Perhaps when they are considering owning something, they watch or assist its maker, always thereafter connecting her wares with her, her unique personality and gifts, and the personal connection they made with her. This closeness—in world view as well as in geography—to the actual maker and to the process of creation gives them an appreciation of the abilities that are required, causes them to honor the maker, her talent and labor, and to rejoice in the use of her creation. Their enjoyment of owning is in this way based upon entirely different criteria from those applied in exchange cultures.

In this society, because everyone's resources and talents are free to everyone else, not only do the gifts create a luxurious abundance for everyone of everything, but the members of the community also give one another the most precious gift of them all, an abundance of time. When they broke the tyranny of money in this town, they also ended the tyranny of Father time. They are now in control of their own lives and therefore they are in control of their own time. They feel no frenzy and are never "beside themselves." Instead they are always "inside themselves"—centered, alive, and experiencing themselves and others entirely in the present.

Controlling time, they do not allow time to force them on a mad march from this side of the day to that and off into the night where it reluctantly drops them, raw and unfinished, on their beds in the dark, They do not obey the clock here or live by its dictates. No one wears a wristwatch. They make no appointments. Healers, hairdressers, tailors, dentists—all who supply services to the community—are available during certain parts of certain days. When townspeople drop by then and find someone waiting before them, they stop and chat or sit and rest in the sunshine or read awhile in the library or plant some bulbs along the path or write a poem until their turn.

They know that having not just enough but an abundance of time is the cornerstone of their freedom.

I began this chapter with thoughts about time, Father time in particular, and how patriarchy manipulates time (which is both life and money) to create the scarcity necessary for oppression. But I have other, happier, more hopeful thoughts about time and its relation to plenty and peace.

I believe that for hundreds of thousands of years before patriarchy, time was "Mother time," perceived by humans as rich, abundant, and shimmeringly alive, loosely spiral, deeply and freely associative, sensorially satisfying, connective and restful—like dancing effortlessly in warm space among stars.

I long for a world governed again by womb time, warm time, free time, life time, gift time, Mother time. I long for a regulation-free world of self-governing people. I long for anarchy, and I believe there is only one way to have it.

It seems to me, as it has seemed to women before me, that only by combining our dreams, our energy, and our material and cultural resources in self-designed and self-created communities with one another can we hope to free enough time for enough women to restructure the hologram and make tyranny an anachronism.

That we will do this, that we will begin now, and that because this is our appointed hour we will succeed beyond our wildest expectations—this is the dream that sustains me.

THIRD WORLD DIVA GIRLS
POLITICS OF FEMINIST SOLIDARITY

BELL HOOKS

Coming from a Southern black working-class background, one
that remains a place I consider "home," I brought with me to
feminist movement a certain style of being that grows out of
black cultural traditions, like signifying. In the P.C. (politically
correct) world of feminism, signifying tends to provoke negative
feedback, as there has been so much emphasis on a notion of
friendship and sisterly bonding that is based on principles of
"seamless harmony." No one really speaks about the way in
which class privilege informs feminist notions of social
behaviors, setting standards that would govern all feminist
interaction. Often the "nice, nice" behavior privileged white
women had rebelled against in their relationships with white
men was transposed onto relations between white women and
women of color. It was a common occurrence at feminist events
for women of color to be accused of having said or done the
wrong thing (especially in confrontational encounters where
white women cried). Feelings of social awkwardness intensified
when black women found that our social and cultural codes
were neither respected nor known in most arenas of feminist
movement. Moving in academic circles, space often inhabited
by not too interesting smart people, a few intellectuals here and
there, and in artistic circles peopled mainly by folks from
privileged class backgrounds or the up and coming greedy folk
who are wanting as much as they can get for as little cost, I
often feel my class background. I struggle with the politics of
location—pondering what it means for individuals from

Copyright © 1990 by Gloria Watkins   265

underclass and poor backgrounds to enter social terrains
dominated by the ethos and values of privileged class experience.

Assimilation makes it very easy for those of us from
working-class backgrounds to acquire all the trappings that
make us seem like we come from privilege, especially if we are
college-educated and talk the right kinda talk (every time I try
to get clever and throw some vernacular black speech into my
essays, they are perceived as errors and "corrected"). Until
recently I felt that was alright, I'd been happy to keep that
speech for private spaces of my life. Now, I recognize how
disempowering it is for people from underprivileged backgrounds to consciously censor our speech so as to "fit better"
in settings where we are perceived as not belonging. It's easy
enough for folks of working-class backgrounds to step into the
world of privilege and realize we've made a mistake and to go
right back where we came from. There's a certain inverse status
to be had by retreating back into one's problematic roots
bearing the message that it's really better there, a more
righteous place (where you might not be fully understood but
where you at least have ties). Better to be there than to be with
those privileged "others" who don't have a clue where you're
coming from.

Faced with the choice of assimilating or returning to my
roots, I would catch the first train home. There is another more
difficult and less acceptable choice, that is to decide to maintain
values and traditions that emerge from a working-class
Southern black folk experience while incorporating meaningful
knowledge gained in other locations, even in those hierarchical
spaces of privilege. This choice makes a lot of people
uncomfortable. It makes it hard for them to put you in a neat
little category and keep you there. In a troubled voice, my
grandmother asked me the last time I saw her before she died,
"How can you live so far away from your people?" In her
mind, "my people" were not synonymous with a mass of black
people, but with particular black folks that one is connected to
by ties of blood and fellowship, the folks with whom we share
a history, the folks who talk our talk (the patois of our region),
who know our background and our ways. Her comment
silenced me. I felt a pain in my heart as though I had been
pierced by a sharp blade. My grandmother's words were like
that; they felt to me like little knives. My silent response was

tacit agreement that only misguided confused folks would live away from their people, their own.

I often think about my people, especially the womenfolk, the way we were raised, when I participate in feminist meetings and conferences. I am startled by the dichotomy between the rhetoric of sisterhood and the vicious way nice, nice, politically correct girls can deal with one another, do one another in, in ways far more brutal than I ever witnessed in shoot and cut black communities. With no body of feminist theory shaping her actions, my mama was determined to raise her daughters to value our connections to one another. Often she would "preach" on the subject of sisterhood. She would tell us about households of women, sisters usually, where they were always quarreling with one another, fighting, back-stabbing, working out some "serious" female rivalry. Mama made it clear there was gonna be none of that in our house. We were gonna learn how to respect and care for one another as women. It was not an easy task; her six girls were very different. Despite her efforts, now and then envy and little hatreds would surface, but for the most part we learned how to bond as sisters across our differences. We all had to become grown women to look back and see the importance of this early home training 'cause it takes being a woman to know just what we can do to wound one another. Now that we are grown black women, we can sit on the porch at family reunions and groove on the strength of our ties, that we are close despite differences of class, experiences, values, attitudes, sexual practice, education, and so on. At those times I remember mama's hard work, teaching us tolerance, compassion, generosity, sisterly ways to love one another.

Growing up in a household full of black females, it was impossible to cultivate any sense of being "exotic." 'Cause folk will laugh at you in a minute and tell you your shit is just common. This does not mean that within our collective family setting one's uniqueness was not acknowledged or valued—it was—but it did not give anybody the right to assert dominating power over other folks. Moving in and out of segregated black communities into predominantly white circles, I have observed how easy it is for individual black females deemed "special" to become exoticized, objectified in ways that support types of behavior that on home turf would just be considered out of control. Basically in white culture black women get to play two roles. We are either the bad girls, the "bitches," the madwomen (how many times have you heard folks say that a particularly assertive black woman is "crazy") seen as threatening and treated badly, or we are the supermamas, telling it like it is and taking care of everybody, spreading our special magic wherever we go. Certainly the most outstanding contemporary example of the way this particular image is codified in popular culture and commodified is the construction of Oprah Winfrey as beloved black "mammy" icon. Everyone tries to destroy the bad girls, who are constantly checked and kept in line, and the supermamas, who are sometimes "vamps" (witness the change in Oprah's image after she lost weight—take the 1989 Revlon ad, for example) on their off time, and get to do whatever they want; after all they are "special." Unless we remain ever vigilant about the ways representations of black womanhood (especially those of successful individuals) are appropriated and exploited in white supremacist capitalist patriarchy, we may find ourselves falling into traps set by the dominant culture.

In the past few years I have received greater attention for my feminist writing, more public recognition, and it makes me understand how easy it is to become self-enthralled, to believe that somehow one deserves to be set apart from others and in some cases to "lord it over them" especially those who seem to be less enlightened, less knowing. Now and then I have to "check" myself, look at my behavior and engage in some downhome critical feedback, or I have to check things with comrades to make sure I'm not getting out of line. It seems to me that one of the real danger zones is that space where one encounters black women/women of color outside home communities in predominantly white space. Often we meet in these arenas and treat each other as adversaries. Often in white settings we are like siblings fighting for the approval of "white parents" whose attention we now have. It's serious. Recently I attended a major conference on "Third World feminism" where I was one of several "women of color" invited to speak (I put that label in quotes because I rarely use it. I mostly identify myself as a black woman.) When I arrived at the conference, I was mingling and heard a number of participants talk about how they had come to see the fireworks, the negative confrontations that they were confident would take place

between women of color there. Their comments and
expectations reminded me of the many scenes fictively
portrayed in African-American literature where black people,
most often males, fight one another publicly, to entertain white
folks, making of themselves a dehumanized spectacle.

Fearful that just such a happening might take place at this
conference, I was particularly sensitive to whether or not I and
other women of color were relating to one another with
recognition, care, and respect, appreciating those women who
were engaged in a similar process. We were acting out an
ethical commitment to feminist solidarity that begins first with
our regarding one another with respect. Throughout most of
the conference, as though by collective mutual consent, Third
World feminist speakers maintained an impressive positive
interaction with one another even in situations where dialogue
was rigorously critical. Folks disagreed but not in ways that
were trashing of one another, silencing, or disabling. On the
final day of the conference, the sense of care was completely
disrupted by the actions of one Third World woman
scholar—behaving towards women of color, particularly black
women, in ways that were disrepectful (for example she was
always quick to point out perceived intellectual inadequacies in
their comments) setting the stage for the competitive spectacle
many of us had worked hard to avoid.

In the aftermath of this encounter, as folks were digging up
the bodies and trying to lay blame, I was chastised by many
people for having behaved in a positive respectful manner
towards this critic throughout the conference. She is a scholar
whose work I respect and from my cultural tradition an "elder"
whom I should respect on principle. I was surprised by all this
criticism directed at me for being "too nice." Suddenly the usual
bourgeois insistence on decorum that is a tedious norm in most
public academic settings was deemed non-applicable to this
situation and participants seemed really glad to have had an
occasion to witness the spectacle of one woman of color
"putting down," in very fancy ways, black women and black
people. Indeed the girl was out of control. Of course, in the
aftermath, she placed the blame on "us," more specifically me,
saying it was something I said that just upset her. Naturally she
could have decided to work out with me, in another setting,
whatever was bothering her, but dare I say "that would have

been too much, right." The point however is that this business
of blaming the black women for why "you have to abuse us":
sounds so familiar. Similarly, when black women challenge
racism within the feminist movement the dominant response is
one of hostility and anger. We are most often accused of
inviting this hostility whenever we confront to resist. Black
women resisting racism within feminist movement were trashed
and then told "You made me do it." Frequently white women
use this tactic to mask their complicity with racist structures of
domination. A parallel paradigm is often enacted in interactions
between powerful Third World elites and black Americans in
predominantly white settings. This was certainly taking place at
the conference, nor was it surprising that it was initiated by the
Third World woman scholar whose work has received the most
extensive legitimation in privileged white academic circles.

The current popularity of post-colonial discourse that
implicated solely the West often obscures the colonizing
relationship of the East in relation to Africa and other parts of
the Third World. We often forget that many Third World
nationals bring to this country the same kind of contempt and
disrespect for blackness that is most frequently associated with
white western imperialism. While it is true that many Third
World nationals who live in Britain and the United States
develop through theoretical and concrete experience knowledge
of how they are diminished by white western racism, that does
not always lead them to interrogate the way in which they enter
a racialized hierarchy where in the eyes of whites they
automatically have greater status and privilege than individuals
of African descent. Within feminist movement Third World
nationals often assume the role of mediator or interpreter,
explaining the "bad" black people to their white colleagues or
helping the "naive" black people to understand whiteness. For
example: in a women's studies program where the black woman
is seen by white colleagues as hostile and angry, white women
go to the Third World national and express concern saying,
"Why can't she be like you." She responds by saying: "In my
country we have a long tradition of diplomacy; therefore I am
in a better position to cope with the politics of difference."
Confident that she cares about the fate of her black colleague,
she then shares this conversation with her and offers advice.
Unwittingly assuming the role of go-between, of mediator, she

re-inscribes a colonial paradigm. Such an action disrupts all possibility that feminist political solidarity will be sustained between women of color cross-culturally. Certainly many of us left the conference on Third World feminism feeling as though a rift had been created between black women and Third World nations that remained unexamined and unresolved.

Weeks after the conference ended, I was still defending my position that it was important for women of color to treat one another with respect, even if that meant extending oneself beyond what might normally be seen as appropriate behavior. Audre Lorde makes this point again and again in her insightful essay "Eye to Eye," reminding readers that in patriarchal white supremacist context, this gesture, whether it be black women dealing with one another with respect, or women of color in general, is an act of political resistance. It is an indication that we reject and oppose the internalized racism that would have us work against one another.

Feminist solidarity between black women/women of color must be constructed in ways that enable us to engage in meaningful critique and rigorous intellectual exchange, without brutally trashing or negating one another. To maintain this commitment to solidarity we must be ever vigilant, living as we do in a society where internalized racism and sexism make it a norm for us to treat one another harshly and with disrespect. So often we are in settings with well-known Third World feminists, writers, thinkers who are able to be gracious to white women (even if they consider them racist) but who completely downgrade or dismiss the women of color in their midst, especially if they are perceived as not showing proper deference. I was told a very disheartening story recently that demonstrates the behavior I am describing. A little-known black woman scholar participated in a summer institute for college professors in an ivy league university setting. She went to the program already in conflict about her place within the academy. She was hoping to have a learning experience that would reassure her that her presence, her voice mattered. Bonding with another black woman participant helped. Together they attended a lunch for a celebrated black woman writer with white women feminists.

At one point her black woman friend was speaking, sharing ideas, when she was suddenly aggressively told by the famous

black woman writer to "shut up." This dismissal shocked and
wounded the black women. The white women present acted as
though they did not hear this comment and were apparently
completely enthralled with the writer. Feeling erased and
humiliated on two accounts, first that their presence was not
seen as important and second that it was not important that
their voices be heard, they left feeling all the more alienated.
Ironically, the well-known black woman writer may have
responded as she did because she is probably accustomed to
being the only black woman in such settings, the "voice of
authority," and she may have been threatened by the presence
of other voices with potentially equal authority based on shared
knowledge and experience. And these black women may not
have been giving her the same quality of "adoration" that white
women give. It's difficult to know what her experience was.
Often well-known black women find we are present in settings
where white audiences hang on our every word, and it may be
difficult to move into settings with people of color where this is
not taking place. Of course we need to interrogate "reverence,"
for idolization can be another way one is objectified and not
really taken seriously. For example: some famous black women
receive standing ovations even if they give talks that are
generally perceived to be lacking in power or uninteresting. In
such cases, audience feedback does not enable the speaker to
accurately interrogate her impact. While this incident describes
conflict between the well-known black woman and the
unknown audience and/or peers, where power was used to
hurt, often the opposite occurs.

Sometimes it is easier for well-known women, feminists, to
be most caring and protective towards individuals who do not
share the same status and are not in a position to claim the
limelight. In such circumstances a benevolent hierarchy surfaces,
where power-over becomes the occasion for the assertion of a
generosity, even as the hierarchy is maintained. Usually the
famous or well-known person accepts the assertion of
dominating power as part of her cue, as the rewards of status.
Within the United States this is part of what lets you know
you've made it, you're a star. One of the perks is that you are
often allowed to treat others badly, to be offensively
narcissistic, and though folks may hate you, they rarely call you
on your shit. In this culture we are socialized to believe that

really important people have a right to be self-absorbed, to think
their needs and concerns are more important than others'. This
may be especially problematic for black women who become
stars because there are so few of us in any arena. It is difficult
because stardom on a broad scale means simultaneous isolation
and fame. This then breeds fierce territorialism since we operate
within a social matrix that is always telling us that only one of
us can be at the top. Since many black women/women of color
have usually overcome grave obstacles to arrive at a point where
we receive recognition, we can easily have a false sense of
entitlement.

Working as we do in a capitalist environment, writers,
especially well-known women of color, are acutely aware that
white people represent the largest possible group of consumers
for the "products" we make. This can translate into: "they" are
the people who should receive attention and feedback. How
many times have we heard the woman of color feminist talk
privately about how much easier it is to relate to white women?
Often it is easier to make connections with white women
because they may be acting out of a kind of racial fear and guilt
that leads them to respond positively to negative behavior
and/or accept any kind of treatment to keep a friendship with a
woman of color. Often white women agree uncritically about all
issues pertaining to race when speaking with an individual black
woman/woman of color. This limited deference allows them to
feel anti-racist and yet be intellectually domineering and
condescending around their perceived area of expertise. Usually
a black woman involved in this kind of relationship is invested
to some degree in assimilationist white-identification leading her
to believe that this kind of tokenism will enhance her status. On
another level it may at times be easier for progressive white
women scholars to accept differences in perspectives among
themselves even as they and women of color police women of
color about women of color. While no woman of color wrote a
harsh unrelenting critique of Elizabeth Fox-Genovese's work
Within the Plantation Household, similar work by black women
scholars has been brutally trashed. How often does one hear
that the work of Rosalyn Terborg-Penn or Paula Giddings is
somehow less then adequate, not sufficiently academically
rigorous.

Writing about the way black women relate to one another,
about policing that leads us to vent an anger deeper than any we

let loose on other groups, Audre Lorde raises these questions:
"Why does that anger unleash itself more tellingly against
another Black woman at the least excuse? Why do I judge her
in a more critical light than any other, become enraged when
she does not measure up?" Black women may "police" one
another because many of us were raised in communities where
we were taught that it was a gesture of care to "oversee" each
other's actions. When many of us were growing up it was
common for elders to monitor the behavior of those younger.
Sometimes this monitoring was helpful, but it was often
repressive. In different locations such gestures may be less an
expression of care and more an attempt to maintain the status
quo. Black women often police one another to maintain
positions of power and authority, especially in professional
settings where it is easy to begin thinking of oneself as different
from and superior to other black women. Many of us are
repeatedly told by white "superiors" that we are different,
special. Internalizing this message can make it difficult to share
space with another black woman. Hooked on being the
"exception" this individual may need to expose or undermine
other black female peers, to show that she is better. This can
lead to horribly negative interactions in work settings. Since
black women (like almost everyone raised in this society) are
usually taught to believe competition is necessary for success,
it's easy for folks to feel particularly gratified by having
one-upped a colleague; that may be even more the case if that
person is another black woman/woman of color. Also we
appear more qualified and trustworthy in the eyes of white
people when we function as overseer, willing to crack the whip
harder on each other.

When asked to submit a list of ten names from which three
would be chosen to evaluate me in a tenure process, I felt most
wary of naming black women. I named only one, whom I felt
could be trusted not to judge my work unfairly, which is not to
say that I thought she would only make positive comments. My
wariness is a response to negative encounters with black
women peers, who often see differing opinions and lifestyles as
reason to viciously trash, excommunicate, and ostracize other
black women. This seems ironic since most black women,
especially those of us who are reluctant to advocate feminism,
often chauvinistically insist that we have had this tradition of

mutual support and closeness and did not need feminist
thinking to create such ties. There is some truth in this
assertion, although it is usually forgotten that these ties often
emerge in a homogeneous setting. Many of us learned how to
bond with females who were like us, who shared similar values
and experiences. Often these close-knit groups used the power
of their intimacy to trash women outside the chosen circle.

Like all women within patriarchal society, black women have
to develop oppositionally feminist strategies that will indeed
enable us to accept, respect, and even honor peers who are not
like us. We must understand that through active work, such
solidarity should lead to the formation of different strategies
that make productive communication possible. Many women
who are high achievers have learned the rugged individualist
model of success. This is true of many black women. They may
feel that any gestures of bonding with other women threaten
that success. Sometimes black women in positions of authority
and power impose internalized racist assumptions on those
folks whom they have power to influence. They may share
downgrading messages that they once received and used as a
challenge, a goad for further productivity. Unfortunately, that is
not the way most of us respond to negative feedback. In Nikki
Giovanni's "Woman Poem" she has a line that reads, "I ain't
shit, you must be lower than that to care." Confronting
internalized racism and sexism must be a central agenda for
both feminist and black liberation struggle. An important stage
in this process is developing skills that enable us to look at
ourselves critically and observe how we behave towards others.

Recently, at a dinner where a well-known black woman
writer was present, I said in conversation with the person I was
sitting next to that I had sent a novel to several publishers and
it had been rejected. The famous black woman writer (whose
work has inspired and excited me both as a writer and a
teacher) interrupted the conversation she was having to say
loudly to me, in a hostile tone of voice, "Probably it's just a bad
novel." Since she had been behaving all evening as though no
one had anything to say worth listening to but herself, I was
not surprised by this not-so-subtle attack. I was grateful,
however, that I had not met her at a time in life when I was
longing for a black woman mentor, for affirmation that I
should continue writing. No interaction between us indicated

that she was familiar with my writing. I pondered how damaging this negative feedback could have been for a fledgling writer. Her hostility saddened me. Though we were in a group that was predominantly white and were hearing many of the usual comments made in such settings (some of them naively racist), she did not direct critical comments to these speakers. In fact she was most gracious to the white men present. Audre Lorde's question "Why does that anger unleash itself most tellingly against another black woman at the least excuse" came to mind. To answer that question we would need to critically examine the dynamics of black female interaction from a feminist perspective.

When I later spoke with other guests, who had again relished this spectacle, I was told that I must have done something to invite such hostility. Their need to absolve the well-known writer of responsibility for her actions seemed linked to the longing to maintain their idealized notions of powerful black womanhood. When you are well-known, surrounded by fans and adoring followers, few people offer critical feedback. Most folks tend to graciously overlook abusive and dominating behavior by famous "feminist" thinkers, even if our work is based on a critique of domination. Feminist analysis of the way patriarchy manifests itself in everyday life highlights the subtle and seemingly trivial incidents where men exercise coercive control and domination over women as important arenas of political struggle. Individual men changing their dominating behavior serve as necessary examples for their peers. Often women engaged with feminism critique behavior in men that is acceptable to them when done by women. Much of the dominating and abusive behavior that happens in feminist circles where there are gradations of power would be immediately challenged and critiqued if the perpetrators were men.

As feminist movement has progressed and individuals have even begun to talk about post-feminism, many women are forgetting one of the most important dimensions of feminist struggle, the focus on feminist ethics. That focus was rooted in the recognition of the way in which patriarchal sexist thinking distorts women's relation to one another. Commitment to feminist politics was a corrective process. Consciousness-raising groups were once settings where women engaged in dialectical exchange about these issues. Nowadays there is a tendency to

act as though it is no longer important how women deal with
one another. In the place of the community-based
consciousness-raising group, we have feminist stars who are
leaders in that they shape feminist thinking and action. Yet
these women are often the least willing to participate in sessions
where their feminist practice might be interrogated. The
emergence of a feminist star system, one that has concrete
material rewards (royalties from book publication, paid
lectures, high-paying jobs, etc.), means that women jockey for
power within feminist circles, and women of color are most
often competing with one another.

When feminism becomes a means for opportunistic self-
advancement, it means that prominent spokespeople can easily
lose sight of the need to share critical feminist thought with
masses of people. Much of the small amount of feminist writing
done by women of color is directed towards a white audience.
Thus it comes as no surprise that we are not working as hard
as we should be to spread the feminist message to large groups
of people of color. It also means that we are rarely engaged in
the types of mentor relationships that would produce a new
group of feminist thinkers and theorists who would be women
and men of color. Those who are deeply committed to feminist
struggle must be ever mindful of the reality that this
commitment is actively manifested when we share knowledge,
resources, and strategies for change with those who have the
least access.

Working with a brilliant group of young women of color
who are struggling to deepen their critical consciousness, to
learn ways to be politically active, who are striving to develop
intellectually, I lovingly called them "Third World diva girls," a
title which gives expression to their uniqueness and importance.
We use the word "girl" in that way it is used in traditional
African-American culture as a sign of intense womanist
affection, not as a put down. It is an evocation to and of
intimacy, based on proud recognition of gender. And we use the
term "diva" because of the special role women have had in
opera.* It both names specialness but carries with it the
connotation of being just a bit out of control, stuck on oneself.

---

* See Catherine Clement, *Opera: The Undoing of Women* (Minneapolis:
University of Minnesota Press, 1988).

We wanted it as a reminder of how easy it is to imagine we are
superior to others and therefore deserve special treatment or
have the right to dominate.

I began to think about writing this essay when one of the
diva girls called me weeping wildly after she had been at a talk
given by a prominent black feminist thinker. The audience was
predominantly white. During the question period she spoke
even though she was terrified to do so in a public setting. The
speaker ridiculed and dismissed her words. She felt crushed. On
another day yet another diva girl called to share a painful
interaction between herself and a black Third World national
whose scholarship is grounded in analysis of the experiences of
African-American women. All her attempts to critically engage
this scholar, especially in encounters where she seeks
recognition of their different cultural standpoint, are heard as
attempts to usurp power and are rebuffed. She too left this
encounter feeling crushed, wondering why prominent black
women scholars of all ethnicities so rarely mentor black women
students. How can prominent women of color engaged in
feminist movement be surprised that there is so little
participation in the movement by folks like us if we behave as
though feminism is a turf we have conquered, a field of power
where we can maintain authority and presence, and reap
rewards only if there are a few of us present, if we are always a
rare commodity.

A clear distinction must be made between receiving the
respect and recognition exceptional women of color active in
feminist movement rightfully deserve and the misuse of power
and presence. Speaking about this in relation to black women,
Lorde reminds us:

> Often we give lip service to the idea of mutual support
> between black women because we have not yet crossed
> the barriers to these possibilities, nor fully expressed the
> angers and fears that keep us from realizing the power of
> a real Black sisterhood. And to acknowledge our dreams
> is to sometimes acknowledge the distance between those
> dreams and our present situation.

If "Third World diva girls," whoever they may be—emerging
women writers and thinkers or the already famous and
well-known—want to know whether we are cultivating the

kind of sisterhood based on feminist solidarity and informed by
feminist ethics, we must look and listen, observe and hear the
response around us. We must engage in ongoing self-critique.
When I give a talk and no one raises challenging questions,
then I consider how I've represented myself. When I'm doing
talks and folks tell me that I'm not the way they thought I
would be, I ask them to explain. Sometimes they want to let me
know that I'm not power tripping like the way they thought I
might, since so many of us do. I am especially gratified when I
receive a letter that clarifies how I am perceived. One came
recently. After hearing me speak at the university where she
works, a black woman listener wrote these words:

> Your lecture raised my consciousness of the world in
> which we live to a much higher level. I was so deeply
> touched by your words and your obvious "black pride."
> I have had no female or male black role models. . . So
> hearing you speak was monumental. . . I don't see you
> as the "celebrity figure" you are but as a true sister who
> knows her roots and herself and is proud of it. I believe
> you have appeared in my life for a reason.

This letter inspires me, strengthens the conviction that
feminist solidarity has reality and substance.

Sometimes I act like a diva girl in the worst way—that is
narcissistic, self-focused, or wanting others to serve me. Home
with my family recently I was wanting attention and my sisters
let me know it was getting out of hand. Tired from intense
months of teaching, writing, and being on the lecture circuit, I
did indeed want to be pampered and waited on, to get that
special care the divas of our imagination merit because they are
so unique. My sisters were willing to give that care, to affirm
my specialness, even as they let me know there were limits,
boundaries beyond which I would be placing them in the role
of subordinates. The difficulties women of color face in a white
supremacist capitalist patriarchy are intense. We can only
respect and admire all among us who manage to resist, who
become self-actualized. We need to cherish and honor those
among us who emerge as "stars," not because they are above us
but because they share with us light that guides, providing
insight and necessary wisdom. To be a star, a diva, carries with
it responsibility; one must learn to know and respect

YOU CAN KILL THE SPIRIT[*]

AN ARGUMENT AGAINST THE SELLING OF OUR SOULS

LAURA BURROWS

For a number of years, I have been noticing what is to me, an increasingly disturbing trend within the women's community: the trading of money, and quite a bit of it, for spiritual help, information, training, and tools. The amount of money that some are willing to pay indicates that there is a market for "getting spiritual" and that there is a growing awareness of the spiritual in many of us. We recognize the centuries-long denial of a deep and elemental part of ourselves. We recognize a need to touch that part of ourselves in order to heal and become whole. This is good. However, it has never felt right to me that money is being made off of our search for something that has been stolen from us. To me, the marketing of spirituality feels contrary to the woman- and earth-centered world view of Wicca and other Old Religions. Being a Libra and wanting to be fair, I still go back and forth on this issue, but my gut reaction has remained constant. I make no claim to having an answer. Issues of money are complex and emotionally charged. I merely offer my thoughts as food for the thoughts of others.

I have heard both European traditionalists and American Native elders say that the trading of money for spiritual help is not correct, nor even necessary. Doreen Valiente says in her book *Natural Magic*:

---

[*] This title is paraphrased from the song "Like a Mountain" by Naomi Littlebear.

Copyright © 1993 by Laura Burrows

Magic . . . is all around us . . . [A]ll we need is that
ability to see and understand. We do not need to join
high-sounding "secret" fraternities [sic], swear frightful
oaths and pay fees in order to become magicians . . . still
less do we need to buy a load of expensive paraphernalia
such as ceremonial swords, wands and so on, which can
be seen advertised for sale today.[*]

She goes on to quote an old Wiccan saying, "The adept owns
nothing yet has the use of everything."

The concept of money and the trading of money have been
used against women and the earth for a long, long time. In
Western Europe, the development of a profit consciousness or
motivation (land-for-gain as opposed to the feudal
consciousness of land-for-use) has been a major factor in the
loss of our connection to the land, as well as the loss of much
of our joyous, free, and life-loving women's heritage.[**] This
developing profit-consciousness inspired such acts as the
expropriation and enclosure of common land, the rise of
professionalism with its buying and selling of knowledge, and
the attacks on traditional healers and midwives.[***] Profit was
used as both justification and rationale for an all-out physical
and psychic attack upon the independent and strongly
decentralized pagan culture. This war—this persecution of
Witches and of women as Witches—went on for hundreds of
years, peaking in the sixteenth and seventeenth centuries, the
Burning Times. The escalation of persecution coincides
chillingly with the early voyages of Spain and other European
powers to the Americas in search of gold and silver.

Until the time of Columbus, two thirds of European gold
came slowly—by land and through numerous middle-man
merchants—from the west coast of Africa. As Jack Weatherford
documents in his book *Indian Givers*, "The Europeans sought
desperately for ways to increase the trickle of gold that flowed
up so slowly from the Gold Coast. . . . Every step in the
discovery and conquest of America was spurred on by a greed

---

[*] Doreen Valiente, *Natural Magic* (Cusher, WA: Phoenix Publishing, Inc., 1985), p. 14.

[**] Starhawk, *Dreaming the Dark: Magic, Sex, and Politics* (Boston, Beacon Press, 1982), pp. 183–219.

[***] Barbara Ehrenreich and Deidre English, *Witches, Midwives, & Nurses: A History of Women Healers* (New York: The Feminist Press, 1973).

for gold that overshadowed the quest for silver, spices or souls."* Columbus was after gold but found little. Following him were Hernando Cortes and his conquistadores, then Francisco Pizarro and Hernando de Soto. Between 1500 and 1600, many American Natives were killed, their nations and cultures destroyed in the European search for gold.

When there was no more gold, the Europeans went after silver. Weatherford says,

> Never before in the history of the world had so much silver money been in the hands of so many people. . . . Now for the first time people had massive amounts of silver and gold. Quickly and inexorably the traditional mercantile system of Europe changed. With so much money, the old system mutated into a true money economy. . . . Precious metals from America superseded land as the basis for wealth, power, and prestige.**

I have heard women say that money is a power like any other, a tool that can be used for good or ill, depending on our choices. They say that we must not be afraid to take this power that has been used against us and turn it around—use it to free ourselves. But I wonder who among us is clear enough to be able to dismantle the master's house with the master's tools.*** I am not convinced that it is possible.

Weatherford sees a money economy as being tainted from the start:

> Europe . . . paid the price for its greed. Spain, the greatest beneficiary of [American] silver, soon bankrupted itself. By 1700, Spain was reduced to a minor power of neither economic nor political importance . . . The silver of [the Americas] helped to destroy Spain almost as though it carried with it a curse written in the blood of the legions of Indians who died to supply it. And the curse did not stop with Spain. The money passed into the hands of the greedy Dutch, British and French traders and pirates. . . . They used it to build large, modern

---

* Jack Weatherford, *Indian Givers: How the Indians of the Americas Transformed the World* (New York: Fawcett Columbine, 1988), p. 6.
** Weatherford, pp. 13–15.
*** This phraseology is Audre Lorde's.

navies and armies that colonized almost every country in
the rest of the world. . . . But they also fought with each
other in war after war. By the middle of the twentieth
century, these empires too had fallen. . . . By then,
economic power on the European continent had shifted
to Germany and the Soviet Union, the two nations that
had participated in and profited the least from the blood
money of (America).[*]

The search for material wealth and profit has been the
motivating factor behind the near destruction of our entire
planet, not to mention the unnecessary suffering and misery of
every living being. Given this energy attached for millennia to
the trading of money, I again wonder who among us is clear
enough to be able to use money for good?

▲ ▲ ▲

The trading of money for spirit troubles me. Now that circles
of women are re-forming, we present a very old and therefore
"revolutionary" world view, in which the earth is respected,
everything is possessed of spirit, women are divine, and all have
equal voice, equal access to power, and equal access to the
abundance of the universe. The trading of money sets up an
immediate hierarchy and scarcity consciousness. It reinforces a
belief in "experts"—that someone else knows more, is worth
more, has something that we don't have. I think we need to be
acting against this programming. We need to seek out those
who share power and information freely, who do not accept
expert status and who make themselves ultimately unnecessary
by helping us to unblock our own awareness and find all that
we need within ourselves.

The trading of money seems to perpetuate every "ism"
that I can think of—race, class, sex, age, sexual preference,
religion. . . . After all, who in this country has control of and
the most access to money? Rich white men. Should spiritual
help and training be available only to those who can afford
the high cost of workshops, classes, readings, and "tools of
the trade"? An earth-centered spirituality would, by definition,

[*] Weatherford, pp. 19–20.

be like the earth—who gives in abundance to all, asking in return only life, love, and respect. It is told that in the ancient days of Western Europe, coveners worshipped sky-clad (weather permitting). One purpose behind this custom was to eliminate class barriers between the celebrants. All women were to be recognized as Goddess.

It seems to be that the power of money is the ultimate illusion in our Anglo-European-centered culture. Money is not power! Money is a symbol for power and can represent, at best, the ability we all have within us to meet our needs for physical survival, safety, and comfort.

It also seems to me that we have been intentionally and seriously misled. We have been taught that money is our only tool, our only way of relating to the material world. We have been led to believe that money will meet all our needs and ensure our survival. We have been taught to rely on money alone for our food, shelter, clothing, comfort, and pleasure. Because of this, we simply are not free. We have not been taught how to truly survive. When we rely on money, we limit our creativity and freedom.

I have heard women say that our spiritual teachers and leaders are valuable and honored members of our women's communities and that we must, therefore, support them financially in order that they can be free to perform their services. That a leader or teacher should be honored, respected, and valued is beyond question. But could there not be ways of doing this that do not involve the trading of money?

I realize that we live in a world operating on a market economy—we must pay for housing; we cannot all grow our own food or make our own clothes or live on love—but we could put some energy into moving in that direction. If you want to learn something that another woman knows, think of a way to be useful to her and propose an exchange. (In older days, such an arrangement was known as an apprenticeship.) Get together with friends and form study groups to share skills and information. If you perceive the need for a magical tool, try making it yourself. The power of a tool comes from the energy of the maker as well as the user. To make our own tools in a meditative and intentional way, no matter how seemingly simple or crude, is the best way to have them be useful to us.

One called to teach or be of service can find ways to do so in any situation. It is not necessary to form a class, do a workshop, give a lecture—because it is difficult to put a monetary value on learning (or, really, on most things). One called to teach must want to teach in the most effective manner: by example. If one is to teach the truth, then one must have access to one's own wellspring and be able to draw power from the source within, replenish oneself from within, and respond to need from that deep, all-encompassing compassion and love that exists inside all of us. I am a teacher any time a woman recognizes me as such. My reward is like that of the earth: respect and the furtherance of life and love.

It is often said in Wicca that all time is now. If that is true—that this moment is the most important because it is the only one we can count on—then it is also true that the way of doing something is more important than any end result. I wish that we could move away from a money economy and toward something else. A gift economy, which is in keeping with the nature of women and of the earth and which encourages creativity and thinking of others, is one idea. Many women are heading in this direction, and I am glad to see it. One example is a women's community in Texas called Stonehaven Ranch. In their statement of philosophy, they say, "We can counter or dissolve the greed, ego-mania and fear that are part of the competitive exchange system. A world where five billion people freely satisfy each other's needs has more probability of success and happiness than a world where everyone is trying to be me first at the expense of others."* Makes sense to me. Let us all try to imagine such a world and then make it so.

---

* "Stonehaven: An Attempt to Preach What We Practice," in *HOT WIRE: A Journal of Women's Music & Culture*, vol 4, no 3 (July 1988), p. 59; another version of this article appears in this book on pages 293-296

LESBIAN ECONOMY

A FIRST STEP

JANET MILLER

The following idea was sparked by a talk given at the Mountain Moving Coffeehouse for Womyn and Children in Chicago by Sarah Hoagland, author of *Lesbian Ethics*. In a group discussion following her talk, she challenged us to come up with some concrete ways to create a lesbian economy. I couldn't come up with any ideas on the spot, but a few months later thought of a limited start toward this goal. Rather than providing a solution to jump to, it assumes the limits of today's world, namely that right now, lesbians are not in a position to be able to leave the patriarchal economy completely behind. What follows is a realistic, if small, first step, not the end solution.

The idea requires a conceptual jump from the way we are used to thinking about property.

Lesbians with excess goods would bring them to some central space, preferably one already near lesbian traffic. Any lesbian who wanted anything at this space would take it. The goods ordinarily wasted by lesbians who had no use for them would now be funneled back to benefit other lesbians.

Let me start by talking about how goods would get into the space. As a middle-class lesbian, I have access to goods I don't need, or don't want. Only with the most valuable of these do I actively search for someone in the community who can use them. The time and energy expended to find someone who wants, say a pair of shoes, brand new, bought on sale (and therefore unreturnable), but too small, is not worth it, and I

Copyright © 1993 by Janet Miller

287

usually just donate such items to patriarchal charities, or eventually throw them away. Many lesbians have access to excess goods through their jobs: gifts from vendors, overruns, discarded or obsolete products, scrap. Often a vegetarian gets an "xmas" turkey from her boss, or a lesbian with a scent-sensitive friend gets a free bottle of perfumed soap with her gas fill-up. Aunt Beatrice sends her annual holiday gift, a brand-new laminated plaque, featuring a flower-framed religious tract. A lesbian's neighbor moves, leaving behind usable furniture, another lesbian changes weight and doesn't need some of her clothes of the old size...the important point to note here is that all of these goods are *excess*, goods that normally would not be used by the donor/source. NO lesbian should "sacrifice," or give up goods to which she has any attachment. The foundation upon which this system is based is the assumption that the lesbians who are the source of the goods will have absolutely no concern about what happens to them.

Once the goods are in the space, let me explain how they will benefit lesbians. Any lesbian would be free to come to the space, and take anything/everything she likes. This would not be based on need. The idea is not to establish a "charity," or necessarily a funneling of goods from one economic group to another (although this would probably happen). Rather this is a recycling of wasted goods back to other lesbians who can benefit from them. Any lesbian would take any and all things that interest her, regardless of her income. In fact, all lesbians would be encouraged to take everything they could possibly be inclined to want. Taking would not be based on reciprocity; no donations of time or money, or assumptions of future donations, would be necessary to receive goods. The premise is that any movement of the goods that benefits a lesbian is positive. If a lesbian gets something at the space she would ordinarily buy in the patriarchy, and instead spends the money on the community, lesbians benefit. If a lesbian obtains goods she needs, and usually could not afford to buy, that benefits a lesbian. If a lesbian who has always spent money each holiday season to buy her grandmother a gift gives her grandmother something she has obtained free from this lesbian space (that another lesbian brought in when Aunt Beatrice sent it to her), then she saves money for herself, and this benefits a lesbian. If a lesbian takes something and then sells it, she receives the money, and this also benefits a lesbian. The only limit on the goods flowing out would be to assure that the flow benefits lesbians.

As far as logistics go, it would take relatively little to try this first step, which is providing a space near or at the site of other lesbian activities. The only restrictions needed are those that assure that lesbians are the only people who know about it. It is imperative not to publicize it, so that straight womyn don't use the space to obtain goods for themselves or their men, and to avoid sabotage of the process by men or their sympathizers, either on an individual or governmental level. The only "rules" about the space that I thought would be helpful are housekeeping suggestions:

1. Respect the organization of the goods, and put things away that you don't want so that other lesbians can easily find them.

2. Don't bring in items that will attract bugs. Wash dishes and securely package foodstuffs.

3. Don't donate problem items. Accepting perishable goods would be labor-producing, as a lesbian would have to cull spoiled foodstuffs frequently. Goods that are larger than can fit into the average car may become cost-of-disposal liabilities if no one takes them. For these two categories of goods, I recommend posting these items on a bulletin board. These goods can then be obtained directly from the source lesbians.

Politically, this space benefits all lesbians, as a group, a community, regardless of any other characteristics. It in no way benefits men. It is not vulnerable to men's typical methods of appropriating womyn's goods and money, because it is not based on money or on reciprocity. No "membership" records mean nothing on paper for men to use to track down lesbians who have benefitted. It can be done within lesbians' current economic realities, and is not dependent on any other political or economic progress being made first. The risk involved should not be a deterrent to many lesbians, since the goods given to the space are already excess, by definition, and there is no cost tied to taking goods.

This plan does have some drawbacks, and operates under some restrictions. One restriction is that it is based on an assumption of excess, which will not always be accurate, particularly outside the US.

The idea is based on every lesbian acting from a sense of entitlement—knowing that she deserves anything and everything in the space—and should therefore take it if she wants it. A friend of mine (Mary Hauck) pointed out that different lesbians, due to differences in class backgrounds and other factors, have differing levels of sense of entitlement. It may be difficult to "educate" lesbians enough to get them to freely take from the space. If a lesbian doesn't take something she wants so that it will be available for another lesbian "who deserves it more," that other lesbian might never materialize, causing the good to be discarded. On the other hand, a lesbian who "needed" it less but who had a larger sense of entitlement might choose to take it. (This is not meant to imply that I believe that larger senses of entitlement are always paired with lesbians of more class privilege; "middle-class" guilt can cause a middle-class lesbian to have a very small sense of entitlement, and some lesbians who have always been poor can have large senses of entitlement. There is no rule that applies to all lesbians.) The result would be that lesbians with larger senses of entitlement would benefit disproportionately.

One side effect of the plan, as Sarah Hoagland pointed out to me, is that lesbians may learn the value of things that come free, that you can get something without spending money, and it can still have worth.

Thinking about this idea, one year I gathered some jewelry and ritual objects that I had not used and were no longer necessary for me, and took them to the Michigan Womyn's Music Festival. I put them in a basket, with a sign reading "Gifts—Feel Free to Take!" and left the full basket in the meditation circle space. When I came back the next day, sure enough, womyn had taken all the things I'd left, and others had left some stones, driftwood, and other gifts to pass on. It felt *great*!

Perhaps a regular give-away area could be set up at festivals, in addition to the occasional "barter" area. It would be great if we could begin with this first step, taking advantage of festival woman-only space. I have helped organize this at one festival

already and am willing to discuss details with any festival
organizers who are interested.

THE PHILOSOPHY BEHIND STONEHAVEN

AN ATTEMPT TO PREACH WHAT WE PRACTICE

GENEVIEVE VAUGHAN

Stonehaven is a meeting place for peace and justice and feminist groups. The big house is alcohol-free, to provide a space where thoughts and feelings are clear and we can know and respect ourselves without alteration. The groups that come here are asked to network with each other whenever possible and inform themselves about each others' ideas and purposes.

Founded in 1985, Stonehaven is based on the idea that women's nurturing is a basic value system that provides an alternative to the prevailing value system in U.S. culture. The present value system has led—through competition, manipulation, exploitation, and self aggrandizement—to war, famine, and the threat of nuclear annihilation. We feel that because values motivate behavior, by stimulating a better value system, recognizing it, and promoting it as a viable solution, we can increase the momentum of a natural trend toward its use.

Women's nurturing is free gift-giving and does not require an equivalent repayment. Stonehaven is an attempt to extend this principle outside the family and show that in fact gift giving, concentrating on satisfying needs rather than on receiving payment, is a normal, healthy way for human beings to behave. If we can overcome the embarrassment giving and receiving sometimes engenders, and keep it free from the taint of bribery or blackmail, we find that giving and receiving are pleasurable and satisfying. We can counter or dissolve the greed, ego-mania,

Copyright © 1987 by Genevieve Vaughan

and fear that are part of the competitive exchange system. A world in which five billion people freely satisfy each others' needs has more probability of success and happiness than a world in which everyone is trying to be me-first at the others' expense.

The gift-giving principle may be called a gift economy, as opposed to the exchange economy. *Gift economy* means the gift goes from one person to another without being paid back—it just goes on and on. When we receive kindness, it is easier to be kind.

At Stonehaven we are not to be repaid even for food, or *especially* for food, because food is representative of women's nurturance, mother's milk—which is free—and is stronger, more empowering because it is free. Just think if babies had to pay back their mothers' milk. We *need* interdependence. Being mammals means not only that we have mammaries but that we have mothers. Snakes don't have mother–child relationships.

The exchange economy denies nurturing and dependence and therefore mothering. It's as if society wants to make us look like reptiles instead of like mammals—"every man for himself." But we are all reciprocally dependent, even if we deny it: The salary you earn and say gives you independence only allows you to have access to dependence on others—for example, on those who produce and sell food. Then what you pay them allows them access to dependence on others—for example, on producers and sellers of clothes. They are dependent on you and others like you for earning your salary; otherwise they would have no one to sell their products to, and so on.

By refocusing, you can see that what is usually called independence in the exchange economy is actually multiple and extensive dependence. In the exchange economy, independence has been given a positive connotation and dependence a negative one, so people do not usually view dependence/independence from the Stonehaven perspective. By concentrating on our own property, egos, whatever, we block our natural altruism and impulses by which we would satisfy others' needs. We overvalue independence, and we devalue and look away from dependence.

In mother–child relationships, dependence is evident and cannot be covered over. Nurturing and the satisfaction of needs (free gift-giving of milk, food, caretaking) produce bonds that enhance life and growth. This kind of altruistic behavior, when it coexists with the exchange economy (which requires repayment and centers on the independent ego), is necessarily in conflict with it. The two are opposites, and the me-first, competitive behavior inherent in the exchange economy succeeds in hiding the altruistic behavior and denigrating it. It does not succeed in abolishing it, for altruism—nurturing and interdependence—is essential to human life. Unfortunately it often does succeed in co-opting it. By denying the importance of their dependence on others and of the nurturing they receive, many people make it seem that their power comes from themselves alone and independently. This makes the others, who have been co-opted or used, seem powerless and, in fact, become powerless.

So at Stonehaven we don't have people pay us. We ask them to personally give the price they would have paid us to somebody else who either uses it or passes it on. We're doing this to foster and recognize a value system that does not lead to war and famine.

We as women are learning to respect gift giving, both as a principle and in ourselves, and to stop putting ourselves down for doing it. We are often blind to our own generosity because in fact generosity is best when it isn't pointed out. When it is pointed out, it sometimes stops being a virtue and starts being an ego trip. We tend to put down our own generosity in favor of the mindless issue of exchange that rules our society. This wrong rule says that we may only give in order to get something back.

Exchange comes from the patriarchal economic mode, which also retains the power of definition. It defines itself as the norm and teaches us to denigrate gift giving as not normal because gift giving is its contradiction and can undermine the structures of greed. The female mode that gives in order to satisfy a need fosters a knowledge of others' needs and creates bonds of trust and reciprocal support, on a practical plane beyond definition.

▲ ▲ ▲

We live in a world of immense injustices with which most of the middle class in the United States never come into contact.

The news media does not inform us of what is happening to poor people either inside or outside our country's borders. This artificial, manipulated blindness is like the denial of an addiction: it permits it to keep happening. Our government, together with big profit-motive business, creates havoc worldwide—both economically and militarily destroying the poor and those who want to self-determine. People often do not know, or do not grasp, or do not really believe this—but it is true. Perhaps we do not believe it because we feel powerless to stop it.

Many of the people who come to Stonehaven are overcoming their feeling of powerlessness and are trying to stop it. In their experience and work, and because they care a lot, they have acquired information about the injustices that are happening.

The philosophy of Stonehaven is that altruism—other-orientation—is good and normal, and that the altruism of the people in the United States is being thwarted and stymied also because our government makes others inaccessible to our knowledge and to our other-interest, and then exploits and kills them. The reason our government, big business, the system, does this is that it is based on the me-first, short-term profit motive, and the profit motive is based on the exchange economy.

Stonehaven is an attempt to foster something that is not based on the profit motive or the exchange economy. The gift economy is just the opposite and is already widespread throughout the world—as widespread as mothers—though it has been unrecognized even by those who are engaging in it, including ourselves. By informing ourselves and validating our altruism, we are trying to promote and empower a motive that is an alternative to the me-first profit motive and already lies ready and waiting to emerge in the human spirit, and in women's free labor and daily practice.

The experiment of Stonehaven is to give to each, according to her ability, the ability to give again. So we ask women who come to Stonehaven to seek out someone and give him or her or some organization a gift. The gift should be something that the receivers can use to satisfy a need (or that they can pass on if they do not need it), on a sliding scale according to what the visitors would have paid at Stonehaven. The motto of the gift economy is—if you don't need it, then "Pass it on, no backfire."

We trust that by stimulating this alternative way of doing things we are taking a step toward a world based on women's nurturing altruism rather than patriarchal me-first egotism, in which what goes around will come around whenever anyone needs it.

The objection has arisen that people may take advantage of us if we give away things free. We hope to be able to defend ourselves against this if anything really negative comes up. But we trust in the capacity of all people to respond to trust responsibly and to self-regulate so as not to exploit us. If people keep the money they save here instead of giving it again, this means that in their estimation they need it themselves more than others, or that our society's habitual rules of etiquette have triumphed once again over a gesture of the heart. We hope that most, if not all, of our visitors will take the risk of trying this new, small, practical thing for peace.

1994 UPDATE

Stonehaven continues to be a project of the Foundation for a Compassionate Society, an organization that includes a number of projects and is based on the values expressed in this article. Over the years, literally hundreds of groups have used Stonehaven (including the Foundation, which has used it for innovative projects of its own, such as the Feminist Media Pool). A series of Goddess workshops has recently been initiated, including one that was videotaped by the women working on the Foundation's "Let the People Speak" and WATER (Women's Alternative Technological and Electronic Resources) video projects. Economic difficulties have made it necessary to charge those who can pay a small amount. However, Stonehaven's fees are generally very low, and many workshops and weekends are still given on the gift economy basis.

AUNT LUTE BOOKS

THEORY AND PRACTICE IN ACTION

JAMIE LEE EVANS
WITH INPUT FROM THE STAFF AT AUNT LUTE BOOKS

As I sit down to tell you the story of Aunt Lute Books, I begin to feel a conflict between myself the writer and myself the marketing director. As a writer I want to tell you things I find funny or interesting beyond the normal curiosity conjured by a press like Aunt Lute. As the marketing director, I want to tell you all the wonderful things that make our press a great book publisher, not only unique in its practice, but superior in its production of fine literature. The combination of roles confuses me. I also have to look at the world we live in: when talking with Carol Seajay of *Feminist Bookstore News*, she said, "if you can't be honest with feminist booksellers, then who can you be honest with?" I ask myself, "what would keep me from being honest as a marketer *or* a writer to *feminists*?" The answer is, of course, that the climate which surrounds me and Aunt Lute, and includes feminists at times, is in a period of significant backlash against those who try to do things differently, and especially against those who strive to put women of color at the center and achieve true multicultural harmony.

If I had to say it in a few sentences, I would tell you that Aunt Lute Books is a book company filled with feminists who believe in true multicultural vision. And, overall, our idea of multiculturalism goes far beyond what is currently being passed as such. For example, if a press of any size is being run predominantly by white men or women, but the publication list

Copyright © 1994 by Jamie Lee Evans

is filled with people of color, this does not make that press
multicultural. It may mean that said company has a great list, it
may mean that said company is exploiting people of color for
profit, it might mean any of several things, but it does not
constitute a multicultural work environment.

For twelve years, Aunt Lute Books has been growing and
changing, from a very *small* small press started by two white
lesbians, Joan Pinkvoss and Barb Wieser, to a multiracial,
multiclass, nonprofit *large* small press with ten women and a
tiny office. Publishing works by Audre Lorde, Gloria Anzaldúa
and Paula Gunn Allen, Aunt Lute has always had a hand in the
theory and practice discussion. But the discussion was never
limited to the books we published. Aunt Lute's staff and
management practice has been evolving with the dialogue.

Aunt Lute has operated as a for-profit sole proprietorship
(although in the feminist publishing world we know that the
literal distinction of not-for-profit and for-profit publishers can
be quite slight), a merged for-profit partnership (Spinsters/Aunt
Lute, 1982–1990), and finally as the Aunt Lute Foundation, a
full-fledged 501 (c)3 nonprofit corporation. Since 1990, Aunt
Lute has gone from a staff of three white women and one
woman of color to a staff that includes African American,
Iranian, Southeast Asian, Latina, European, Jewish, Chinese,
and mixed heritage lesbian, bisexual, and heterosexual women.

Once Joan Pinkvoss left Spinsters and formed Aunt Lute as a
nonprofit corporation—specifically to remove the "ownership"
of Aunt Lute titles from white women and put it into the hands
of a public institution—old and new staff had the opportunity
to reformulate Aunt Lute's mission, reorganize its personnel
policies, and change the basic structure of the organization to
facilitate long-range change. In 1991, with grant money secured
for consultation and organizational development, Fabienne
McPhail and Joan, Aunt Lute's current codirectors, led the
group into a strategic planning retreat that would determine the
staff/power structure of the future Aunt Lute. During the
retreat, staff, volunteers, and board members mapped out
long-range plans and a mission statement for Aunt Lute that
focused on the empowerment of disenfranchised women
through the publishing of their works. Although the press and
prior staff had already shown a commitment to these voices, it
was now on paper that Aunt Lute would be a "multiracial

women's press committed to the publication and distribution of
high quality, culturally diverse works."* Among the women
who would find a place in Aunt Lute's catalogues would also
be lesbian, working class, Jewish, fat, and immigrant women.
Aunt Lute would never again be the same: the staff would
always be diverse in culture and race; the main power would no
longer rest with one woman, but in two codirectors. The grants
we write, the books we publish, the marketing of the books,
etc. would always contain a community voice, i.e., all would be
unique to Aunt Lute's long-term goal of empowering women
by acting as a link within and between communities of women,
and creating new dialogues and discussions. With renewed
commitment, we were ready for the next steps.

The staff, volunteers, and board of Aunt Lute had a unique
opportunity with the retreat to create the vision of the company
together. Of course, then there was the work of making it
happen. No one at Aunt Lute would tell you that we work in a
feminist utopia, but, overall, there is a feeling that through
conflict and struggle comes the energy and new possibility for
change. Now we have a management team that makes the core
decisions of the press. The team includes the two codirectors
(senior editor and development director) and the heads of our
three departments: Chris Lymbertos, our managing editor;
Melissa Levin, our operations director; and myself, the
marketing director. Whether the decisions are about what
building to move into, what health care to choose, or
troubleshooting around a company issue like distribution of our
books, the management team meets and all members have equal
space and power in laying out their positions.

We're taking some time adjusting to the new roles we're each
playing in the company, and we schedule three-hour meetings
twice a month to ensure that all decisions have as much time to
be presented and discussed at our meetings as possible. During
the meetings, we rotate facilitation, and someone brings food (a
task we also rotate), and, key to our sense of equal power
during these meetings, all team members make the same
amount of money during the meetings.

---

* from the Aunt Lute Mission Statement, 2a.

Of course, trying to build a feminist business in a capitalist world is a difficult task. A perfect example of that difficulty is around the scheduling of six hours a month for five staff members. Sometimes going to management meetings means working overtime to get your basic job done, or sometimes it means falling behind. In working together we often have issues around trust and the breaking down of old hierarchical patterns from both "sides" of the power structure. We constantly have to realize that we are not a feminist discussion group, nor solely a political action group, but a business with bills, payroll, taxes, deadlines, etc. Capitalist patriarchy doesn't allow much space for power to be shared: there simply isn't enough time in the work week, or even beyond, if we want to put a final product out. So, our management team is both an exciting opportunity and, in some ways, an experiment, the end result being something we're not sure of.

In addition to a diverse staff, Aunt Lute has also instituted a seven-member, equally diverse Manuscripts Development and Acquisitions committee (MADEVA). MADEVA, under the leadership of our first reader, Cristina Azocar, and our senior editor, reads all incoming manuscripts and makes recommendations to our management team on the manuscripts we will publish. MADEVA meets once a month, and its members reflect the communities we seek to reach with our books. Having a community-based MADEVA committee is an important part of being a multicultural organization, as we know that the real impact of our press is the manuscripts we publish. Other community-based work at Aunt Lute includes our publishing internships, which provide women who have traditionally been excluded from the publishing world an opportunity to get work experience and training. Often our interns end up working for income at Aunt Lute or moving on to work in publishing in other ways.

The way we market our books is also affected by our community focus. Instead of the traditional marketing approach of making consumers want your product, and placing them in mainstream venues, Aunt Lute publishes books that the community needs, and in addition to the feminist and mainstream bookstores, we sell our books where the particular cultural community goes. For example, *Our Feet Walk the Sky*, a collection of writings by South Asian Women, is being sold in

major bookstores and also Indian grocery stores. The three
authors of *Tight Spaces* read in African American churches and
NAACP meetings, and our Jewish titles have been sold at both
Jewish book fairs and Hillel Houses.

Along with our marketing, our author readings take place
not only in bookstores or universities, but also in community
centers, libraries, and community gathering spots. As a
long-term goal, Aunt Lute would like to create larger, more
diverse audiences and will do so by touring several different
community authors together. This will hopefully further
coalition work and alliance work by gathering diverse
communities together.

Aunt Lute is now in the process of building a strong and
active, diverse board of directors that will act as a support team
as well as give some financial guidance and stability to our
future. In two years, five years, ten years . . . as theories and
practicality continue to change, the women and books of Aunt
Lute will also be evolving, and for all experiments, those
successful and abandoned, we will know that our work was
forging a different way, and for that, none of it a loss.

AN ALTERNATIVE TO THE ECONOMICS OF THREAT

MARY KAY BLAKELY

As a writer, I understand my culture primarily through its literature, the stories of its people. My friend Mary Lou Weisman, another writer, suggested that one of the reasons I'm experiencing such immense alienation from American politics right now is that I tend to read life as a character-driven novel while other people, George Bush for example, lead plot-driven lives. The story currently being serialized in the daily newspapers, "Kinder, Gentler Nation," offers a strong economic argument in favor of spreading fear and concentrating wealth. The plot depends on the domination of a Third World, CIA deceits, hostage deals, an expensive war to roust a drug czar out of Panama, a chapter in which an undetermined number of Middle Eastern people have been killed to keep oil at $17 dollars a barrel, and so on. A happy ending would be that the president and his friends end up rich, with plenty of killing machines to keep it that way. The title is apparently intended to be ironic.

My unhappiness with this plot is roughly equivalent to what a character from a 19th-century novel of manners might feel, say, finding herself in the middle of *American Psycho*. It was in this state of despond that I arrived at a conference called "Women and Economic Development" in Peachtree, Georgia, in September 1991.

It was the fourth annual, multi-national conference on economics organized by the Ms. Foundation for Education, featuring many distinguished speakers and executives from

Copyright © 1992 by Mary Kay Blakely

world banks and lending organizations. The all-female faculty held advanced degrees from Harvard and Michigan and Berkeley; fellowships from the MacArthur and Rockefeller and Ford Foundations; and resumes that, if offered to Solomon Brothers or Citibank, would have attracted six-figure salaries. Their daunting mission was to teach the nuances of credit and debt, labor and unions, taxes and legislation, wealth and investment to about 250 activists and community organizers who felt compelled—some, like me, under duress—to improve their "economic literacy." The general feeling among the participants seemed to be that if we had to live through the hostile takeovers and violent wars of "Kinder, Gentler Nation," we had best learn the language.

We were all excruciatingly aware that another presidential election was coming up in which the economy was destined to be a major issue, and none of us had a particularly wonderful time during the last election. Standing in a voting booth in 1988 was, as Whoopie Goldberg described it, "like being in Disneyland on bad acid." The gap between what we knew to be true and what the Bush fiction asked us to accept required a mind-bending suspension of disbelief. While we were observing more poverty and homelessness than any other period in memory, for example, *The Wall Street Journal* and *The New York Times* were reporting that after eight years of Reagan/Bush Republicanism we were experiencing a "rebounding economy." Rebounding for whom? Rebounding us where? If it is possible to have a "rebounding economy" in a society where one must step over near-corpses on the sidewalks every day, a sight so common in urban areas today that most citizens can no longer afford to grieve over each casualty, could we really claim to understand the language of economics? No.

Duty brought me to Peachtree, but I did not expect to enjoy myself for a minute: these were, after all, economists. It is their job to remind us, whether serving on city councils or listening to impassioned debates at cocktail parties, that although justice and peace and equality are charming ideas, the pursuit of those goals is bound to cause "major economic problems." For most of these community organizers, usually identified as "bleeding hearts" in the Bush canon, major economic problems are a brick wall against which we have repeatedly cracked our heads.

I had come to understand the field of economics as a system of immutable laws beyond human control, a kind of financial bubonic plague that could inflict megadisasters through mysterious cosmic forces. These insidious influences could cause billions of dollars to leak out of the Savings and Loan industry without anyone knowing exactly where the money went. Economists asked us to understand that the $500 billion that American taxpayers will have to repay over the next five years was not actually deposited and then embezzled by old-time crooks. It never existed in actual dollar bills but comes to us through deregulation, double-digit interest rates and falling real estate values, a speculative fortune that has become real debt. We are asked, too, not to attempt to pay this imaginary debt with imaginary taxes and call it even. This is the smoke-and-mirrors language of economics, and I anticipated being gaslit in Peachtree for three days.

Imagine my surprise, then, when the conference opened with a burst of song from Jane Sapp and Mary Haitz at a session called "Discovering Common Ground." These economists felt the only way to eliminate fear of "the other" was to get to know her. To that end, Latin and African and Native and white American women alternated at the microphones with women from other countries, each telling moving stories of her people. Despite repeated accounts of homelessness and forced prostitution and the egregious results of toxic waste and inadequate health care, nobody applied the brakes to this discussion for the sake of averting "major economic problems." The consensus here was that these were major economic problems. In a wild departure from the themes of power-driven economics, where money flows in great abundance to the strongest site, these thinkers imagined a compassion-driven economics, where money is carefully distributed in small increments wherever it is most needed.

They did not seem disturbed that, under their system, people at the top end of the income charts might face a tough period of profit withdrawal in order to halt the drain on the bottom. In the U.S., for example, "the top one percent saw an average family income grow by 75 percent, from $313,206 in 1980 to $548,970 in 1990," Thomas Byrne Edsall and Mary D. Edsall reported in "Chain Reaction," while families in the bottom ten percent experienced a nine percent decrease during the same

decade, "from $4,791 to $4,295." According to the conference
members at Peachtree, many of whom were mothers and
grandmothers as well as economists, it was time for the top one
percent to be gracious guests at somebody else's party.

Nor were they losing sleep over creating a possible bomb
shortage by converting military budgets into funds for food,
clothing, shelter and—why not?— "rest and relaxation" for
working classes everywhere. They noted the arms race that
collapsed the economy of the Soviet Union had severely
damaged the U.S. as well, and the Third World is now handily
summarized as "debtor nations" in the daily newspapers.
Economist Ann Markusen pointed out that "two-thirds of the
national deficit in this country was accumulated under Reagan
and Bush, and a very large share went for defense build-up."
She challenged the standard claim that our bloated military
budget, now at $300 billion a year, has simulated the economy
by providing employment for thousands of Americans.
Translated, that really meant "lots and lots of jobs for white
men, particularly, well-educated white men, because the defense
industries employ lots of scientists and engineers," she said. Few
companies in the private sector have a $300 billion budget to
compete for that talent, and "consequently, the defense build-up
has debilitated other industries."

Indeed, the notion of spending any more money on arms was
flatly rejected as an effective means of ensuring national
security. Planting missiles in silos all over the globe has not left
any nation, on any side of the Cold War, feeling particularly
secure. Instead of "deterrence" (giving other countries explosive,
megaton reasons to fear us), the conference favored a policy of
"concurrence" (giving other countries nourishing, generous
reasons to like us), which caused far less wear and tear on
human relationships and could achieve the same results. Instead
of death, or the threat of death, currently the main
government-subsidized export from the United States, the
women at Peachtree would like the $300 billion military budget
spent on almost anything else. Therapy, for example. If their
budget had been in place last January, instead of "kicking butt"
and decimating explosives over Baghdad, soldiers would have
been commissioned to penetrate the enemy—however
resistant—with food, medicine and, very probably, intensive
workshops on "Getting to Yes."

Their appreciation for "merger-mania" and "hostile takeovers" was likewise dim. Administrators from the Women's World Bank and the Ford Foundation at Peachtree talked enthusiastically about "micro-enterprise." Jean Pogge of the Woodstock Institute in Chicago explained that "micro-enterprise development—and micro-credit lending, a critical component—came to America from the Third World." In Latin America and Asia, socially responsible investors in ACCION and FINCA have provided millions in credit to the self-employed poor, allowing market vendors, backyard mechanics, seamstresses, shoemakers, carpenters, and others to free themselves from loan sharks charging interest rates so high it was impossible to break the cycle of poverty.

The most famous program is administered by the Grameen Bank in Bangladesh, "which alone serves some 884,000 borrowers, with repayment rates between 98 and 99 percent," Pogge reported. "As of January 1991, this unusual bank has disbursed over $300 million in loans to micro-enterprises." The concept of peer lending groups, which makes borrowers accountable to one another as well as to their bank for loan repayments, is responsible for much of the success. "Access to capital may be what attracts women to our borrowing groups," said Beverly Smith of the Women's Self-Employment Project in Chicago, another micro-credit fund, "but many say that the support they get is even more valuable than the loan."

Working Capital provides loans to entrepreneurs in rural Massachusetts, Vermont, and New Hampshire, while The Good Faith Fund services the working poor of Arkansas. The Good Faith Fund was "initially structured exactly like the Grameen Bank, but we have adapted the model over time to fit the local environment," said Julia Vindasius, the manager. "In our experience in Arkansas, the poorer the population you target, the more technical assistance and other support you have to provide."

Workshops and training are required for recipients of loans from The Lakota Fund, which administers a $900,000 grant from the Ford Foundation to launch a micro-lending program in South Dakota. Even before the "Kinder, Gentler Nation" left the Lakota tribe with unprecedented levels of unemployment, alcoholism, and illiteracy, they lived for generations on a thin trickle of money dripping through the pale green buildings of the reservation's welfare offices. Mary Scouts-Enemy, an administrator of the Lakota Fund, said that long-term dependency cannot be reversed with a $500 loan; education is essential. She and her colleagues often have to go door-to-door on the Lakota reservation with announcements about workshops and meetings because many of the residents have no phone. Imagine: banking administrators who make house calls.

Despite the immense size of the economic problems they faced, the participants did not encourage each other to settle for micro-solutions. At one of the eight "Talking Circles" on Friday evening, women from Australia, Puerto Rico, and the U.S. were still debating labor issues well past midnight. Sinith Sitthinaksa of Thailand said it wasn't enough to organize workers in South Carolina or Ohio. Since American businesses had become multi-national largely to find the cheapest labor, union organizations also had to become international to ensure fair wages everywhere. Discussion leaders Maria Riley and Pam Sparr of the Women's Division of the United Methodist Church agreed: as long as labor can be exploited anywhere in the world, we can depend on somebody to do it.

There was universal recognition that their plans for a character-driven economy were up against big money, big power, literally, big guns. They would need capital, and plenty of it. The best news of the conference: money is coming. As the baby-boom generation approaches middle-age, the same group that is currently swelling the market for alternative medicine, a movement toward "socially responsible investing" is growing every year. An increasing number of investors are buying shares in large mutual funds that screen capital away from companies that produce armaments, pollute the environment, mistreat workers, or conduct business with oppressive regimes. Many church groups and foundations are becoming "pro-active investors," diverting portions of their holdings into community development credit unions and micro-enterprise funds, where modest profits keep housing and business loans affordable for the poor. The Resource Center for Women and Ministry in the South, Inc., in Durham, North Carolina, reported that "today, more than $500 billion are invested with social criteria." If this movement doubled its capital by the year 2000, peace would be as profitable as war in the new millennium. The women at Peachtree did not consider this an impossible idea—especially if everyone kept holding workshops on "economic literacy."

According to their economic theory, which might be called "Beyond Bush Country" if it were ever seriously reported in the *Times*, profits and being Number One are not the only, or even the most important, measure of success. In the economic story they are trying to write, employment, health care, a safe environment, and world peace would be universally valued. A happy ending would be that people everywhere, fed and rested, had no use for junk bonds. The Peachtree economists believe in this vision, even while knowing that Ivan Boesky gave a talk entitled "Greed is Good" to an enthusiastic Wall Street audience in 1985. They do not see their plans as unreal, any more than it was unreal to suppose, ten years ago, that decent citizens should accept thousands of homeless on their city sidewalks as inevitable facts of life.

The unreal happens every day. We see it, for example, on the Supreme Court. The same folks who packed the court have been appointing the Federal Reserve Board. Like most people, I had assumed only bankers and Wall Street financial experts were qualified to serve on this elite committee which shapes the national economic policy, until Ann Markusen observed that ideally, in a democracy, everyone affected by the economy should be represented: single moms, nurses, senior citizens, and so forth. Appointing only bankers to the Federal Reserve Board is rather like naming members of the National Rifle Association to draft our gun-control laws.

"The economy is a man-made thing," Markusen declared, throwing the curtain back on the Wizards of Wall Street. "We have suffered ten years of the grimmest, most inhumane economic policy that this country has seen in the 20th century, and it is time to reverse it." Inspired by the idea of a Federal Reserve Board by, of, and for the people, I started a list of candidates as I wandered from seminar to seminar.

Lyzette Perez, a single mother of eight who was homeless three years ago and now runs a community education program for teenagers at the Camden Urban Women's Center as well as an import business of handmade jewelry, would be a useful advisor on how to stretch a little capital a very long way. Cindy Marano, the executive director of Wider Opportunities for Women in Washington D.C., and Peggy Powell of Cooperative

Home Care Associates, a worker-owned health service in the Bronx, know how to plant ambition and raise expectations in the most arid deserts of the economy. My expert on home improvement loans would be Lynda Wright, Executive Director of the Public Welfare Coalition in Chicago, who spends her vacations building houses for the poor in FourCorners, Louisiana, as a cure for burnout. My foreign policy advisors would be Felicia Ward and Kalima Rose, editors of an international economic journal called *Equal Means*, because they know how to analyze profits and losses in human terms. Of course I would need Mary Scouts-Enemy of the Lakota Fund to oversee the door-to-door evaluation program. Nobody on the People's Federal Reserve Board would want to carry on without knowing how their policies are affecting people who can't be reached by phone from Washington.

As my imaginary list takes shape, I see that I have appointed a Federal Reserve Board heavily represented by "special interest groups." Back to the old language problem, I know that a special interest group—women, minorities, laborers, the handicapped—is any population outside the main group—able-bodied, educated white men. At election time, when the President speaks harshly against the SIGs, voters are trained to think of small, rabid factions of opportunists out for themselves rather than people like themselves. They will not think of the president and his lucky one percent.

By the end of the second day, arms full of brochures and newsletters and resource materials—more homework in "economic literacy" than you could do in a month—you need a little break. Two days with these impassioned, intelligent women have created such an immense swelling in your soul, such a fierce rekindling of faith in the possibility of change, you feel slightly ungrounded. An intense yearning to live the dreams you've been so earnestly debating provokes a familiar ache. Relief for that ache is usually what propels you into marches and campaigns. You are vulnerable to conscription, in a crowd of 250 persuasive women with a thousand urgent things to do. You decide to slip into the auditorium for a screening of *Hearts and Hands*, a safe little documentary film about quilts. What emotional trouble can you get into with quilts?

As other, similarly paper-laden women file into the auditorium you can't help smiling, remembering your anxiety about
what to pack. A conference on economics suggested that you
should wear the uniform: a suit and silk blouse, high heels, and
pantyhose. Perhaps because of your acute alienation, you
packed your sweats and jeans, figuring you'd try to pass for a
maintenance worker. Instead, you blend right in. Everyone's
wearing work clothes. You see colorful caftans, loose-flowing
robes, embroidered vests, handcrafted jewelry, batik prints,
spangled sweats and cotton shirts; the styles are artful and
attractive but the dominant fashion statement is, "Be
comfortable." Since you are now in the habit of thinking
micro, what women wear strikes you as suddenly significant.
You suspect that the remarkable clarity of thought, the
purposefulness and energy of the last two days is somehow
connected to the fact that nobody's feet hurt. With no shoulder
pads or pinched waists, no whale bone or wire cups, we were
women unbound.

Coming straight from Manhattan—particularly, the
publishing industry—you notice immediately: there are no
emaciated bodies here. It was a solidly middle-aged crowd,
many directing large national and international operations and
managing multi-million dollar budgets. Professionally and
physically, these women had heft. This assembly looked like it
never heard of "Ten Weeks to Thinner Thighs." Suddenly, you
see why a culture that keeps women's minds glued to their
bodies, that keeps us mourning the loss of youthful beauty, is
so incredibly costly. We can't grow up. We can hardly grow at
all.

The diet industry consumes a bloated $30 billion annually,
the absurd price of our cultivated body shame. Comedian Jetta
Jones recently told an audience at The Improv that a California
diet spa estimated a 35-pound weight-loss program would cost
her $35,000. "For that amount of money," she said, "I could
hire someone else to go out in public and be me for a year."
Yet these women have somehow escaped the pervasive body-
loathing. Their enjoyment was palpable around the buffet
tables at dinner, as if food were not the enemy but a delicious
life-force. Everything about them was hearty—their appetite,
their laughter, their passion, their charisma. Their size. How did

they learn to feel entitled to so much "space"? Fully grown, full
of purpose, their middle-aged beauty was electric.

The soft-voiced narrator in *Hearts and Hands* interrupts
your musings on how to spend the $30 billion we could save
by eliminating body shame, and you turn to the history of
women's sewing, a major thread in the story of female
enterprise. In previous generations the quilt was like a market
share traded for vegetables or grains or, in the case of one black
seamstress in the South, for freedom. The beauty of the quilt
was that, when materials were in short supply during wars and
famines, it could be made from scraps. Women cut up their
wedding dresses and ball gowns during hard times and sewed
nonstop through revolutionary wars, Midwestern droughts,
months of travel in covered wagons. Their quilts were sold to
raise money for the temperance movement, hung in yards with
coded messages for underground railroad conductors, raffled in
fund raisers for frontier hospitals. A period of "crazy quilts"
emerged during the settlement of the West, when women were
without patterns and had to invent. With a needle and thread
and a few scraps of fabric, enterprising women supported large
families, saved farms, and kept a whole country warm.

You come for a simple story about quilts, and you get a
provocative history of sacrifice, struggle and unimaginable
human courage. Several other women besides you are discreetly
mopping their cheeks when the lights come up. You file damply
out of the auditorium and pass the wall of quilts from South
Dakota, products from one of the successful micro-enterprises
launched by the Lakota Fund. Stitch by stitch, workshop by
workshop, the women keep talking, patching together a
humane economy from small co-ops in South Carolina and
micro-miracles in Bangladesh. But if they include no CIA plots,
no exciting wars, no hostile takeovers in their literature, can the
authors of "Beyond Bush Country" attract fans from "Kinder,
Gentler Nation"?

Opinion polls showed that after the spectacular televised war
in January 1991—the "surgical strikes" covered by "surgical
news" that omitted pictures of dead human beings and referred
to them only as" collateral damage" and "air losses"—netted the
president the highest approval rating in history. If Greed is
Good on Wall Street, War is Fabulous for the White House. In
the ten months since, however, a kind of national malpractice

suit seems to be forming. For all the expensive, splendid
equipment used, the main enemy is still at large. And the
hospital bill has now arrived . . . just as we are discovering how
many of us have no health insurance.

A proposition on a recent Chicago ballot indicated 73% of
the voters wanted to reduce military spending to provide more
funds for housing, education and social programs. And in a
New York Times/CBS poll in October 1991, 66% of those
surveyed rated the condition of the national economy "fairly
bad" to "very bad." The *Times* reported that "the number of
Americans who say 'things' in the country have 'pretty seriously
gotten off on the wrong track' has doubled since January."
Many voters didn't understand precisely what the president
meant during his last campaign when he confessed to trouble
with "the vision thing." Now, it appears, they know.

Even with public support for a compassion-driven policy,
however, its proponents are still up against a trillion dollar
deficit, a $500 billion S&L bailout, a $300 billion military
budget. Trying to dismantle this superstructure with workshops
and newsletters seems so futile. Another picture of enormous
vulnerability comes to mind, a lone protester standing in an
empty street as a tank rolls toward him. All odds in the
forthcoming collision favor the tank. The man's only weapons
are his unshakable belief and a firm stance that says, No more.
And then a miracle, broadcast all over the world from
Tiennaman Square: with less than five feet between them, the
tank stops. What made it happen? Behind all that metal and
armor, some human impulse stirred. The unreal happens every
day.

At Peachtree, it happens to you. Though you suspect the
economic battles to undo the greed of the 1980s could easily
stretch over the whole next decade, you enlist as a seamstress in
the crazy quilt army. Before you go home, you subscribe to
newsletters, put your name on mailing lists, sign up for more
workshops on socially responsible investing and economic
development. You know you will be speaking up passionately
at cocktail parties again . . . but you will not let "major
economic problems" silence you anymore. You will meet myths
with facts.

You wave goodbye to the woman from Montana and
remember her comment at the closing ceremony. Quoting her

eight-year-old son, who declared solemnly at dinner one night that he had "come to a pitchfork in the road," she said the conference had changed her life. You, too, have been forked in Peachtree. By the time you get on the plane to go home, your acute alienation has given way to commitment. You want to believe that by taking up our pitchforks, one by one, women could turn the face of the earth.

RELATED READING

This is by no means an exhaustive list of book on women and business or women and money; it is a list of books we found interesting in our exploration of the woman-centered economy, and we think you might find them interesting too.

Chappell, Tom. *The Soul of a Business: Managing for Profit and the Common Good.* New York: Bantam, 1993.

Godfrey, Joline. *Our Wildest Dreams: Women Entrepreneurs Making Money, Having Fun, Doing Good.* New York: HarperBusiness, 1993.

Hawken, Paul. *Growing a Business.* New York: Simon & Schuster, 1988.

Helgeson, Sally. *The Female Advantage: Women's Ways of Leadership.* New York: Doubleday, 1990.

Henderson, Hazel. *The Politics of the Solar Age: Alternatives to Economics.* Indianapolis: Knowledge Systems, Inc., 1988.

Lulic, Margaret. *Who We Could Be at Work.* Eden Prairie, MN: Blue Edge, 1994.

Orsborn, Carol. *Inner Excellence: Spiritual Principles of Life-Driven Business.* San Rafael, CA: New World Library, 1992.

Penelope, Julia, Ed. *Out of the Class Closet: Lesbians Speak.* Freedom, CA: The Crossing Press, 1994.

Scollard, Jeannette R. *The Self-Employed Woman: How to Start Your Own Business and Gain Control of Your Life.* New York: Pocket Books, 1985.

Sinetar, Marsha. *Do What You Love, The Money Will Follow: Discovering Your Right Livelihood*. New York: Dell, 1990.

Wilkens, Joanne. *Her Own Business: Success Secrets of Entrepreneurial Women*. New York: McGraw-Hill Book Company, 1988.

Whitmyer, Claude, ed. *In the Company of Others: Making Community in the Modern World*. Los Angeles, CA: Jeremy P. Tarcher/Perigree Books, 1993.

Whitmyer, Claude, ed. *Mindfulness and Meaningful Work: Explorations in Right Livelihood*. Berkeley, CA: Parallax Press, 1993.

Wolf, Naomi. *Fire with Fire: The New Female Power and How It Will Change the 21st Century*. New York: Random House, 1993.

CONTRIBUTORS

LISTED ALPHBETICALLY BY FIRST NAME

ANN HARRISON is a writer and radio reporter who divides her time between Boston and Northampton, Massachusetts.

ALICE LOWENSTEIN is a writer for *5-Star Investor*, a Chicago-based investment newsletter published by Morningstar. She also drums with the Women's Action Coalition Drum Core (yes, that's the actual spelling).

bell hooks is author of many books, including *Outlaw Culture: Resisting Representations; Teaching to Transgress: Education as the Practice of Freedom; Sisters of the Yam: Black Women and Self-Recovery; Yearning: Race, Gender, and Cultural Politics;* and *Feminist Theory: From Margin to Center.*

CAROL SEAJAY is editor and publisher of *Feminist Bookstore News.* She has worked in and around feminist bookstores since 1975. She edited feminist newsletters and did abortion counseling in Michigan in the early 1970s, started working at A Woman's Place Bookstore in 1975, opened Old Wives Tales Bookstore in 1976 (with Paula Wallace), and has worked full time on *FBN* since 1983.

DEBORAH RENEE LEWIS studied English rhetoric at the University of Illinois at Urbana-Champaign. Her short fiction and poetry have appeared in *Little America,* and she is currently at work on a novel, *The Oonagh Journals*. She eeks out a living at a bookstore and reads voraciously.

ELEANOR MORTON earned a B.A. in Women's Studies from Earlham College in 1994. Currently, she is living in Bloomington, Indiana, and working for the rights of senior citizens. She continues to write.

GENEVIEVE VAUGHAN is the founder of the Foundation for a Compassionate Society and is now working on a book about the gift economy as women's economic way.

GLORIA I. JOSEPH, social scientist and essayist, is a Black feminist activist of West Indian parents. She is professor emeritus from Hampshire College, Amherst, Massachusetts, and resides in St. Croix, Virgin Islands. She is actively engaged in women's organizations in the United States, the Caribbean, and South Africa. In addition, she is an avid gardener and raises honey bees.

JAMIE LEE EVANS is a lower-class, 27-year-old, lesbian feminist of Asian descent. She currently rages, loves, and builds community in Oakland, California, where she is a core member of the Lesbian Emergency Action Fund (Lavender LEAF). Her community of lesbians is actively involved in sharing resources and redistributing lesbian wealth.

JANET MILLER is a radical lesbian feminist concentrating on using her energy to create what she would like to see in the world.

JOANI BLANK is the founder of Good Vibrations, a retail and mail order concern that sells products to enhance people's sex lives. She also publishes books that teach sex education in a sex-positive way, as owner of Down There Press.

KARIN KEARNS is a licensed midwife in private practice serving the Tampa Bay area. Herself a home-birth mother of a 15-year-old son, Roman, Karin has been a long-time activist for reproductive rights. Karin also lectures and presents numerous workshops on midwifery, pregnancy and childbirth, and well-woman-care topics.

KAREN RUDOLPH has raised funds for feminist and Native American organizations. She is currently cowriting *Making the River*, a book about American Indian Jimi Simmons.

KAREN WILLIAMS, known as the Diva of Comedy and the Queen of Improv, is a comic and writer. She is creator and facilitator of the Humor-at-Large Workshop Series, author of the playbook *Let's Laugh About Sex*, columnist for *Lesbian News* and *Outlines*, and producer of the National Women's Comedy Conference.

LAURA BURROWS is a Dedicated and Consecrated Diannic Wiccan priestess and member of the Re-Formed Congregation of the Goddess. The views expressed in her article do not necessarily reflect the views of any other Diannic Witch. She is a lesbian currently living and working as a tradewoman in Bozeman, Montana.

LAURA POST writes a nationally syndicated arts column and was a regular contributor to *HOT WIRE: Journal of Women's Music and Culture* for many years.

LORAINE EDWALDS is a poet, a singer, a friend, a lover, and a book production manager for a medical association. She is striving to keep these roles in balance.

MARGARET VanARSDALE is a lesbian of Dutch-German heritage who runs a small business and believes in supporting all women in every way possible.

MARY BYRNE is producer of the National Women's Music Festival, which is held the week after Memorial Day every year at Indiana University in Bloomington, Indiana.

MARY KAY BLAKELY's essays and articles on social and political issues have appeared in the *New York Times*, the *Washington Post*, *Vogue*, *Life*, and *Mirabella*. She is a contributing editor at both *Ms.* and the *L.A. Times* Sunday magazine. She has numerous books to her credit, including *Pulling Our Own Strings: Feminist Humor and Satire* (with Gloria Kaufmann), *Wake Me When It's Over*, and *American Mom*.

MARY WALLACE is a teacher and writer. She works daily with people of widely differing economic means, in far-flung areas of her city. A quiet subversive, she works to free the power of women in all the realms she encounters.

MIDGE STOCKER founded Third Side Press in 1991 and is working diligently to keep it running, as part of the woman-centered economy. She is editor of the *Cancer as a Women's Issue: Scratching the Surface* (Women/Cancer/Fear/Power series, volume 1) and *Confronting Cancer, Constructing Change: New Perspectives on Women and Cancer* (volume 2).

MINNIE BRUCE PRATT is author of *Rebellion: Essays 1980–1991* and of *Crime Against Nature*, which received the Lamont Poetry Prize in 1989 and the American Library Association Gay/Lesbian Book Award in 1991. Her most recent work is *S/HE*, a collection of autobiographical nonfiction prose.

NETT HART is a country dyke who does salvage, writing, community organizing, and administers a nonprofit organization for lesbians on land, Lesbian Natural Resources.

PELICAN LEE is a lesbian activist and organizer focusing on women's and lesbian land communities and accessibility for low-income lesbians.

PHYLLIS CHESLER is a psychologist and the author of six books: *Women and Madness*; *Women, Money and Power*; *About Men*; *With Child: A Diary of Motherhood*; *Mothers on Trial: The Battle for Children and Custody*; and *The Sacred Bond: The Legacy of Baby M*. She is Professor of

Psychology at the College of Staten Island, City University of New York, and editor-at-large of the feminist magazine *On the Issues*. She is one of the founders of the Association for Women in Psychology, the National Women's Health Network, and an APA Custody Training Institute. She is writing a book on women and self-defense that focuses on the case of the nation's so-called first female serial killer. She has been ill with Chronic Fatigue Immune Dysfunction Syndrome for a year and a half.

REBECCA HENDERSON grew up in a Norwegian Quaker farming community in Iowa in the 1940s and 1950s. For part of her 30 years as a lesbian, she lived in Iowa City; then she moved to New Mexico in 1985. Her work has centered around land, lesbians, and community organizing.

SONIA JOHNSON (PhD, Rutgers, 1965) was excommunicated from the Mormon church for uppityness in 1979 and has been uppity ever since. In 1981, she was presented with the Playboy First Amendment Award with its $5,000 prize, which she refused. In 1984, she ran for the presidency of the United States as the nominee of the Citizens Party, the Consumer Party, and the Peace and Freedom Party. She is a nationally prominent speaker and author of five books, *From Housewife to Heretic*; *Going Out of Our Minds: The Metaphysics of Liberation*; *Wildfire: Igniting the She/Volution;*, *The Ship That Sailed Into the Living Room: Sex and Intimacy Reconsidered;*, and *Out of this World: A Fictional True-Life Adventure* (cowritten with Jade DeForest).

THERESA CORRIGAN has owned and operated Lioness Books in Sacramento, California since 1981 and is a member of the Feminist Bookstore Network. She has also taught in the Women's Studies Program at California State University, Sacramento for more than 20 years. She is a writer and co-editor of a two-volume anthology about women's relationships with other animals (Vol. 1, *With a Fly's Eye, Whale's Wit and Woman's Heart* and Vol. 2, *And a Deer's Ear, Eagle's Song and Bear's Grace*) published by Cleis Press.

She is active in the struggle to keep independent bookselling
and publishing alive and well.

TONI ARMSTRONG JR. was publisher for many years of
HOT WIRE: Journal of Women's Music and Culture.
She continues to participate actively in women's music and
culture as a musician and as publisher of *Women's Music
Plus: Directory of Resources.*

INDEX

People of color, 45. *See also* African American women

Perez, Lyzette, 311

Performing arts organizations, 240-241

Phillips, Layli, 65

Pietila, Hilkka, 72

Pine Ridge Inn, 212-214

Pinkvoss, Joan, 300

Pogge, Jean, 309

Politics of the Solar Age: Alternatives to Economics, The (Henderson), 250

Pollution, 71-72

Post, Laura L., 127

Powell, Peggy, 312

Pratt, Minnie Bruce, 8, 27

Presses, women's. *See also* Publishers, feminist history of, 77-86

Pride and Joy, 117, 120

Priorities, 215-218

Producers, 156-157

Proposals, 140

Provincetown, Massachusetts, 122-123

Provincetown Business Guild, 124

Psychiatry, 127-129

Psychic economics, 73-76

Public Welfare Coalition, 312

Publishers, feminist, 181, 299-303. See also Presses, women

Publishers, lesbian, 181

Purple Cactus burrito bar, 123

Q

Questionnaires. *See* Surveys

R

Racism, 50, 63, 146, 270, 271, 275

Raffles, 90

Reader's Feast, 186

Reagan, Ronald, 306

Recession, 70

Reed, Ann, 156, 157

Reproduction economics, 68-72

Resources, 233-242

Responsibility, 139-140, 144-145

Riley, Maria, 309

Roberts, Kim, 159-165

Rose, Kalima, 312

Rosenblum, Barbara, 107

Rosengarten, Theodore, 36n

Rudolph, Karen, 9, 95

S

S/M, 154-155

Sage: A Scholarly Journal on Black Women, 64

Scouts-Enemy, Mary, 309, 312

Seajay, Carol, 9, 77, 184, 299

Segregation land issues and, 102-103

Self-censorship, 152

Sewing industry, 314

Sex business, 205-208

Sexism, 50

Sexism, internalized, 275

Sharing and necessity, 100

Signifying, 265

Silent auctions, 90

Sisterhood, 79, 265-280

Sliding-fee scale, 87-94

Smith, Beverly, 309

We gratefully acknowledge the following for permission to reprint previously published work:

ANN HARRISON: "Big Business: Lesbians Deal with Personal Profits and Collectives Action" appeared previously in *One in Ten*, a supplement to *The Boston Phoenix* (September 1994). Reprinted by permission of the publisher.

bell hooks: "Third World Diva Girls: Politics of Feminist Solidarity" appeared previously in *Yearning: Race, Gender, and Cultural Politics* by bell hooks (Boston: South End Press, 1990). Reprinted by permission of the publisher.

CAROL SEAJAY: "20 Years of Feminist Bookstores" appeared previously in *Ms.*, vol 3, no 1 (July/August 1992). Reprinted by permission.

GENEVIEVE VAUGHAN: "Stonehaven: An Attempt to Preach What We Practice," appeared previously in *HOT WIRE: The Journal of Women's Music and Culture*, vol 4, no 3 (July 1988). Reprinted by permission of the author.

KAREN RUDOLPH: "Feminist Fundraising Phobia" appeared previously in *Sojourner: The Women's Forum*, vol 18, no 4 (December 1992). Reprinted by permission of the author.

JAMIE LEE EVANS: "Aunt Lute Books" appeared originally in a slightly different form in *Feminist Bookstore News*, vol 7, no 1 (May/June 1994). Reprinted by permission.

JANET MILLER: "Lesbian Economy: A First Step" appeared previously in *Lesbian Ethics*, vol 3, no 3, and in *Hag Rag*, November/December 9989 (1989). Reprinted by permission of the author.

MARY KAY BLAKELY: "Quilting New Networks" appeared previously in *Ms.*, vol 2, no 5 (March/April 1992). Reprinted by permission.

MARY KAY BLAKELY: "Psychic Economics" originally appeared in *The New York Times*, March 19, 1981.

MINNIE BRUCE PRATT: "Money and the Shape of Things" was presented originally for the Society of the Humanities at Cornell University, and at Hamilton College, on April 10 and 13, 1989, and appears in *Rebellion: Essays 1980–1991* by Minnie Bruce Pratt (Ithaca, NY: Firebrand Books, 1991). Reprinted by permission of the publisher.

NETT HART: "Taking a Slide" appeared in a shorter form in *Feminist Bookstore News* (May/June 1992). Reprinted by permission of the author.

PELICAN LEE and REBECCA HENDERSON: "Lesbian Land Patterns" previously appeared in *Maize* (Winter 93). Reprinted by permission of the authors.

PHYLLIS CHESLER: "All We Have is Each Other" originally appeared in *On the Issues* (Winter 1992). Reprinted by permission of the author.

SONIA JOHNSON: "Lilies of the Field" appeared in *Wildfire: Igniting the She/Volution* (Albuquerque, NM: Wildfire Books, 1989). Reprinted by permission of the author.

THERESA CORRIGAN: Feminist Bookstores: Part of an Ecosystem" appeared in *Sojourner: The Women's Forum*, vol 19, no 3 (November 1993). Reprinted by permission of the author.

OTHER BOOKS FROM THIRD SIDE PRESS

FICTION

Hawkwings   by Karen Lee Osborne.
   A novel of love, lust, and mystery, intertwining Emily Hawk's network of friends, her developing romance with Catherine, and the search throughout Chicago for the lover of a friend dying of AIDS. $9.95   1-879427-00-1
AMERICAN LIBRARY ASSOCIATION
1992 GAY & LESBIAN BOOK AWARD FINALIST

The Sensual Thread   by Beatrice Stone.
   Life in the country as a sensually aware woman finally takes hold of Leah Kirby. $10.95   1-879427-18-5

On Lill Street   by Lynn Kanter. $10.95   1-879427-07-9
   "Watching everyone struggle with her/his feelings, politics, impulses is truly engrossing and a joyful experience."
                              —Bay Windows

AfterShocks   by Jess Wells.
   The Big One hits San Francisco. An 8.0 on the Richter scale and everything falls apart. $9.95   1-879427-08-7
   "This book kept me up all night."   *—Kate Millet*

Two Willows Chairs   by Jess Wells.
   Superbly crafted short stories of lesbian lives and loves.
$8.95   1-879427-05-2

The Dress/The Sharda Stories   by Jess Wells.
   Rippling with lesbian erotic energy, this collection includes one story Susie Bright calls "beautifully written and utterly perverse." $8.95   1-879427-04-4

DRAMA

She's Always Liked the Girls Best   by Claudia Allen.
   Lesbian plays by two-time Jefferson-award-winning playwright. $11.95   1-879427-11-7
AMERICAN LIBRARY ASSOCIATION
1994 GAY & LESBIAN BOOK AWARD FINALIST

1994 LAMBDA LITERARY AWARD FINALIST

MYSTERY

Timber City Masks   by Kieran York.
Royce Madison tries her hand at sleuthing and is determined
not to let bigotry take over her town. $9.95   1-879427-13-3

HEALTH

SomeBody to Love: A Guide to Loving the Body You Have
by Lesléa Newman.
Looking at ourselves as beautiful, powerful, and lovable—
challenging what society teaches us. Empowering women to
rethink our relationships with food and with people.
$10.95   1-879427-03-6

Cancer As a Women's Issue: Scratching the Surface
Midge Stocker, editor.
Personal stories of how cancer affects us as women,
individually and collectively.
Women/Cancer/Fear/Power series, volume 1 $10.95   1-879427-02-8
*"If you are a woman, or if anyone you love is a woman, you
should buy this book."*   —*Outlines*

**Confronting Cancer, Constructing Change:
New Perspectives on Women and Cancer**
Midge Stocker, editor.
*"Written from an unabashedly feminist viewpoint, these
essays provide much food for thought, touch the heart, and
supply useful information on making decisions regarding
healthcare."*   —*Library Journal*

Women/Cancer/Fear/Power series, volume 2 $11.95   1-879427-09-5

**Alternatives for Women with Endometriosis: A Guide by
Women for Women**   Ruth Carol, editor.
Overview of non-Western therapy alternatives for pain relief
from endometriosis. A dozen women share their personal
experiences. $12.95   1-879427-12-5

AUTOBIOGRAPHY

Enter Password: *RECOVERY*   by Elly Bulkin.
   Autobiography about transforming the self through language,
detailing with uncommon courage the author's experiences with
trashing in the feminist community, facing memories of
childhood sexual abuse, exploring Jewish identity, and ending a
long-term relationship. $7.95   1-879427-10-9
   *"a gift to all of us struggling to overcome the silences of our
lives."*   —Sojourner

 Third Side Press
The book you are holding is the product of work by
an independent women's book publishing company.

To order any Third Side Press book or to receive
a free catalog, write to Third Side Press, 2250 W.
Farragut, Chicago, IL 60625-1802. When ordering
books, please include $2 shipping for the first book
and .50 for each additional book.